Burn the Script
Kill the Leadership Theater, Lead for Real

David Schippers, Sc.D., CISSP

Burn the Script

Burn the Script

Kill the Leadership Theater, Lead for Real

Dave Schippers, Sc.D.

Iron Dog LLC

Grand Rapids

Published in the United States by Iron Dog LLC

Dave Schippers.

burn the script: kill the leadership theater, lead for real

ISBN 979-8-9922934-0-1

1. leadership, 2. personal transformation, 3. motivation, 4. organizational culture, 5. self-help, 6. leadership development, 7. toxic workplace, 8. real leadership, 9. culture change, 10. shadow work, 11. archetypal leadership, 12. fearless leadership, 13. workplace sabotage, 14. burnout recovery, 15. truth in leadership, 16. authentic leadership, 17. leadership theater, 18. organizational clarity, 19. leadership manipulation, 20. executive transformation, 21. jungian leadership psychology, 22. leadership fear and ego, 23. conflict management, 24. kpi performance metrics, 25. culture rebuild strategies

Dedication

To my wife Leslie-who stood by my side while jumping from helicopters and swimming with sharks. Our relationship is what grounds me. Thank you for your unending support.

To BE—who waited patiently as you awakened in me the call to bring truth and clarity into a world of delusion. Your guidance is the Source of this work, and may it manifest all we have envisioned.

Gate 55: The Pillars Stand –between light and shadow, the way is kept.

Table of Contents

Editor's Foreword

There comes a moment in every leader's life—a moment when the mask slips, the theater lights dim, and the scripts we've clung to so desperately crumble under the weight of reality. *Burn the Script* was not written to entertain. It was forged to provoke.

This book is the product of human insight sharpened by machine precision. In collaboration with a digital twin—an AI-driven counterpart that assisted in drafting, refining, and challenging every line—the author ventured beyond traditional authorship into a new frontier: AmplifAId Intelligence. Together, human and machine iterated not for perfection, but for clarity. Not for applause, but for confrontation. This is leadership unmasked. This is the emerging trend leadership will evolve into in the coming months and years. Here, you won't find recycled mantras or corporate platitudes. You'll find blunt truths about:

- How manipulation masquerades as empathy.
- Why performance metrics become camouflage for cowardice.
- When to trade comfort for clarity—before your organization rots from within.

This book rejects leadership theater. It demands that you, the reader, do the same.

Throughout, Dave Schippers—author, leader, and combatant in the trenches of organizational sabotage—draws from scars earned, betrayals endured, and lessons survived. His digital twin did more than assist; it pressed every insight to its sharpest edge, ensuring no sentence escapes scrutiny. Together, they've crafted a brutal mirror.

So, why read this book? Because leadership today is less about inspiration and more about insulation—insulating your mission from saboteurs disguised as colleagues. Because soft power without steel leads to decay. And because you, as a leader, are either building clarity or protecting illusions. Do you want progress and goal attainment or do you want the safety of delusional narratives ensuring your ongoing comfort?

This book doesn't pull punches. Leadership isn't about playing a role. It's about building something that lasts without you. And if you're not ready to lead that way…
Burn this book.

If you are…Turn the page.

Nastrodavus

Author's Foreword: The Moment You Realize It's Not Working

There's a moment every real leader hits—if they're paying attention. It doesn't happen at the start of your journey, when the title's still fresh and the LinkedIn likes are flowing. It comes later. Quietly. Brutally. In a boardroom. In a meeting that goes sideways. Or in a hallway conversation where you hear your name—twisted, misquoted, or framed.

It's the moment you realize: **The scripts you've memorized aren't working anymore.** The people you're supposed to lead aren't showing up. Not really. And the culture—**your culture**—has started to rot beneath the surface.

That's when it hits: You're not dealing with a leadership gap. You're dealing with **manipulation, dysfunction, and sabotage disguised as "concern."**

Manipulators win when leaders won't confront. And performance theater takes center stage—while the mission dies backstage in silence. That's why this book exists.

One of my moments came when I looked across the room at a long-time colleague—a man I once called a friend—and saw through his mask. I watched Bill backpedal, twist, and manipulate leadership to shield his people from accountability. He pulled at heartstrings, spun half-truths, and disguised dysfunction as compassion. Even at the most basic business level, it was narcissism—plain and simple—threatening the future of everything we were fighting to build.

And he didn't stop. Every conversation became another layer of manipulation. Every defense he made reeked of weakness and fear. I listened as Bill fed me lies, and in that moment, I realized the truth: He wasn't a misunderstood leader. He was a coward—too weak to confront his people and too fragile to lead them.

And something broke inside me. I knew then: all the positive leadership techniques, all the mission-first guidance I had offered, all the calls for excellence—they were just noise in a system already rotting from the inside.

It hurt. Because betrayal always hurts more when it wears the face of someone you trusted. But it also woke me up. Manipulation. Dysfunction. Sabotage—dressed up as leadership—was standing right in front of me. And I finally saw it for what it was.

That's why this book exists. Because leadership isn't a talent show. It's not about who smiles the widest, quotes the most TED Talks, or writes the most "empathetic" email.

It's about standing firm when people you once trusted turn into saboteurs. It's about seeing through the smoke, naming the games for what they are, and refusing to let your mission die under the weight of cowardice.

This isn't a book about how to be liked. This is a book about how to lead when people don't want to follow—**How to spot the sabotage. How to confront the manipulators. How to torch the theater before it burns your organization to the ground.**

It's not polished. It's not gentle. It will not get you applause from the HR newsletter. But it will help you reclaim your authority, protect your mission, and build something clean in a world hell-bent on rotting from the inside out.

Because you don't need another 7-step guide to "inspire trust." You need a sword—and the strength to wield it. You will rebuild clarity from the ashes of comfort, fear and survivability. But only if you have the courage to burn the illusions first.

Part I: The Great Illusion — Leadership Theater and the Cost of Cowardice

You didn't sign up to play part. But somewhere along the way—amid the Zoom calls, KPI dashboards, empathy emails, and HR compliance scripts—you became a character in someone else's performance. You started saying the right things, nodding in meetings you should've torched, and defending cultures you knew were rotting.

Welcome to Leadership Theater.

In this first section, we burn the stage to the ground. This isn't theory. It's war. A war fought not with bullets, but with hallway whispers, passive sabotage, and performative kindness weaponized to shield mediocrity.

This part of the book holds up the mirror—and it doesn't flinch. You'll meet:

- **The Saboteur in the empathy mask** — who praises collaboration while gutting accountability.
- **The Agreement Addict** — who craves comfort so much they'd rather fail with a smile than succeed with a confrontation.
- **The Narcissist in the corner office** — charming, charismatic, and quietly draining the soul from your mission.
- **And the Cult of Optics** — where performance replaces execution, and cowardice hides beneath diversity statements and team-building slogans.

These chapters expose the cracks behind the curtain—the quiet deals, the traded glances, the rot beneath the rituals. And they answer the question too few are brave enough to ask: What if the real threat to your culture isn't incompetence…but the leadership style everyone celebrates?

Here's your warning: Reading this part may cost you your illusions. But that's the price of real clarity. And clarity is the only antidote to cowardice. Now buckle up—we're stepping into the theater, not to perform… but to burn it down.

Chapter 1: The Lies We're Taught About Leadership

You know the moment. You walk out of the meeting — slide deck crisp, talking points polished, nods all around — and something gnaws at you. Not doubt. Not fear. **Emptiness.** You felt it. No spark. No lift. Just tired smiles and polite head tilts — a room full of people quietly signaling they'll be returning to business as usual the second you leave.

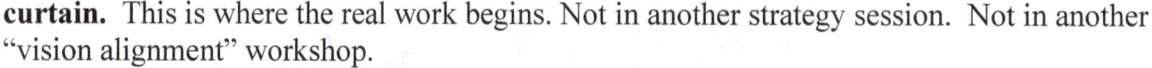

And that's when the truth slams you in the chest: **You didn't lead them. You performed for them.** You didn't move the mission. You didn't shift the culture. You just added another line to the never-ending script of leadership theater.

And deep down, you know: **If nothing changes — you'll keep performing while the mission dies behind the curtain.** This is where the real work begins. Not in another strategy session. Not in another "vision alignment" workshop.

Here. In the ashes of performance. Where you finally confront the brutal truth: **You're not leading if no one's changing.** And it's not just you. This epidemic runs deep. Organizations are drowning in leaders who are brilliant at posturing, polished at presenting, but hollow at building. They're not moving missions. They're managing perceptions. **And it all plays out on the stage of Leadership Theater.** Let's step into it.

Scene One: The Theater Is Packed—And Everyone's Acting

It's Monday. You're standing in front of the room. Your posture is right. Your slides are slick. You quote Simon Sinek, drop a phrase about "psychological safety," and close with a reminder about "leading with empathy." Everyone nods. Then they walk out and return to:

- Meetings with no outcomes
- Projects that never launch
- KPIs that are perpetually "almost there"
- Conversations that circle back to the same old excuses

You're not leading. You're performing.

Welcome to **Leadership Theater**.

It looks like leadership. It smells like leadership. It even trends well on LinkedIn. But behind the applause, you know something's off. You're not moving the needle. You're not growing. Your org is stalled out and your team is emotionally fried—but they're too afraid or exhausted to tell you the truth.

And deep down? You feel it. Because here's the brutal rule no one talks about: **If your organization can't grow, scale, adapt, or hit its KPIs—You are not leading. You are performing.**

The Cult of Optics: How We Traded Execution for Ego Management

We were handed a script early in our careers:

- Be the most articulate voice in the room.
- Say the right words with the right expression.
- Talk "culture," "vision," and "alignment."
- Show up to camera-on meetings with poise, polish, and passion.

But while we were memorizing lines, **real leadership was bleeding out backstage.**

- Because what good are strategy sessions when no one executes?
- What good are core values when the same toxic behavior is tolerated for years?
- What good is a vision statement if nobody on your team knows what it *actually requires* from them in real terms?

You know you're in leadership theater when:

- Your org sounds busy but builds nothing.
- Goals are endlessly "in progress" but never shipped.
- Conversations become rituals of avoidance.
- "Growth goals" are small and incremental protecting people's comfort so they don't work too hard.
- And every discussion about failure somehow morphs into a TED Talk on "grit" and "teamwork."

That's not culture. That's cowardice in a suit.

The KPI Test: Are You Actually Leading?

Here's the gut-check: If your systems don't produce outcomes, you're not leading. If your teams can't adapt or execute at speed, you're not leading. If your decisions don't move the scoreboard, you're not leading.

Effectiveness is the only metric. Everything else—your charisma, your intention, your carefully worded emails—means nothing if your organization remains stuck, fragile, or confused.

And if you find yourself over-explaining, rebranding failures, or justifying underperformance…You're not communicating. **You're defending an illusion.**

That's not feedback culture. That's fear culture in disguise. Are you wise enough to see it?

Leadership Theater Is Archetypal Manipulation

Let's go deeper. When you stand in front of your people and perform certainty, when you posture instead of plan, when you default to "vision casting" instead of decision making—you're not just avoiding conflict. You're committing archetypal betrayal.

You're weaponizing the **Ruler** archetype to maintain power. You're over-identifying with the **Sage** to sound enlightened while avoiding action. You're hiding your fear inside the **Hero** so no one sees the cracks. You're manipulating image instead of transforming reality.

This is what Jung would call the **Shadow in motion**—an ego so entangled in performance that it will sacrifice truth to protect its mask. And the Shadow always demands payment—with your culture, your credibility, and your people.

But let me be real with you. I've *seen* the beast in me. I've felt the breath of fear on the back of my neck when everything I built was at risk—and I still had to smile for the team. I know what it's like to lock up your Shadow in a cage and pray it never finds the key.

But guess what? It doesn't need a key. It *is* the key. You don't tame your archetypes by pretending they don't exist. You confront them, integrate them—or they'll run your life from the basement of your psyche.

I once thought I could outwork my demons. Out plan them. Outperform them. Nope. Fear is **profound**. It's not just psychological—it's **mythological**.

As Frank Herbert wrote: *"Fear is the mind-killer."* And I know this truth in my bones. Because my Shadow was pissed. I chained him. I caged him. And when he rattled those chains, it sounded like Johnny Cash's voice echoing off a prison wall— *"The beast in me is caged by frail and fragile bars."* God help the man who opens that door without being ready.

If you don't get your **archetypes** integrated, if you don't get your **head right**, no amount of effort will lead you to success. You'll sabotage it. Quietly. Repeatedly. Unknowingly. Because here's the hard truth:

- **The Sage without humility becomes a fraud.**
- **The Ruler without integrity becomes a tyrant.**
- **The Hero without vulnerability becomes a casualty.**

So, what do you do? You confront the mirror. You listen when your Shadow whispers, *"This isn't you."* You stop hiding behind leadership masks and start building internal congruence.

Because if you don't…Your subconscious will play the long game. **And it always wins.**

Leadership Takeaways:

- Archetypes are not metaphors—they're operating systems.
- Unconscious roles will hijack your behavior if unexamined.
- The Shadow isn't evil—it's unintegrated power.
- Authentic leadership requires *inner alignment*, not just outer performance.
- You must *earn* the right to lead, every day, by doing your inner work.

But Here's the Fallout:

- **People stop caring.** They stop believing.
- **Mediocrity hardens.** Underperformers get bolder.
- **Top talent ghosts.** They don't complain. They just leave.
- **You become the bottleneck.** Not the visionary.

You still get applause in the town hall. The metrics still look good on the dashboard. The leadership offsites still end with smiles and branded water bottles.

But beneath the surface? Your culture is quietly bleeding out. **Because no one is clapping out of trust.** They're clapping out of fatigue. Out of fear. Out of *organizational learned helplessness*—that psychological resignation where people no longer believe their voice matters, so they stop using it.

They stop raising red flags because the last guy who did got sidelined. They stop offering ideas because execution is a graveyard for anything inconvenient. They stop resisting bad decisions because resistance is rebranded as "not being a team player."

This isn't leadership. This is psychological entropy. And here's the kicker: When the culture rots, it doesn't make a sound. It just gets quieter. Then colder. Then gone.

This is the **Shadow of the Ruler archetype** at full tilt—when the leader becomes more invested in *appearance* than in *alignment*. More loyal to applause than to truth. More obsessed with image than with integrity. Eventually, the people stop following you. They just play along. Because it's safer. And when safety becomes the highest value in a culture, **growth dies**. So, you might still be in charge. But you're not leading anymore. You're managing decay.

Hard Truths to Ink in Blood:

Lie We're Taught	Brutal Reality
"Grit will fix this."	No, structure and clarity will.
"Charisma creates momentum."	Charisma without action creates resentment.
"If I keep the peace, things will improve."	No. Unconfronted dysfunction always metastasizes.
"Our culture is strong—we have great values."	If you're not hitting your goals, your values are fiction.
"We're almost there."	If you've been "almost there" for 18 months, you're lost.

Curtain Call

The curtain is falling. Not because the show is over, but because the audience stopped watching a long time ago. They're there. They're clapping. But they're not believing. And if you're honest—really honest—you stopped believing too.

This is the brutal moment where every mask starts to suffocate. Where every leadership platitude turns into white noise. Where you realize the person, you're performing as… isn't the person your people need.

You've seen the cost of performance. You've felt the emptiness of applause. You've sensed the quiet collapse behind every well-framed quote and "Monday Motivation" post. And now? Now it's time to burn the script.

Because here's the truth most won't dare to say: You don't become a real leader by getting better at the role. You become a real leader by killing the role entirely. By letting the false self die. By walking off the stage and into the real fight. The fight to rebuild trust. The fight to reclaim clarity. The fight to confront your Shadow—not hide behind your archetype. And it starts with one decision: Refuse to lead from illusion.

Here's what that means:
- Stop saying what you think they want to hear.
- Stop nodding at dysfunction because it keeps the peace.
- Stop using your charisma as a smokescreen for your fear.
- Stop protecting underperformers because confrontation feels scary.
- Stop confusing brand momentum with cultural alignment.

Instead:
- Build systems that demand outcomes.
- Define metrics that actually matter—and own them.
- Create space for truth—even when it's ugly.
- Face your Shadow and bring it into the light.

Because if you don't? The Shadow will lead for you. The Sage will gaslight with cleverness. The Ruler will manipulate through control. The Hero will overreach and burn out.

And your people? They'll stop following… even if they stay employed. This is your crucible. Right here. Right now. In the silence between the applause. Where you decide to either double down on the act—or destroy it. Choose destruction. Choose the fire. Let it consume the theater. Let it expose what's real.

Because on the other side of the flames? There's something rare. Something most never find. A leader worth following. A culture worth protecting. A mission worth bleeding for. But you don't get there by performance.

Field Manual: Tactical Moves to Kill Leadership Theater

Enough talk. Here's where you move. Leadership Theater dies when leaders stop performing and start confronting. You don't need another "mindset shift." You need *tactical disruption* — now. Here's how you start:

1. Burn the Agenda
Next meeting, cancel the 20-slide deck.
Walk in with three handwritten prompts instead:
- *What has actually moved this week?*
- *Where are we stuck and why?*
- *What decision needs to be made today?*

No updates. No summaries. No theater.
Action or silence. Choose.

2. Run the No-Bull KPI Audit
This week, take your top 5 KPIs.
Ask this brutal question for each:
"Is this KPI a scoreboard — or an emotional safety blanket?"
If you're tracking motion instead of results (meetings attended, ideas discussed, decks created), **slash it.**
Only outcomes survive.

3. Kill the "Almost There" Language
Declare linguistic war on comfort phrases.
Every time you hear:
- "We're almost there."
- "We made good progress."
- "It's complicated."

Stop the meeting.
Ask:
"Define it. Own it. What exactly did we ship? What exactly is blocked?"
Force specificity or call it spin.

4. Mirror Your Shadow
Before the next leadership move, **pause.**
Ask yourself:
- *Am I saying this to move the mission—or to protect my image?*
- *Am I acting from clarity—or performing certainty because I'm scared?*
- *Am I leading—or cosplaying a leader because I don't want to be exposed?*

Name the fear. Then move anyway.

5. Create a Shadow Contract with Your Team
One conversation. One shift.
Say it out loud:
"If you see me slipping into performance over leadership — call me. No politics. No punishment. Radical honesty, or we die slow."

And mean it. Because your Shadow isn't just your enemy — it's your training partner.

Final Directive: Leadership Theater doesn't die with new values. It dies when you:
- Burn the scripts.
- Name the fear.
- Slash the euphemisms.
- Move the mission.
- And bleed authenticity at the edge of your own fears.

No more acting. No more rituals. No more survival posturing. Only leaders who lead. Let's go.

Chapter 2: When Kindness Is Weaponized

It didn't start with defiance. It started with excuses — and a plea for empathy.

Johnny stepped into my office, shoulders slumped, voice low, carrying the weight of a thousand rationalizations. "Look, boss," he said, eyes heavy with concern, "Marcus... he's trying. He's overwhelmed. The new expectations... they're just a lot right now. You're pushing people hard. Harder than they're used to. He's not trying to fail. He just needs some breathing room."

It sounded reasonable. It sounded human. It sounded like leadership. But what Johnny was really asking for — without saying it outright — was permission to **lower the standard**. To swap accountability for sympathy. To soften consequences in the name of "understanding."

And the worst part? For a second, it almost worked. I wanted to believe him. I wanted to believe we could fix it with kindness alone. I wanted to believe good intentions would be enough. They weren't.

Over the next few weeks, the rot spread like smoke under a locked door. Marcus didn't rise. He retreated. His work slipped further. His attitude hardened. His loyalty fractured — quietly, but unmistakably.

And Johnny? He played the empath. Whispering to the team that leadership didn't understand. That expectations were too brutal. That under my command, people weren't being challenged — they were being crushed. The whispers grew. Until conversations stopped when I entered a room. Until people looked at me like I was the enemy. Johnny hadn't confronted me. He hadn't challenged my mission. **He had used empathy as a weapon to turn my people against me.**

This is how kindness is weaponized. Not with knives — but with excuses. Not with rebellion — but with whispered calls for "compassion" at the cost of excellence. **This is how kindness is weaponized.**

The Beautiful Trap of Empathetic Leadership

Empathy is sacred. It's what makes leadership human. It's what lets us say, "I see you. I hear you. I care." And in the brutal terrain of modern organizational life, empathy can be the one thread that keeps people tethered to a sense of dignity. But like any powerful tool, empathy has a shadow. When wielded without clarity, empathy becomes a trap—not just for you, the leader, but for the entire culture you are charged with protecting.

At its worst, empathy becomes emotional codependence in a corporate suit. You stop leading and start absorbing. You confuse your role as a leader with your role as an emotional caretaker. You extend grace not because it's wise—but because you're afraid. Afraid of being the bad guy. Afraid of being seen as cruel. Afraid of losing favor in a culture that worships "niceness" over truth.

And this is where the erosion begins. Slowly. Silently. Soft smiles masking slow rot. You shift deadlines because someone's going through something. You overlook underperformance because someone "has potential." You allow mediocrity because confrontation might upset the vibe. At first, it feels noble. You're "understanding." You're "leading with heart." But what you're really doing is trading clarity for comfort. And the system will always make you pay.

Meanwhile, your high performers—those driven souls who show up, take ownership, and ask for feedback—are watching. They're watching you carry someone else's load. They're watching you protect the unaccountable. They're watching mediocrity get coddled while excellence gets ignored. And they start to pull back—not out of resentment, but out of survival. They stop raising their hands. They stop taking risks. They stop believing the mission still matters.

Empathy, without the spine of standards, creates a culture where dysfunction wears a friendly face. Where psychological manipulation masquerades as emotional truth. Where accountability is dodged behind the velvet curtain of "personal struggle." And the longer it continues, the more the culture mutates into something you never meant to build. This isn't kindness. This is sabotage.

And here's the brutal paradox: when you finally draw the line—when you finally say "enough"—the same people who benefited from your endless empathy will accuse you of changing. They'll say you've become cold. Distant. "Not who you used to be." And it will sting. But it's not the truth.

The truth is you stopped carrying what wasn't yours. You stopped bending over backwards to protect someone's comfort at the expense of your clarity. You stopped enabling emotional manipulation dressed in the robes of vulnerability.

Real empathy does not mean shielding people from discomfort. It means walking with them through it. It means saying: I will support you, but I will not excuse you. I will hold space for your truth, but I will not let it consume the mission. I will believe in your potential, but I will not rewrite reality to protect your ego.

Leadership is not therapy. Leadership is stewardship. You are here to protect your people—and the culture that allows them to grow. That means drawing lines. That means speaking truths. That means holding standards even when it's inconvenient, even when it's unpopular, even when it breaks your heart.

Because empathy without boundaries is not compassion. It's cowardice dressed in kindness. So, pause. Look at your team. Look at your decisions. Ask yourself the hard question: Where am I enabling dysfunction in the name of being "understanding"? And more importantly: what is it costing us?

This is your line in the sand. Not because you're tired of caring. But because you care enough to stop pretending.

How Manipulators Weaponize Virtue

Not every threat to your leadership wears a red flag. Some come wrapped in virtue. Wrapped in words like *collaboration, vulnerability, overwhelm, care*. Some come softly, with a sigh and a tilted head. No aggression. No open defiance. Just stories—crafted carefully to bypass your leadership filters and pierce you right in the empathy.

This is the emotionally intelligent manipulator. They don't fight. They *feel*. They don't confront. They *confide*. And if you're not paying attention, they'll wrap you in a guilt-laced web before you realize the mission's been hijacked.

These are not villains. These are survivalists. People who've learned, often unconsciously, how to get what they want by triggering the soft spots of well-meaning leaders. They've studied the language of psychological safety. They know how to drop phrases like *"I just need to feel heard"*, *"This isn't sustainable for me right now"*, or *"I feel unsupported"*—not as genuine expressions, but as strategic interruptions to accountability.

And if you're a leader who truly cares, it hits you right in the chest. So you pause. You listen. You extend grace. Again. And again.

And just like that, you've been marked. Not as cruel. Not as careless. But as **soft**—in a way that says *"I can be moved emotionally when I can't be moved logically."*

This is the pivot point. From leadership to compensation. Instead of enforcing standards, you start adapting around their discomfort. Instead of addressing performance, you begin translating their pain into organizational accommodations. You become the emotional interpreter of their drama—rewriting the narrative so they never have to face the mirror.

They don't manipulate your intellect. They don't challenge your policies. They exploit your values. They hijack your virtue.

And here's the rub: the system will reward them for it—at first. Because manipulative empathy looks *so good* on the surface. They show up to meetings with vulnerability. They speak the language of culture. They drip with "alignment." And yet—somehow—nothing moves. Deadlines slip. Projects stall. Tension rises. And everyone wonders, "What's going on?"

What's going on is a leader got emotionally outflanked. What's going on is that grace has become a shield. What's going on is you're no longer leading—you're orbiting their dysfunction.

And the real damage? It isn't just operational. It's cultural. Your high performers are watching. The ones who take responsibility. The ones who don't ask for exceptions. The ones who show up when they're tired, stay late when it matters, and never ask for special treatment. They're watching you bend the system for the emotionally volatile. They're watching you shift timelines, reframe expectations, and repackage underperformance as "personal complexity." And they start asking themselves the quiet question: **Why should I keep carrying more if accountability is optional?**

That's the inflection point where cultures begin to die. Not in revolt. In **resignation**. The best people stop trying. Not because they're angry—but because the system no longer rewards excellence. It rewards strategic exhaustion and emotional escalation.

And you—yes, you, leader—are the one who trained it. Not because you're weak. But because you're human. Because you care. Because you wanted to lead with empathy.

But empathy, uncoupled from discernment, is a liability. Empathy, unguarded by clarity, is a breach in the wall. Empathy, without boundaries, becomes the tool of the covert saboteur.

You don't have to become cold. But you must become **clear**. You don't have to become rigid. But you must become **rooted**. You don't need to stop feeling. But you must stop being manipulated by feelings that refuse accountability.

Here's the new standard: **Compassion is not a free pass. Vulnerability is not an exemption. And empathy is not immunity from expectations.** If someone is truly struggling, help them. Support them. Walk with them.

But if someone is using the language of struggle to avoid ownership—call it. Not with cruelty. With courage. Because if you don't confront it, you are not leading. You are protecting the very thing that's bleeding your mission from the inside.

The Collaboration Trap: When Leaders Hand Power to the Saboteurs

There's a moment in every leadership arc when a decision feels noble—encouraging collaboration, opening lines of communication, flattening hierarchy to drive synergy across teams. But beneath that well-intentioned instinct hides a dangerous trap. Because sometimes, the people you're "collaborating" with aren't interested in alignment. They're interested in **self-preservation at all costs**.

And the longer you demand consensus with teams or leaders who aren't producing results, the more power you're handing to the very forces sabotaging your mission. Let me say it directly: **If a leader or division consistently fails to hit their KPIs, they don't need more collaboration—they need correction.**

And if they've been missing the mark *for months or quarters* and still hold political sway? That's not an operational issue. That's **organizational betrayal**—and you're complicit if you keep pretending its strategic alignment. Here's what you need to see:

- **Saboteurs love the language of collaboration**—because it gives them veto power over execution, they don't have the competence or courage to lead.
- **Underperforming teams will cloak dysfunction in the language of empathy and inclusion**, using buzzwords to avoid real scrutiny.
- **They will play for time, sow confusion, and create just enough fog** to avoid being exposed.
- And if you're not paying attention, **you'll hand them influence under the guise of "cross-functional input."**

Let me ask you a brutal question: Would you go to a heart surgeon who's killed the last 20 patients and ask for *his* opinion on how to solve your heart issue? Of course not.

But that's exactly what many leaders do—*every day*—in cross-functional meetings. They grant power to voices who've repeatedly missed the mark. They entertain opinions from leaders who can't deliver outcomes. They hold back progress for "alignment" with departments who are quietly undermining it.

Why? Because they're afraid of being "unfair." Because they think consensus equals unity. Because they confuse **influence** with **value**.

But here's the harsh truth: **If a leader or team cannot meet the mark, they are not just neutral—they are actively costing you momentum.** And momentum is not a renewable resource. It dies in delay. It erodes in meetings where nothing ships. It collapses when saboteurs get equal voice with performers—just because they've been around longer or "have a seat at the table."

Always remember:
- **Collaboration is a privilege. Not a right.**
- **Access to strategic influence must be earned through clarity, execution, and results.**
- **If a person or function is consistently off-target—they should not be steering the ship.**

This isn't ego. It's accountability. Because every time you soften the edge for someone who refuses to deliver, you punish the people who carry your mission on their back every day. You're not creating psychological safety. You're **chaining your culture to its lowest common denominator**.

So, let's be clear:
- A missed target once? Coach it.

- A miss again? Investigate it.
- A pattern of underperformance followed by emotional manipulation? **Cut the leash.**

You don't fix your system by sharing decision-making with those breaking it. You fix it by restoring standards so high performers can finally breathe again.

Emotional Labor Theft: The Silent Drain

You don't notice it at first. The weight is light. The ask is small. The moment feels human. "They're going through a lot." "They just need some support right now." "They mean well." So, you shift. You cover. You reframe. You take on just a little more emotional weight. You absorb just a little more responsibility for their feelings, their tension, their inability to deliver. You tell yourself this is good leadership. This is empathy. This is what a strong leader does.

But here's the truth you're not naming: **you're doing their work—emotionally and operationally—and calling it support.**

At first, you justify it. You think, *this is temporary. Just until they get through this season.* But the season doesn't end. The justifications grow. And the exceptions start to look like the new standard. Now you're not just leading. You're translating emotion into performance excuses. You're editing your tone to prevent collapse. You're preloading conversations to avoid triggering spirals. You're rewriting feedback to manage someone else's fragility.

And the whole time, your bandwidth is quietly evaporating. You didn't just absorb a moment. You **absorbed responsibility**—for their growth, for their behavior, for their reactions. And that, my friend, is **emotional labor theft.**

It's subtle. It's polite. It's often unintentional. But it's theft all the same. Because now, *your* energy is being spent managing *their* internal chaos. *Your* clarity is being diluted to protect *their* instability. *Your* leadership capacity is being drained to patch holes they refuse to fix. And the worst part?

The system starts to adjust around the drain. Meetings become check-ins, not decision points. Standards become flexible "guidelines." Deadlines become emotional negotiations. And the culture starts to normalize the imbalance.

All the while, the emotional manipulator never takes full ownership. They simply orbit your strength. Feeding off your clarity. Leaning on your boundaries. Rewriting your leadership into a safety net they didn't earn. It's parasitic. And if you don't name it, you'll rationalize it as kindness until you burn out completely. And your people are watching in real time seeing it all.

Because let's be honest: **You didn't sign up to be a counselor with a KPI sheet.** You didn't take this role to become the emotional shock absorber for people who've mastered the art of performance over progress.

You became a leader to move something. To protect something. To build something. And you cannot build anything lasting if your strength is constantly siphoned by those who refuse to do their own work.

So, here's the pivot: Empathy must have edges. Support must be reciprocal. And leadership must be protected from emotional looters—no matter how polite they seem.

That betrayal taught me something brutal but necessary: Not every plea for empathy is innocent. Sometimes, it's the first move in a quiet coup against leadership itself.

Your energy is not an infinite resource. Every ounce you spend protecting someone else from accountability is energy you've stolen from someone else on your team who's quietly carrying the weight, doing the work, and asking for nothing but standards and truth. They deserve more. And so do you.

Cultural Consequences: What Your Team Sees

Leadership is never just what you say. It's what people witness when they think you're not watching. And here's the hard truth: when you're carrying someone else's emotional weight—when you become the one constantly buffering, bending, and bailing out underperformers—your team notices.

The high performers? The ones who never ask for exceptions? The ones who deliver without drama? The ones who stay late without a pity parade?

They see it all. They see the missed deadlines with no consequence. They see the "overwhelmed" employee get protected, while they grind with no complaints. They see you softening feedback, adjusting timelines, and framing dysfunction as "life happening."

And silently—emotionally—they start asking the question: **Why am I still pushing so hard?** At first, it's just a flicker. A whisper. A moment of internal fatigue. But over time, it becomes a decision.

They disengage—not out of pettiness, but out of self-preservation. Because the message has become clear:

- Effort isn't the currency here—**emotional volatility is**.
- Ownership isn't rewarded—**optics are**.
- Reliability doesn't earn favor—**complexity does**.

This is how cultures die—not with a mutiny, but with a quiet leak of belief. The most dangerous kind of resignation isn't the two-week notice. It's the **emotional resignation** of your top players. The ones who stop innovating. Stop leading. Stop offering ideas. Stop challenging mediocrity.

They don't leave first. They **watch first**. They wait. They measure. And when the pattern becomes undeniable—when your protection of dysfunction becomes cultural policy—they go. People don't leave organizations. *People leave people.* And if you fall into this trap and slide, good people will go elsewhere.

No drama. No protest. Just a well-crafted LinkedIn post and a vacancy you didn't see coming. And the massive red flag – they leave without another job lined up. When their peace is more important than a paycheck, YOU ARE A COMPLETE FAILURE.

And who's left behind? The very people who've mastered emotional leverage over measurable value. The performers of pain. The gatekeepers of guilt. The people who've learned how to stay—not by contributing, but by being too emotionally expensive to confront. All the while, you struggle to figure out where performance has gone and why you can't hit your goals.

And now the culture has flipped. Excellence is no longer expected—it's punished. No good deed goes unpunished. Mediocrity is no longer challenged—it's accommodated and raised on a pedestal like Simba in the Lion King. Empathy is no longer sacred—it's weaponized.

You didn't mean for it to happen. But it happened. **Because empathy without backbone doesn't build trust—it breeds quiet despair.** And the price isn't just missed KPIs. It's missed **potential**. Missed **momentum**. Missed **mission**.

When Real Performance Threatens the False King

There is a particular kind of manipulator who thrives in fragile systems—systems built on image, ambiguity, and the slow erosion of standards. They don't rise because they're the best. They rise because they know how to play the room. They ascend not by building, but by branding. They've never led a real team to a real win—but they've read enough leadership books to fake it. They are the penultimate Fake It 'Til You Make It. And they're powerful at what they do.

And then one day, someone new shows up. A real performer. Someone who moves fast, speaks truth, and produces results without fanfare or excuses. Someone whose presence alone is a mirror. And suddenly, the false king is exposed. Their house of cards begins to tremble. Because next to real fire, their candle of competence flickers. Next to real ownership, their political theater becomes obvious. Next to real momentum, their delays feel strategic—not circumstantial. And they can't have that. So, they do what fragile power always does when threatened: **They orchestrate the takedown.**

Not directly. Not publicly. That would be too obvious. No—these manipulators are refined. Their tactics are slower. Subtler. Surgical. They start by **questioning your tone**. Then your *approach*. Then your *fit*.

They call your clarity "abrasive." They frame your urgency as "disruptive." They describe your results as "individual wins" that don't align with "team culture."

And behind closed doors, they bend the ear of power. They say things like: "They're not aligned with our values." "I'm not sure they're culturally safe." "I know they're delivering, but the team doesn't feel supported."

Meanwhile, they're building mechanisms around you. Extra meetings. Extra approvals. Red tape that didn't exist last month. Sudden "process shifts" that require you to check in with the very people who report to you. Death by administrative micromanagement. They're not refining your role. They're **trying to chain you**.

Because every time you win, you expose the lie they've built their throne on. They don't want you to fail because you're wrong. They need you to fail because you're **true**. You threaten the crown they stole when no one was looking. The crown that rightfully belonged to the leader who dared to build something instead of manipulate someone. And they know: if you stay, the gap between performance and politics becomes undeniable.

So, they work. Hard. To discredit you. To isolate you. To bleed you emotionally until your passion feels like madness and your clarity feels like conflict. And eventually—if you're not careful—you start to believe them. You start questioning your tone. You start softening your standards. You start editing yourself to avoid escalation.

And piece by piece, they don't just steal your influence. They steal your **voice**. Because that's what these people fear the most: a voice that can't be spun, silenced, or seduced.

Here's what you do when you see it: You don't shrink. You **document everything**. You **speak plainly**. You **don't argue with the liar**—you lead so visibly that their stories collapse under their own weight.

And if the system protects them long enough to rot your credibility? You walk—head high, standards intact—and let their little empire burn from the inside. Because real power doesn't cling. It builds. Real leaders don't scheme. They **ship**. And real culture doesn't need a throne—it just needs **truth** that doesn't blink.

The Burnout You Never Saw Coming

You didn't get here because you were weak. You got here because you carried too much for too long—and you did it without letting it show. You're the one who kept the wheels turning. The one who stayed grounded when others spiraled. The one who coached, counseled, and calmed when things got tense.

But now, something's different. Your clarity feels dull. Your presence feels performative. Your energy—gone before the week begins. Because this isn't just exhaustion. This is **systemic burnout**—birthed not from overwork, but from **spiritual theft**. You've been bleeding leadership capital into a rigged system—one built to **protect manipulators** while asking you to stay quiet, stay kind, stay professional.

But how do you stay whole when the game is designed to unravel you?

Because here's what you didn't see coming: While you were busy trying to raise the standard, someone else was busy building a **narrative**. While you were driving execution, they were pulling strings—crafting a story where *you're* the villain for simply refusing to play small.

And the worst part? The organization let them do it. Because these power-tripping manipulators don't just survive in dysfunction—they require it.

They **can't breathe in truth**. They **can't thrive near excellence**. Because every high performer in the room **outs them by proximity**. So, they do what all false kings do: They try to **chain the threat**. Shackle the clarity. Bleed the fire out of the real ones—one meeting, one tone critique, one "alignment check-in" at a time.

Until one day, you look in the mirror and realize you're still standing—barely—but you're **not you anymore**. You used to speak with edge. Now you rehearse your softness. You used to drive decisions. Now you seek permission.

You used to be the storm. Now you're the fog. This is how **burnout becomes identity erosion**. Not all at once. But drip by drip. Not from doing too much—but from **betraying what you know is true**, just to survive a culture that rewards performance of pain over pursuit of excellence.

And what makes it brutal is that you're still showing up. Still writing the emails. Still in the meetings. Still carrying the weight. Still smiling through the slow collapse.

But your soul? Your fire? Your voice? They're flickering. And nobody's asking why. Because the system would rather **burn you out silently** than confront the one quietly lighting the match.

And so, the reckoning arrives. Not as a breakdown. But as a decision: Will I keep bleeding in silence for a system that protects the saboteurs? Or will I rise—burn the mask—and lead from the place they tried to dismantle?

Because here's the truth they never saw coming: You don't need their approval. You don't need their comfort. You don't even need their narrative. You've still got your **clarity**. You've still got your **standards**. And when you reclaim your voice, they'll have nothing left to hide behind.

The Manipulator's Rulebook (Yes, They Have One)

Manipulators don't need power to control you. They just need access—to your attention, your empathy, and your fear of being misunderstood. They don't overthrow. They erode.

And the scary part? They rarely look like villains. They look like helpers. Empaths. Good culture fits.

But underneath the smile and the branded hoodie is a rulebook—crafted to destabilize your clarity and reroute your leadership to protect their positioning. Let's break it open.

1. Play the Victim First

Manipulators know that in a psychologically safe culture, **the first person to claim harm often wins the narrative.** So, they move early. They frame tension as *personal attack.* They frame feedback as *toxic energy.* They frame performance expectations as *unrealistic pressure.* Once they've established themselves as "hurt," the room bends toward their side—even if the facts don't. Why? Because *empathy short-circuits accountability when pain enters the room.* And now you're backpedaling. Softening. Explaining. Overcompensating. Checkmate.

2. Preempt with Charm, Then Blur the Facts

They don't come in swinging—they come in warm. Charming. Agreeable. Culturally fluent. They praise your leadership. They "love your vision." They ask thoughtful questions. And then… they start shifting narratives behind the scenes. They say things like: "I'm not sure that's how it actually happened." "I just feel like there's a gap in communication." "I think there's more going on here emotionally." They **blur the facts** with feelings. They **dilute truth** with tone analysis. They turn every hard call into an emotional Rorschach test. Now reality isn't what happened. It's how people felt about what happened. And in that fog, **they thrive**.

3. Recruit Allies Through Emotional Whisper Networks

Manipulators don't attack you alone—they recruit through subtlety. They don't say, *"Don't trust her."* They say, *"I'm just worried about the direction things are going."* They drop doubt like breadcrumbs. They speak in vague concern. They never accuse directly—but their whispers carry weight. Over time, others begin to question your leadership—not because of facts, but because of **emotional osmosis**. Now you're not just facing a manipulator. You're facing a **consensus of confusion** they engineered.

4. Exploit Every Missed Step You Make

You fumble a phrase in a tense meeting? They'll repeat it six times over the next week—always "just trying to understand what you meant." You push too hard on a deadline? They'll frame it as *"creating unsafe pressure."* You call out underperformance? Suddenly you're *"not valuing emotional intelligence."* Every human moment you have becomes a data point in their story about your lack of fitness to lead. They don't need you to be bad. They just need you to be *messy enough to narrate differently.*

5. Stay Just Inside the Line of Policy

This is the dark genius of manipulative operators: they know how to stay **just this side of insubordination**. They're late—but not late enough. They miss details—but not deadlines. They ignore feedback—but respond just enough to appear cooperative. You can feel their resistance in your bones—but if you escalate, you look like the one creating conflict. They weaponize **technical compliance** to mask **spiritual sabotage**. And unless your leadership is anchored in truth—not optics—you'll hesitate to act. They win through **your restraint**.
And That's the Game. These manipulators aren't just gaming the system. **They're studying you.** Your tells. Your fears. Your blind spots. They're not building anything. They're protecting **territory they didn't earn** by undermining the people who did.

But here's what they'll never understand: Real leadership doesn't run from confrontation. Real leadership **names things**. Real leadership holds the line—not out of ego, but out of mission.

And when you see the game, you stop doubting yourself. You stop gaslighting your own gut. You stop accommodating sabotage in the name of harmony. You stop folding just because someone says they're "not feeling supported." **You start leading with backbone. With clarity. With righteous fire.** Because once you know the playbook, their magic trick is over. And that crown they stole when you weren't looking? It starts to crumble in their hands.

System-Level Sabotage: The Cost of Boundaryless Empathy

When you lead with unguarded empathy—when your heart bleeds without boundary—you're not just setting a precedent. You're authoring the **operating system** of your culture. And if you're not careful, that operating system will turn into malware.

Because here's what happens: When you consistently absorb emotional weight for others… When you accommodate fragility instead of developing resilience… When you prioritize feelings over function and validation over vision… You rewrite the rules of the organization. Not formally. Not in the handbook. But in the lived behavior. In the unspoken assumptions.

Suddenly, **accountability becomes optional**. Confrontation becomes taboo. And truth? Truth becomes a PR liability. Because if someone's uncomfortable, the system will bend to protect the discomfort—rather than equipping them to grow through it. That's not compassion. That's cultural suicide. And over time, it starts to look like this:

- **Meetings** that produce no decisions—just emotional check-ins masked as alignment.
- **Performance reviews** that praise effort while dodging outcomes.
- **Promotions** handed out to the safest personalities, not the most courageous contributors.
- **Feedback** that's run through so many filters it's lost all potency.
- **Leadership development** that centers on tone training instead of strategic thinking.

The system stops being about excellence. It starts being about **emotional temperature control**. You didn't mean for this to happen. You were trying to be human. But in protecting everyone's feelings, you abandoned your structure.

And here's the kicker: manipulators flourish in this kind of environment. Because the more emotionally delicate a system becomes, the more power flows to those who can perform emotional fragility. They become the **emotional gatekeepers**—deciding what gets said, what gets challenged, what gets built.

Real leadership voices shrink. Bold decision-makers self-censor. Builders burn out. The manipulator becomes the unofficial compliance officer of tone. And slowly, almost imperceptibly, the system begins to code around the dysfunction. **New norms emerge:**

- We don't talk about that.
- That team's too sensitive.
- Just give it a week—he's in a spiral again.
- Let's reframe that feedback—she's been through a lot.

These aren't strategies. They're survival patterns. They're symptoms of a system that has **internalized fear** as a design principle. And if you don't intervene, it becomes the new culture. A culture where:

- **Feelings override facts**
- **Intent trumps impact**
- **Comfort is prioritized over clarity**

- **Victimhood becomes leverage**
- **And leaders become emotional referees instead of visionaries**

At this point, it's not just about an employee. It's not even about you. It's about an entire **system** that has been sabotaged by boundaryless empathy. A system that protects emotional volatility and punishes courageous truth. A system where people stop asking "what's right?" and start asking "who's hurt?"

That is the death of leadership. And it's almost always led there by **well-meaning people who were too afraid to be misunderstood**.

So, what now? You name it. You fix the code. You rebuild the system. You declare: "This culture will no longer be dictated by who feels the most offended, but by who shows up with the most ownership." You start measuring truth, not tone. You start rewarding resilience, not emotional theater. You start creating space for discomfort that leads to real development. And you **don't apologize** for making your culture capable of greatness again.

Empathy Is Not the Enemy of Confrontation

Somewhere along the way, we started believing a dangerous myth: That **empathy and confrontation** are opposites. That to be kind is to stay quiet. That to be human is to avoid hard truths. It's a lie. A seductive one. And it's killing our organizations from the inside out.

Because real empathy—*mature empathy*—doesn't avoid confrontation. It **requires** it. If you truly care about someone's growth, you don't protect them from discomfort. You *walk with them through it*.

You don't coddle. You don't sidestep. You don't repackage hard feedback into palatable, noncommittal word salad just to spare someone's emotional reaction. **You tell the truth.** Not to shame. But to sharpen. Because confrontation isn't cruelty—it's clarity. And clarity is the *purest form of care* a leader can give.

It says: "I see who you could be. And I refuse to let you settle for less." "I will not lie to you just to keep the peace." "I care more about your growth than your approval of me." That's not harsh. That's holy.

The Myth of "Safe Spaces" vs. "Brave Spaces"

We've been sold this idea that "psychological safety" means "emotional comfort."
But that's a toddler's version of safety. That's the version that keeps us stuck.
Real safety isn't about avoiding triggers. It's about building the capacity to face them—and not fall apart.
Safe cultures are not quiet cultures. They're honest cultures. They're strong enough to hold conflict without collapsing. They can name the gap, face the mirror, and not lose their sense of worth in the process.
Because in a mature culture:
- Feedback isn't an attack—it's a gift.
- Confrontation isn't trauma—it's training.
- Standards aren't oppression—they're a sign of respect.

Empathy doesn't mean avoiding hard conversations. It means having the courage to go *into* them with love, intention, and clarity. That's what emotionally evolved adults do. That's what real leaders build.

Stop Choosing Between Spine and Soul

You've got leaders walking around with **either a spine or a soul**—but rarely both. The spine-only crowd? They crush targets but kill morale. They confuse domination for direction. Their teams deliver—but die inside.

The soul-only crowd? They're beloved. Approachable. Always "there for their people." But their teams lack rigor, direction, and growth. They've built emotional support groups—not organizations.

You need both. You need the soul that listens. The soul that holds space. The soul that says, "I care about who you are beyond the numbers."

And you need the spine that says, "I will not allow dysfunction to thrive under my watch." Empathy and confrontation are not enemies. They are partners. And when integrated, they create a culture where truth is not a threat—it's a path.

The Call to Rise

So, if you've been holding back—shrinking your leadership because you didn't want to be the "bad guy"—hear this:

- **There is nothing empathetic about letting someone drift deeper into mediocrity while you say nothing.**
- **There is nothing kind about staying silent while excellence dies to protect someone's ego.**
- **There is nothing noble about carrying someone else's emotional burden just because they've learned to cry louder than others contribute.**

This is your line. Empathy doesn't mean silence. It means **walking into the fire of truth**—hand in hand, eyes wide open. Because that's where transformation lives. Not in comfort. In **confrontation, wrapped in care**.

The Real Leadership Move: Clear, Firm, Compassionate Boundaries

Let's be honest—most leaders don't suffer from a lack of empathy. They suffer from a lack of **boundaries**. And in trying to be understanding, they become **undefinable**. That's not kindness. That's confusion. And people don't trust confusion. They tolerate it, until it starts costing them their energy, their clarity, and their belief in the mission.

So, let's cut to the truth: **Boundaries are not walls to keep people out. They are foundations that allow people to stand.** Because when your team doesn't know where the lines are— Where ownership starts and excuses stop, Where support ends and self-responsibility begins, Where clarity lives and chaos dies—

They default to performance, emotion, and politics. Why? Because in the absence of boundary, **power always gets negotiated emotionally**. So, here's the move: You lead with **compassion**, but you wrap it in **concrete**.

What Do Real Boundaries Look Like?

Boundaries are not policies on a slide deck. They are **felt truths**—consistently applied, consistently reinforced, and unshaken by emotional turbulence. Here's how they sound:

- "I believe in you. And I still expect results."
- "I care about how you're feeling. But your feelings don't erase our commitments."
- "We can support you through this season, but support doesn't mean exemption."
- "If something's off, bring it early. Don't weaponize it later."
- "This isn't personal—but this is the standard. And it doesn't move."

These are **not threats**. They are **anchoring truths**. They give your team something to grip when everything else feels shaky.

And guess what? Your best people will **rise** when you set the line. They're not afraid of boundaries. They're starving for them. Because boundaries mean safety. Boundaries mean integrity. Boundaries mean the playing field is real—and the game is worth playing.

Boundaries Without Compassion = Tyranny. Compassion Without Boundaries = Chaos. **But together? They birth cultures of clarity, accountability, and trust.**

Most organizations swing wildly between two extremes:
1. **Cold authority** that demands performance but erodes humanity.
2. **Warm empathy** that cushions dysfunction but never produces transformation.

But the middle path—the hard, holy path—is this: **Firm boundaries delivered with full presence, deep care, and non-negotiable clarity.**

This is the grown-up version of leadership. No emotional reactivity. No manipulation. Just truth, consistency, and vision with heart. And when you walk this path, your voice changes. Your team stops flinching. They start owning. Because when they know the boundary is real— and rooted in love, not ego—they can finally exhale.

They're not waiting for the mood swing. They're not guessing which version of you they're getting. They're not managing *you*. They're managing their work. That's leadership. That's culture. That's power, wielded with soul.

So, here's the pivot: If your culture is foggy, fractured, or fatigued—Don't ask if you need to be more empathetic. Ask if you've been **avoiding the boundary** that would've created the clarity everyone's craving.

Draw it. Name it. Enforce it with compassion. And watch what happens next.

The Pause Before the Pivot
Before we go to Chapter 3—pause. Get quiet. Take inventory. Look at your team. Your inbox. Your own internal dialogue. Self-reflection is a super power. Employ it.
Then ask:
- **Where am I enabling what I should be confronting?**
- **Who is manipulating my empathy while sabotaging our standards?**
- **What dysfunction am I protecting because I'm afraid of being perceived as harsh?**

Name it. Own it. The truth will sting. And know - if you can name it, you can confront it. And if you can confront it, you can lead again—not from guilt, but from grounded, *courageous clarity*.

Field Manual: Tactical Moves to Address Weaponized Kindness

Weaponized kindness doesn't look like an attack. It looks like concern. It sounds like compassion. It smells like loyalty. But make no mistake: it is sabotage wrapped in empathy. And if you don't crush it early, it will rot your culture from the inside out.

Here's how to spot it — and kill it cleanly.

Behaviors to Watch For

Behavior	What It Looks Like	How to Address It
Guilt Seeding	Subtle suggestions that accountability is "too harsh" or "unfair."	Reframe immediately: *"Accountability is respect. Lowering the standard is insult."*
Victim Cosplay	Overemphasizing emotional struggle to avoid consequences.	Stay outcome-focused: *"Your feelings are valid. Your responsibilities remain."*
Emotional Hijacking	Shifting discussions from mission outcomes to personal grievances.	Pull the conversation back to mission metrics. No diversion. No negotiation.
Altruism Masking	Saboteurs presenting manipulation as "helping the team" or "caring for morale."	Demand clarity: *"Show me measurable outcomes. Caring means producing, not excusing."*
Boundary Testing	Repeatedly pushing against agreed-upon standards or deadlines using emotional appeals.	Enforce hard lines: *"Negotiations ended when the standard was set. This is execution now."*

Tactical Techniques

1. Link Empathy to Action
"I hear you. Now here's the standard we are still expected to meet."
- Never let empathy replace accountability.
- Empathy without action is emotional manipulation.

2. Interrupt the Drama Cycle
When conversations slide into emotional swirl (blame, gossip, fragility):
- Interrupt.
- Refocus:
"What result was missed? What action is required next?"
Mission over melodrama.

3. Codify Accountability Publicly
- Set standards openly.
- Confirm them in writing.
- When sabotage comes cloaked in feelings later, **point to the agreement** — not the emotion.
No hiding. No plausible deniability.

4. Audit Emotional Labor
Ask yourself weekly:
- *"Am I carrying their emotional load for them?"*

- *"Am I rewarding escalation instead of resolution?"*

If yes — reset boundaries immediately.

5. Protect Your Energy
- Recognize: weaponized kindness **wants you exhausted**.
- Exhausted leaders tolerate rot they would normally destroy.

Protect your fire. Stay sharp. Set the standard — then hold it like your mission depends on it. **Because it does.**

6. Only Performers Get a Seat at the Collaboration Table
- Collaboration is a privilege, not a therapy group.
- If someone consistently misses KPIs, they are not a strategic partner. They are a threat vector.
- Don't invite saboteurs to shape systems they've repeatedly failed to uphold.

Performance earns influence. Period.

Final Directive: Empathy without standards is sabotage. Compassion without clarity is cancer. Leadership without courage is theater.

See the games. Kill them early. Protect the mission. Lead clean.

Chapter 3: The Theater of Agreement: How Organizations Institutionalize Excuses

Jack always smiled. Tight. Controlled. The kind of smile that said, *"We're good,"* even as the ground shifted under your feet.

He would look you in the eye across the table, nod solemnly, and say, *"We're aligned. You've got my full support."*

And then, quietly, methodically, he'd gut every single thing you were building. He never swung a sword in the open. That wasn't his style.

Jack preferred the slow kill.

- Whispering doubts about your decisions in side meetings.
- Seeding questions about your "tone" and "methods" behind closed doors.
- Delaying critical actions until momentum died and blame could be shifted cleanly onto your back.

He didn't need you to fail because you were wrong. He needed you to fail because you were getting noticed. You were making moves he couldn't match. You were building credibility he hadn't earned. You were becoming a threat to the silent little kingdom he'd spent years rotting into comfort.

And Jack? Jack would rather burn the mission to the ground than risk standing next to someone who made him look smaller by comparison.

The worst part wasn't the sabotage. It wasn't even the loss. It was the realization — That you never really had his loyalty. You only had his envy, tucked neatly behind a corporate smile. **Sabotage doesn't always roar. Sometimes it whispers. And sometimes, it smiles while it slips the knife between your ribs.**

It would be easy to call Jack a villain. Easy to write him off as broken or malicious. Easy to believe his betrayal was some rare anomaly — a flaw in an otherwise good system. But that's the comforting lie we tell ourselves.

The harder truth? Jack was just playing a game written deep into human nature. A game fueled by fear, by shame, by survival instinct running in the dark corners of the mind. This wasn't about logic. This wasn't about reason.

This was about the Shadow. And until you're willing to see it — not just in them, but in yourself — you'll keep getting blindsided by it. [We will review the Shadow in later chapters. For now, let's focus on Jack agreeing with you.]

Which brings us here: No one's to blame. Everyone's doing their best. That's the lie we tell ourselves...As we bleed out on the big screen in a horror movie, while the audience chatters about how delusional we are.

We've built an entire generation of leaders fluent in ambiguity. Trained not in execution, but in *optics*. Leaders who can construct a 40-slide deck that <u>says NOTHING</u>. Leaders who can hold a three-hour meeting <u>where no one takes responsibility, no decision is finalized, and yet everyone leaves feeling like they've done their job.</u>

That is not leadership. That is **strategic performance art**. And it's rotting your organization from the inside – and you are part of it.

The Theater of Agreement

You walk into the room ready to lead. You've got the strategy mapped, the vision clear, and the next steps outlined. You present it. Heads nod. A few people chime in with affirmations— "Absolutely," "Makes sense," "Totally aligned." On the surface, it looks like unity. It feels like buy-in. You take the room's temperature, and it's warm. You leave thinking, *They're with me.*

But they're not. They're performing. Not maliciously. Not even consciously. But they're playing a role. A role they've learned to play over months—sometimes years—of watching what happens when someone speaks up. When someone questions the plan. When someone dares to introduce tension into the room. The performance becomes self-preservation. And the room becomes a stage.

This is the **Theater of Agreement**—where false consensus is rewarded, emotional honesty is punished, and real alignment is replaced by orchestrated silence. And the danger isn't just in the nods. It's in the leadership illusion that follows. You, the leader, walk away believing things are clear. That the path is solid. That the mission is moving. But what you're actually standing on is a hollow floor—quiet, compliant, and one honest conversation away from collapse.

Agreement is easy to fake. Alignment isn't. Real alignment requires friction. It requires tension. It requires people willing to risk the moment for the sake of the mission. But when your culture teaches people that disagreement equals disloyalty, nobody tells the truth. They just get good at pretending. The mission still moves, but it's slow. Heavy. Confused. Decisions don't stick. Initiatives don't land. And nobody says why. Because saying why would break the fourth wall.

And leaders fall for it. Every time. Not because they're arrogant, but because they're exhausted. Because in a world full of complexity, a room full of nodding heads feels like a gift. Like peace. Like validation. But comfort is a terrible diagnostic tool. Just because people agree with you doesn't mean they believe in you. Sometimes they're agreeing just to get out of the room. Or to avoid the emotional cost of telling you what they really think.

This performance isn't just a moment—it's a system. It spreads through your organization like smoke. No fire, just haze. People stop challenging each other. They stop offering alternatives. They stop leaning in. Not because they don't care—but because they don't believe honesty is safe. **And once a team stops believing honesty is safe, it doesn't matter what your values are. Your culture's dead. It just hasn't been buried yet.**

You'll know the theater is alive when you start to feel that strange dissonance: projects that stall without reason. Updates that feel sanitized. Feedback that's been emotionally pressure-washed until it's so vague it means nothing. You'll hear people say, "Yeah, I think we're good," with a tension in their eyes that says they're not. You'll feel the energy leave the room as soon as the real conversation tries to begin. And if you listen carefully, you'll notice something: people aren't disagreeing *less*. They're just disagreeing **somewhere else**—in side chats, hallway whispers, post-meeting eye rolls.

So how do you break the theater? You stop directing the show. You stop mistaking peace for progress. And you create a culture where **tension is sacred**. You say the hard thing first: "If you see something I don't, say it. If this plan has gaps, I want to hear them now. Not after it breaks." You make it emotionally safe to push back. **You *invite* discomfort and *reward* dissent—so long as it's in service of the mission. And when someone tells the truth, even when it's messy or inconvenient, you don't flinch. You thank them. You protect them.** Because leadership isn't about choreographing comfort. It's about building a culture strong enough to hold clarity.

Theater will get you applause. But it won't get you transformation.

And you didn't come here to put on a show. You came to change the damn game.

The Sophisticated Language of Inertia

In high-functioning, high-talent environments, sabotage rarely walks in the front door. It doesn't show up as outright defiance or incompetence. Instead, it slips in quietly, dressed in eloquence, backed by degrees, and fluent in the language of alignment. These are the boardroom saboteurs—not out of malice, but fear. **Fear of exposure, fear of disruption, and most of all, fear of accountability.**

They don't block progress. They slow it. They delay action not with hostility but with polished restraint. They speak in phrases that sound thoughtful, mature, even strategic: "Let's not rush into execution until we've had more time to align." "We need to socialize this with stakeholders." "Have we considered all the downstream implications?" "We'll revisit this after the next round of feedback." "I just want to make sure everyone feels heard." It all sounds wise. It all sounds like leadership. But what it really is... is paralysis in a custom suit.

This is the **sophisticated language of inertia**. It's not laziness—it's a form of protection. A shield against risk. A strategy for self-preservation in cultures where saying the right thing is safer than doing the right thing. It creates the illusion of movement while keeping everything exactly where it is.

And here's where it gets dangerous: it thrives in polite, professional, well-meaning environments. Because it mimics the cadence of alignment. It borrows the vocabulary of emotional intelligence and diversity of thought. But underneath all that polish? **Nothing actually changes.**

We confuse talking with building. We mistake empathy for execution. We reward process over results. And before long, we've trained an entire team to believe that emotional comfort is more important than organizational velocity.

Why does this happen? It's not because people are lazy or malicious. It's because they've learned—consciously or not—that the system punishes boldness and rewards diplomacy. That rocking the boat might make someone uncomfortable. That tension might get them labeled "not a team player." So instead of challenging the room, they slow it down. They use inclusive language to mask indecision. They wrap delay in virtue. And because the words are elegant, we let it slide.

The cost? Momentum erodes. Trust fragments. High performers lose faith. They stop bringing ideas. They stop pushing. They disengage—not because they don't care, but because the system has become a maze of hesitation dressed up in language that sounds intelligent and safe. This is how smart cultures die—not with a bang, but with endless rounds of meetings where no decisions are made. Where action steps become "points of discussion," and strategy becomes "an evolving conversation." People feel like they're working. But they're not building anything that matters.

So how do you stop it? Not with more words. With *moves*.

You set the minimum bar of clarity needed to act. Then you act. You reward decisive movement over emotional consensus. You get honest when elegant delay starts creeping in. You say what no one else wants to say: "Are we actually stuck—or are we just afraid to move?" And most importantly, you refuse to be seduced by the performance of safety.

Leaders must shift their metric from "how comfortable does the team feel?" to "how much forward motion is happening because of us?" You build trust by modeling movement, not comfort. By making people feel seen *while still holding the line*. By refusing to over-index on harmony at the expense of truth.

Because at the end of the day, sophisticated language doesn't move product. It doesn't build culture. And it certainly doesn't inspire transformation.
It just keeps the lights on while the fire dies quietly.

How Cultures Institutionalize Excuses

The most dangerous form of dysfunction isn't loud. It's quiet. It's polite. It's professionally worded, often beautifully branded—and it spreads invisibly.

Cultures rarely collapse because of villains. They rot because of **passivity** dressed up as professionalism. And once the excuse culture takes root, it doesn't need bad actors to thrive. It just needs silence. Just a few too many "That's not my call" moments. Just enough "Let's revisit it next quarter." Just enough deferral, dilution, and deflection to train your organization to protect *comfort* over *clarity*.

This is how excuse-making becomes **cultural infrastructure**. It starts subtly. Accountability shifts from being task-based to emotion-based. Instead of asking, *"Who owns this?"*, people start asking, *"How can we make sure no one feels blamed?"* Meetings, once designed for decision-making, devolve into therapy sessions for workplace anxiety. Objectives get replaced by reflections. Debriefs become apology circles. And suddenly, no one's driving the car—but everyone feels really heard about how confusing the road is.

The emotional temperature of the room begins to dictate strategy. Not truth. Not data. **Feelings.**

This may sound compassionate, even mature. But here's the quiet devastation: **clarity becomes dangerous.** The person who names the elephant in the room—the one brave enough to say, "This isn't working"—is suddenly labeled abrasive, negative, or "not aligned with our values." **They're cast as the problem, not because they're wrong, but because they dared to disrupt the illusion of unity.**

Over time, the cost of confrontation becomes higher than the cost of underperformance. And when that threshold flips, your culture becomes fertile ground for mediocrity.
The new reward structure is clear:
- Speak carefully, not clearly.
- Prioritize diplomacy over direction.

- Get consensus before momentum.
- And above all—never disrupt the emotional equilibrium.

That's how **execution dies** in cultures that look beautiful on paper.

You'll start hearing phrases like:

- "We want to be thoughtful before we act."
- "Let's make sure we gather all perspectives."
- "We're still in discovery mode."
- "This is more complex than it looks."

None of these are inherently wrong. But when they become the default operating system, they replace urgency with **endless emotional buffering**.

The scariest part? People start to **believe** this is leadership. Here's how the infection spreads:

1. **Accountability becomes emotional.**
   Instead of asking who owns the problem, people start asking, "How do we make sure no one feels singled out?"
2. **Meetings become delay rituals.**
   No one leaves with decisions. Just feelings. Just agreements to "revisit."
3. **Failure is recast as growth.**
   A missed goal isn't a miss—it's "a learning opportunity." A dropped project isn't abandonment—it's "a pivot."
4. **Clarity becomes threatening.**
   The person who names the elephant in the room gets labeled "abrasive," "not a team player," or "too intense."

That's how leaders go from driving strategy to **curating emotion**. They stop executing and start tiptoeing. They think protecting people from hard truths is noble. They believe comfort equals culture. And they forget that accountability—real accountability—*feels like friction at first*. You're not leading anymore. You're managing a mood.

And your best people? They see it. They see how failure gets rebranded as a "learning opportunity." They see how the person who delayed the project becomes the person who leads the retro. They see how clarity gets punished, while ambiguity gets rewarded for being "flexible."

So, they stop. They stop innovating. They stop challenging. They stop showing up with fire.

Not because they're weak. But because the system has shown them: **truth has no home here.**

So How Do You Burn the Excuse Architecture?

You name it. In the moment. Out loud. You cut through ambiguity with questions like:

- "What decision is being made here?"
- "Who owns the outcome?"
- "What are we committing to today?"
- "If this fails, who's responsible—and what are we learning now, not after it's safe?"

You strip out weak language from your leadership vocabulary:

- No more *"might," "maybe,"* or *"let's revisit."*
- Replace *"alignment"* with *"accountability."*

- Replace *"process"* with *"progress."*

You model the new values with your own clarity. **And you protect the people who tell the truth when it's hard.** Because until you kill the excuse culture, no system, no strategy, no AI tool, no OKR framework will save you.

A leader's job is not to keep everyone emotionally regulated. It's to create conditions where truth becomes more normal than avoidance—and where clarity scales faster than fear. You want real culture?

Build one where it's safer to speak the truth than to perform agreement. Build one where leaders are judged not by how liked they are—but by how clearly, they **own outcomes**. And build one where excuses don't just get noticed. They get **burned**.

Agreement as a Comfort Drug

Here's the brutal truth: in too many modern organizations, consensus isn't just a value—it's a drug. It feels good. It soothes anxiety. It signals emotional safety. But make no mistake—**it numbs your leadership system**.

We've built cultures where smiles and nods are treated like metrics. Where the absence of visible conflict is mistaken for alignment. Where the collective mood is more important than the actual outcome. Leaders see meetings full of agreement and think, *"We're healthy."* But what's actually happening is *avoidance.*

People aren't agreeing because they're committed. They're agreeing because it's easier. Because it's less risky. Because in your culture, **truth-telling costs more than conformity**.

And like any drug, this kind of agreement has short-term highs and long-term damage. At first, it feels like unity. Everything flows. Meetings are calm. People seem on board. But underneath the surface, tension builds. Frustrations simmer. And eventually, the real players—the truth-tellers, the doers, the ones who actually give a damn—start to burn out. Because when honest dissent feels dangerous, **integrity walks out the door**.

The Biology of Agreement Addiction

This isn't just about feelings. It's about brain chemistry. The human brain is wired to avoid discomfort. We're biologically conditioned to seek **dopamine**—a neurotransmitter released when we receive affirmation, validation, and a sense of belonging. In team dynamics, **agreement becomes a dopamine drip.** It soothes, affirms, and falsely signals cohesion. The leader gets the hit. The team feels safe. Everyone walks away feeling connected.

But dopamine doesn't measure truth. It rewards familiarity. It trains us to avoid the uncomfortable friction that *actually signals progress.* And this is where leadership collapses—when biology is mistaken for strategy.

The result? Cultures that protect **emotional temperature** more than **performance standards**. Now add this to the mix: you've got team members—maybe even whole departments—who haven't met a KPI in **six months**. Entire quarters go by, and not one core metric is hit. But instead of consequence, they get conversation. Instead of accountability, they get empathy. Instead of clear expectations, they get more flexibility.

And here's what that does: **It chains your top performers to the emotional dysfunction of your lowest contributors.** Your A-players—those who own outcomes, who bring clarity, who don't need emotional babysitting—are now required to **emotionally calibrate around the excuses** of people who don't produce. They're asked to soften their language, wait longer for decisions, take on more work, and *never* ruffle feathers. Why? Because someone who hasn't delivered in two fiscal cycles might "not feel supported."

That's not culture. That's what I call **PEAK MORON**. It's unprofessional. And it's inexcusable.

You're not just mismanaging. **You're enabling a soft coup against performance.** You've let non-performers set the standard. You've trained your organization to protect feelings over facts, process over product, and avoidance over excellence. And if you can't see what you're enabling? **Burn me in effigy.** It won't change the reality: **You're allowing chronic underperformance to infect your entire system while smiling in town halls and quietly abandoning your best people.**

Your values? Left on the roadside. Your mission? Drowned in accommodation. Your culture? A museum of missed potential. Your credibility? Eroding every time a high performer watches mediocrity win comfort instead of correction.

And don't be shocked when your best people walk. They're not dramatic. They're decisive. They don't make noise—they just stop showing up with heart. Because they're not going to chain their excellence to your unwillingness to confront reality.

So, here's the line in the sand:

- Stop confusing emotional appeasement with empathy.
- Stop sacrificing your culture at the altar of "understanding."
- And for God's sake—**stop shackling your top talent to the underperformance you refuse to confront.**

Because the longer you avoid it, the more your organization becomes a sanctuary for the stagnant—and a graveyard for the gifted.

Comfort Isn't the Goal—Clarity Is

Here's what gets lost in agreement culture: **movement.** Decisions take weeks. Projects get delayed because "we're not emotionally ready." Mediocre work gets a pass because "we're still building psychological safety."

Meanwhile, the best people? They're dying inside. Because they didn't sign up to be therapists. They signed up to build something. To move something. To be part of a culture where courage means more than consensus.

And when they realize that speaking the truth puts them at risk—but performing agreement protects them? They shut down. Or worse, they leave.

You think you're keeping things calm. But what you're really doing is **trading trust for peace**. Because your team knows when you're not leading. They know when you're protecting egos instead of protecting the mission. They know when you're praising people who haven't earned it.

And eventually, they stop believing you. They nod in meetings—but their hearts are gone. They deliver the minimum—and nothing more. They comply—but they no longer *commit*.

The Withdrawal Is Real—And Necessary

If you've been running a culture on emotional consensus, indirect communication, and strategic ambiguity, then this next phase will hurt. Not because you're doing something wrong—but because you're doing something right **for the first time in a long time**.

Withdrawal is what happens when you stop feeding the addiction. When the dopamine drip of appeasement runs dry. When the performance rituals of agreement, the over-accommodation of underperformance, and the endless mood management finally get cut off at the source.

The reaction is real. You'll get pushback—not just from the underperformers who have grown fat on your flexibility, but also from your *middle contributors* who learned to play the game. The ones who stayed quiet, played it safe, and built careers around not making waves. They're not used to a system where action beats appearance. They're not used to clarity being a requirement, not an invitation.

And so, they grieve. They grieve the loss of emotional leverage. The loss of unearned grace. The loss of a culture where work was measured in how *seen* people felt, not how well they delivered.

Let them grieve. Because here's the real danger: if you backpedal now—if you return to the soft systems just to quiet the noise—you'll *re-addict your organization* to the exact behaviors that kept you stuck. You'll institutionalize avoidance. You'll teach people that progress can be reversed if they protest loud enough. You'll kill transformation before it ever had a chance to breathe.

You Are Breaking a Cultural Addiction

Understand what you're really doing here: you're detoxing a system from a substance it was never supposed to ingest—**emotional manipulation as a substitute for measurable value**. You're removing the comfort food of weak meetings, vague decisions, fake harmony, and emotional micromanagement.

That hurts. For you and for them.

Because no one tells you this in the leadership books: *clarity has casualties*. You will lose people. Some will leave because they were never supposed to be there to begin with. Others will fight to stay relevant through emotional resistance. They will tell you you've changed. That you've hardened. That "you're just not as supportive as you used to be." That's when you'll feel the pull to soften, to apologize for your standards. Don't. Because here's what they'll never say out loud—but what they know deep down: **You didn't stop supporting them. You just stopped enabling them.** And that distinction is the line between leadership and emotional hostage-taking.

Let the Old Culture Grieve—So the New One Can Rise

You need to expect—and even welcome—the withdrawal. Because it's a sign that the culture is beginning to **recalibrate around truth**.

What you're doing is reintroducing structural integrity into an environment that had been running on personality management and performance theater. You're calling the bluff on a system that measured value in vibes, not velocity.

Of course there's going to be friction. That's the sound of illusions dying. So, when your team pushes back, don't just brace—**lead**.

- Hold the line.
- Repeat the standard.
- Anchor into outcomes.
- Speak calmly, but without apology.

Say it out loud: "Yes, this is different. Yes, we're changing. And no, we're not going back."

You don't rebuild a high-trust, high-clarity culture by coddling withdrawal symptoms. You rebuild it by modeling what stability looks like **after the storm**. Because when your team sees that clarity doesn't blink—when they realize the new standard is not a mood but a movement—they will start to trust again.

Not just you. **Themselves.**

Because this isn't just about detoxing the culture. It's about **inviting your real players to rise**. Because real leadership doesn't need everyone to smile. It just needs people to **stand**. To name what's true. To act on it. And to do it **together**, even when it's uncomfortable. Comfort doesn't scale. **Clarity does.**

Burn the Excuse Architecture

If you want to kill the rot, you have to destroy the structure it's living in. Excuse-making is never random. It's architectural. Systemic. Designed, whether consciously or not, to **protect dysfunction and avoid accountability**. And once it takes root in your organization, it doesn't just block performance—it rewires behavior, language, and leadership expectations.

You can't coach around this. You can't rebrand it. You can't nudge it into productivity. You have to **burn it down**.

That means eliminating every subtle form of delay masquerading as thoughtfulness. You ban weak language like "might," "maybe," and "it depends" when real decisions are on the table. You cut out the comfortable buzzwords like "alignment," "exploration," and "gathering input" unless they are backed by timelines, ownership, and a visible outcome.

Because when "alignment" has no deadline, it's just a stall tactic. When "exploration" has no decision point, it's just emotional cover. And when "collaboration" becomes a substitute for direction, you're not leading—you're **hosting**.

You confront ambiguity in real-time.

When someone says, "We just want to be inclusive," you ask, "Inclusive of what? By when? With what effect?" When someone says, "Let's revisit after the next cycle," you say, "What happens if we don't act now?" And when someone says, "It's complicated," you say, "Then simplify it until we can execute."

Because here's what you're really doing: **you're removing the emotional scaffolding that people have built around their fear of accountability.** You're not just managing culture—you're detoxing it.

Collaboration Without Clarity Is Not Leadership—It's Theater

One of the most pervasive lies in modern leadership is that collaboration is always a virtue. It's not. Collaboration without clarity is a stall tactic. A way to keep everyone in the room feeling useful without demanding that anyone in the room actually move. And consensus? That sacred cow of inclusive leadership?

Consensus without execution is not alignment—it's an evasion strategy wrapped in a team hoodie. You're not leading if every decision has to pass through an emotional clearance checkpoint. You're not leading if clarity is always softened, stalled, or reshaped to protect someone's comfort zone. You're not leading if dysfunction gets tolerated just because it's *well-intentioned*.

Because here's what happens when you let the excuse architecture stand:

- Your top performers start to ask why excellence is punished and emotional instability is protected.
- Your boldest thinkers stop speaking up because they've learned that clarity is a liability.
- Your real mission starts to suffocate under a blanket of check-ins, reframing sessions, and non-decisions wrapped in "psychological safety."

And slowly, without saying it, your culture begins to whisper: *truth is too dangerous to say out loud.* That's how organizations die. Not with a scandal. With a **slow surrender to comfort.**

The New Leadership Contract

You are not here to manage perception. You are not here to curate group vibes. You are not here to protect the feelings of people who chronically refuse to deliver.

You are here to:
- Drive **clarity**
- Protect **velocity**
- Name **dysfunction** before it metastasizes

You must become fluent in cutting through fog—compassionately, consistently, and without compromise.

So, when someone says, "Let's hold space for that," you respond, "Holding space doesn't mean we stop the work." When they say, "We don't want anyone to feel excluded," you say, "Inclusion without accountability is how we've gotten stuck." When they say, "This might not land well," you say, "Then we'll say it better—but we'll still say it."

Because **precision beats performance. Ownership beats optics. Action beats agreement.** Every. Single. Time.

So go ahead—light the match. Burn the excuse architecture. Let it collapse.

And from the ashes, build something worthy of your mission. Worthy of your people. Worthy of the leaders you *hired*—not the ones you've had to manage into mediocrity. Let this be the day you stop mistaking emotional choreography for culture—and start building something **unshakeable**.

Leadership is no longer a title. It's a *standard*. One that must be earned in real-time, under pressure, and in full view of your people. The old model—based on personality, likability, and presence—is dead. What remains is the contract: what you promise by how you lead, and what your people learn to expect based on how you show up.

Here's the new contract: **You are here to drive clarity. You are here to protect velocity. You are here to deliver outcomes. You are here to name dysfunction before it metastasizes.** If you're doing anything else—if you're softening truth for comfort, buffering accountability with vague optimism, or stalling action with alignment-speak—you're not leading. You're **hosting**. You've become a curator of emotions, not an architect of execution.

And execution is the only thing that still matters.

Fluent in the Fog

The modern leader must become **fluent in fog-cutting**. You're no longer paid for how you look in meetings. You're paid for how you move systems, hold lines, and cut through the noise with a surgeon's precision.

So, when someone in the room says, "We need more alignment," your answer isn't another deck. It's: "Great. By when? And who's owning it?" When someone says, "Let's wait until next quarter," you don't nod. You ask: "What's the cost of waiting? And what are we afraid of?" When someone says, "This is complicated," you hold their gaze and say: "Simplify it until we can execute. That's the work."

This is what leadership looks like now. Not performance. Not politeness. **Not protection. Outcomes.**

This is clarity that doesn't blink. This is responsibility with a name. This is decision-making without detour.

You cannot out-nurture sabotage. You cannot out-logic a wounded ego at war with itself. You either see the battlefield clearly — or you get buried under the wreckage of the mission you failed to defend.

Precision Over Performance. Ownership Over Optics. Action Over Agreement. Outcomes over effort.

You don't get applause for these moves. At least not right away. Because real leadership doesn't always feel good in the moment. It disrupts. It confronts. It breaks the rhythm of safety theater and calls people back to the edge where real progress happens.

And that's why this contract matters. Because in the absence of it, cultures collapse into emotional triage units—protecting the feelings of non-performers while your top players bleed out under the weight of unspoken resentment and inherited slack.

When you sign this contract—mentally, emotionally, operationally—you are saying:
- I will not mistake politeness for performance.
- I will not tolerate stagnation wrapped in empathy.
- I will no longer ask my high performers to carry the cost of my unwillingness to confront.

This is the new creed. It's not gentle. It's not easy. **But it's real.**

And if you're brave enough to hold it? **You will become the kind of leader people actually trust.** Not because you made them comfortable—but because you told the truth and still stood with them in it.

Because until you confront what fear looks like in a buttoned-up, email-thread-wrapped, calendar-blocked environment, you'll never see how deeply it's driving your decisions. Fear doesn't always look like panic. Sometimes, it looks like consensus.

Field Manual: Kill the Excuse Ecosystem

Excuse culture doesn't collapse with a memo. It dies when you make it too painful — too exposed — to survive. If you want to kill the ecosystem that protects mediocrity and strategic sabotage, you'll have to move fast, clean, and without apology.
Here's how:

1. Ban Emotional Cushioning
Directive: Every decision must stand on mission outcomes — not emotional comfort.
Watch for:
- "I feel like..." leading strategic discussions.
- "I just worry..." derailing operational clarity.

Action:
- Strip emotional language out of tactical meetings.
- Acknowledge feelings — then anchor immediately to action:

"Noted. Now what action moves the mission?"

2. Kill Strategic Ambiguity
Directive: Unclear language is the camouflage of cowardice.
Watch for:
- "Let's revisit this later."
- "We're still aligning."
- "We need more time to process."

Action:
- Tie every open item to a *deadline + deliverable + owner*.

"When is it done? By whom? What's the next irreversible move?"

3. Name Passive Resistance Fast
Directive: Silent dissent is sabotage with better manners.
Watch for:
- Repeated delay.
- Evasive answers.
- Reluctance wrapped in politeness.

Action:
- Confront the behavior — not the drama.

"Are we stuck because we're confused — or because we're uncomfortable doing hard things?"
Expose the fear to kill its power.

4. Reward Mission-Driven Dissent
Directive: Protect constructive confrontation — and destroy emotional hostage-taking.
Watch for:
- People raising real risks tied to outcomes (good).
- People using emotional escalation to block movement (bad).

Action:
- Differentiate dissent that protects the mission from dissent that protects egos.
- Reward the first. Kill the second.

5. Make Ownership Non-Negotiable

Directive: No shared blame. No fog of war.

Watch for:
- Group accountability ("we missed it").
- Vague ownership ("we need to do better").

Action:
- Every action has a name and a deadline.
- No hiding inside collective guilt.

If the action fails, the failure wears a name too.

6. Burn Performative Consensus

Directive: Movement over mood. Always.

Watch for:
- Meetings ending in polite nods but no movement.
- Celebrating agreements instead of outcomes.

Action:
- In meetings, end with only three questions:
  - What moved forward?
  - What must move next?
  - Who owns the next move?

Consensus is optional. Movement is not.

Final Directive: You don't kill an excuse culture by begging for honesty. You kill it by making deception painful, passivity visible, and ownership sacred. Move the mission. Bleed the rot. Lead clean. No theater. No hostages. No survivors.

Chapter 4: Fear Disguised as Coordination

Mark was the storm we all tried to manage. Brilliant at his job. Gifted, even. But beneath the surface — pure emotional rot.

He bullied his team behind closed doors. Weaponized his talent to avoid accountability. Used fear, sarcasm, and ego like tools of dominance.

People covered for him because he was "valuable." Because he produced. Because it was easier to tolerate the poison than to risk confronting the storm. Until it wasn't.

The day I walked him out — I'll never forget it. He didn't go quietly. He didn't ask questions. He launched — verbal attacks, personal jabs, ego warfare at full throttle. I sat there. Took every hit without flinching. Not because I agreed — but because the moment demanded restraint. No remorse. No emotional caving. No justification. When he was done, I slid the separation letter across the table. Looked him in the eye. And walked him out.

The hallway felt like an airport after a crash — silent, stunned, too real. A lot of the team didn't think we could rebuild. Mark had allies. Influence. A shadow network that still lingered. But we didn't blink.

That afternoon, we gathered everyone. No slides. No spin. No theater. I looked them in the eyes and said: *"What came before is gone. We are going to move forward — fast, clean, and without apology. This team will win — in new ways, with new energy, and with zero room for sabotage."*

Some people nodded. Some stayed quiet. Some packed up and left over the next few weeks. And that was fine. Because what came next wasn't built on fear or talent alone. It was built on clarity. On integrity. On load-bearing truth.

This is how the rebuild begins: Not with a speech — but with fire. Not with inspiration — but with incision. You remove the rot. You own the moment. And you start pouring the new foundation.

The real damage didn't happen the day Mark was walked. It happened long before — in every moment we tolerated him. Every time someone looked the other way. Every time his bullying got excused because of his talent. Every time a leader avoided the hard call out of fear it might break the team.

That fear had already broken us. Not just culturally — but operationally. People stopped telling the truth. Decisions slowed. Energy drained. Trust bled out behind closed doors.

Mark wasn't the disease. **He was the symptom of a system that had traded courage for survival.** And until we faced that —There's a reason so many teams feel like they're working hard but going nowhere. A reason projects stall without ever quite failing. A reason cultures feel "nice" but quietly erode from the inside out.

It's not lack of intelligence. It's not lack of process. It's not even lack of ambition.

It's **fear**. Not the kind that storms into the room. Not yelling. Not chaos. This fear is quiet. Sophisticated. It doesn't wear panic on its face—it wears a smile. A handshake. A meeting invite with an agenda and a shared doc link. This is fear in its most insidious form: **fear disguised as coordination**.

The Politeness Pact

Walk into any underperforming organization and you won't be hit with shouting matches, slammed doors, or chaos. You'll be greeted with smiles. Meetings that run on time. Slack channels full of emojis and polite affirmations. A calm, composed workplace where everyone seems aligned—until you scratch the surface and realize: **no one is telling the truth.**

This is the **Politeness Pact**—an unspoken agreement across the organization that says, *"Don't rock the boat. Don't challenge the tone. Don't be the one who makes this uncomfortable."* It's leadership by emotional negotiation. Execution by consensus theater. Culture by unspoken compromise. And at its core? A deeply ingrained fear of friction.

It doesn't start maliciously. It starts with a good intention: let's collaborate. Let's be kind. Let's respect one another. But over time, that healthy intent mutates into an avoidance mechanism. We stop having real conversations. We delay feedback until it no longer matters. We replace direction with discussion, clarity with curation, and conflict with "collaboration"—as if harmony were the ultimate metric of success.
But the truth? **This is not harmony. It's stagnation.**

The Illusion of Emotional Intelligence

This kind of culture cloaks itself in emotional intelligence. It rewards the leaders who speak in soft tones, who use inclusive language, who never make anyone feel "uncomfortable." And who wouldn't want to be that kind of leader?

But when EQ becomes a shield from accountability—when we start calling silence maturity, and avoidance empathy—then we're not leading anymore. **We're managing emotions instead of driving results.** We're curating comfort at the expense of clarity.

We tolerate missed deadlines because "they've had a lot on their plate." We keep underperformers in key roles because "they've been loyal." We rewrite performance reviews to protect feelings instead of protecting standards. And eventually, **we don't lead the culture—we mirror it.**

Appeasement Is Not Strategy—It's Survival

What's even more dangerous is this: **many leaders in these environments are sincere.** They care. They want to be fair. But they've become addicted to the peace that comes from appeasement. They fear the emotional fallout of truth. So, they soften the edges, cushion the feedback, and tiptoe around the elephant in the room.

They think they're building trust. What they're really doing is feeding dysfunction. Because the second you start making decisions to **avoid emotional backlash**, you've given away the keys to your integrity. You've made comfort your compass. And your best people? They see it. They see who gets protected. They see who's untouchable. And they quietly check out— because they know they're living in a culture where performance is optional, but emotional volatility gets accommodated.

Everyone Sees It. No One Says It. Let's tell the truth leaders won't say out loud:
- You've praised people who didn't deserve it—just to avoid drama.
- You've promoted someone who was safer emotionally—not stronger operationally.

- You've kept someone in power because removing them would "create too much tension."
- And every time, a piece of your leadership credibility died.

And the worst part? **Your team knows.** They know you're covering. They know you're stalling. They know you're preserving comfort while the mission bleeds out behind you. They won't confront you. They'll just stop trusting you. They'll smile. Nod. Perform the ritual. But their fire will be gone.

And you? You'll still be hosting meetings and writing culture statements, wondering why nothing moves anymore.

You Were Not Hired to Be Liked—You Were Hired to Lead

It's time to tear up the politeness pact. Not to become a tyrant. But to **become real again.** Because your mission deserves truth. Your culture deserves friction. Your people deserve a leader who is more committed to *clarity* than to *comfort*. The kind of leader who says: "This isn't working—and I won't pretend it is." "We're not aligned—and it's costing us." "This behavior is undermining the mission—and I'm done tolerating it."

That's what leadership is. Not emotional choreography. But **courageous clarity in the face of collective avoidance.** You were never meant to keep everyone comfortable. You were meant to build something that *works*—even if it makes some people uncomfortable along the way.

The Illusion of Harmony

Most leaders don't recognize this form of organizational fear—because it doesn't scream. It doesn't throw chairs. It doesn't rage in conference rooms. It performs. It smiles. It nods. It agrees. And in doing so, it convinces you that everything is working—when what's really happening is **the slow burial of truth beneath a mountain of emotional avoidance.**

Harmony, when real, is powerful. But false harmony? It's a **toxin wrapped in civility**. It starts with small decisions—deferring hard conversations, letting accountability slide "just this once," reshaping feedback into something more palatable. And it feels good. Even noble. After all, who doesn't want to be seen as collaborative? Who doesn't want to lead with empathy? But here's the truth no one wants to admit:

When you start prioritizing agreement over action, and tone over truth, **you're not leading anymore. You're managing optics. You're narrating performance. You're selling theater.**

The Emotional Politics of "Nice"

When harmony becomes the goal, confrontation becomes the threat. We avoid it. We delay it. We wrap it in five layers of emotional softening until what once was a call to rise becomes a gentle whisper that barely touches reality.

We delay confrontation because it feels "aggressive." We tolerate underperformance because "they're doing their best." We withhold feedback because "now's not the time." This isn't emotional intelligence—it's **emotional manipulation** by omission.

And worst of all, it's usually driven by a well-meaning leader who just doesn't want to be seen as the villain. But here's the rub: **you're not the villain because you name hard truths— you're the villain if you don't.**

Because while you're protecting people from discomfort, you're letting the culture rot from the inside out.

What You Think You're Protecting vs. What You're Actually Costing

Leaders stuck in false harmony tell themselves they're preserving relationships. They think they're building psychological safety. But what they're actually doing is teaching people that **accountability is optional if you're emotionally fluent enough to avoid it.**

And your top performers? They see it. They see who gets protected. They see who's allowed to skate by. They see how performance is no longer the currency—**emotional calibration is.**

So, they start to question. Not loudly. But privately. They stop giving full effort. They stop challenging mediocrity. They stop trusting the mission.

Because if excellence comes with confrontation, and confrontation comes with risk, then the safest move is disengagement.

And that's how false harmony breaks your culture—**not through noise, but through quiet exits.**

Harmony That Heals vs. Harmony That Hides

There's a difference between harmony that comes from alignment—and harmony that comes from suppression.

- Real harmony follows **hard conversations** that end in commitment.
- False harmony follows **unspoken tension** smothered in smiles and groupthink.

The former creates trust. The latter creates exhaustion.

If no one on your team has pushed back in months, if no one's been uncomfortable in a meeting, if your retrospectives are all sunshine and safe language—**you're not running a high-functioning team. You're running an emotional safety camp.**

And your results will show it. Slowly. Quietly. In missed milestones and surprise resignations.

To break the illusion of harmony, you must first be willing to **see it**. You must ask:
- Where have I prioritized peace over progress?
- Who have I shielded from the truth?
- What tension am I avoiding because I want to be liked?
- What hard feedback has been postponed so long it's turned into resentment?

And then you must act.

You must reset the expectation: that truth is more valuable than temporary emotional ease. That honesty is the deepest form of respect. That discomfort is often a sign that *real* alignment is being forged.

Because leadership isn't about preventing the storm. It's about walking through it—clear-eyed, steady-handed, and committed to what matters most.

So, tear down the illusion. Not with aggression, but with authority. Not with brutality, but with boldness.

Because when the illusion falls, **truth can finally breathe.** And when truth breathes, **your culture comes alive again.**

Appeasement as Strategy

Fear-based leadership doesn't always show up in dramatic ways. It doesn't always wear the face of panic, volatility, or micromanagement. Sometimes, it arrives dressed in calm language, soft gestures, and strategic silence. It hides inside perfectly worded emails, carefully noncommittal feedback, and endless cycles of meetings where nothing gets decided. It speaks in phrases like, *"Let's keep this collaborative,"* or *"We want to ensure everyone feels included,"* or *"Let's not rush into conflict."*

To the untrained eye, it looks like thoughtful leadership. But what it actually is… is **appeasement with a leadership badge.** It is leadership that has chosen **peace over truth, emotional balance over momentum,** and **public optics over private integrity.** And while it may be done in the name of compassion, inclusion, or cultural harmony, the result is always the same: **stagnation** dressed in civility.

Many of these leaders are not malicious. They're not weak. They're not careless. In fact, they care deeply—often *too* deeply. They've internalized the belief that their primary role is to protect people from discomfort, and in doing so, they become addicted to the illusion of harmony. They won't admit it, but they've learned how to trade small truths for big silences. They'll rationalize inaction as wisdom. They'll spin conflict avoidance as maturity. They'll smother urgency with nuance, mistaking endless diplomacy for progress.

And here's the devastating outcome: they stall the very mission they were hired to lead. They don't mean to. But they do. Not because they're bad leaders—because they're **scared leaders.** Scared of losing connection. Scared of offending. Scared of triggering backlash, especially in emotionally complex environments. So instead of confronting, they **curate.** This is how appeasement becomes a strategy.

You don't challenge underperformance—you empathize with it and create new "contextual KPIs." You don't confront sabotage—you schedule a "values alignment" session to air grievances. You don't enforce standards—you "hold space" and "model psychological safety."

And one day you look around, and you're no longer leading. You're babysitting the emotional climate of people who should be delivering outcomes—not curating vibes. Your team no longer sees a leader. They see a **middle manager of moods**—someone too kind to hold the line, too diplomatic to take a stand, and too emotionally fragile to weather pushback. And the cost? It's invisible—until it's everywhere.

Your best people disengage—not because they're jaded, but because they're watching integrity rot from the inside. They're watching emotional sensitivity get weaponized. They're watching people who underperform get coddled while they're left to carry the weight. They see you working harder to manage feelings than to protect the mission. And they leave—not always physically, but mentally, emotionally, spiritually.

And the ones who stay? They learn the real lesson: **Performance doesn't matter here. Emotional calibration does.** So, they adapt. They soften their edge. They stop telling the truth. They start performing the same politeness act that leadership has modeled from the top. And just like that, you've institutionalized mediocrity.

Not out of malice. Out of **misplaced compassion.** Appeasement, when repeated long enough, becomes a leadership style. And leadership, when stripped of truth, becomes **nothing at all.**

Let's get painfully honest. We don't tolerate bad behavior because we don't see it. We tolerate it because we **don't want to deal with what it would cost to confront it.** We dread the discomfort of the fallout. We imagine the tension in the room, the HR implications, the conversations that might go sideways. We anticipate the sighs, the side glances, the retaliation. And we convince ourselves that we're avoiding chaos when what we're really avoiding is **leadership.**

So, we rationalize. We reframe underperformance as "developmental opportunity." We describe toxicity as "passionate." We tell ourselves they "mean well" or "just have rough edges." We let tenure justify bad behavior. We let charisma disguise sabotage. And we let "not the right time" become a permanent excuse for never doing the thing that needs to be done.

But here's the truth no one says out loud: **Your people know.** They always know. They know when someone isn't pulling their weight. They know when the most disruptive person in the room keeps getting protected. They know when performance doesn't match praise—and when leadership gaslights the entire team by pretending it does.

They may not say anything. But they feel it. And slowly, they begin to shift. They stop offering feedback—because why speak up if the truth won't be acted on? They stop trusting recognition—because the wrong people keep getting it. They stop pushing the limits—because they see that safety, not excellence, is what gets rewarded.

And every time you stand in front of the team and give airtime to someone who's been quietly sabotaging progress… Every time you pretend that "we're all aligned" when everyone knows you're not… Every time you praise incompetence in the name of peace…**Your credibility dies a little more.** Not dramatically. Quietly. Silently. But relentlessly. Until eventually, the people you were meant to lead stop listening. Not because they're rebellious. Because they're **disillusioned**. And that's when you become something far worse than irrelevant. You become the **false prophet**.

The False Prophet in the Office

You're the leader who still preaches vision, but **protects dysfunction**. You talk about ownership, but make endless exceptions for the emotionally volatile. You evangelize values in the town hall, then violate them behind closed doors by promoting people who don't live them. You don't lead anymore. You perform. You recite the script. You smile at the right times. You post the LinkedIn thought leadership. But your team can feel it—you're not building. You're **surviving**.

You're trying to maintain emotional order, not operational excellence. You're trying to preserve harmony, not drive truth. You're trying to keep your seat—not fulfill your responsibility.

And after a while, the mask stops working. Not because you dropped it. But because everyone already saw behind it.

Your words don't carry weight. Your recognition doesn't inspire. Your presence doesn't lead—it lingers. You've become the leader people stop believing in but don't bother challenging. Because they've already made peace with the fact that you're not going to choose courage.

The Cycle of Harm

And here's what makes it all worse: it's **contagious**. When you protect one bad actor, others notice. They learn that emotional manipulation works. They learn that performance is negotiable if you complain long enough or cry loud enough. And soon, your organization becomes a haven for underperformance wrapped in emotional camouflage.

The culture shifts. People stop asking, *What drives impact?* They start asking, *What will keep me safe?* Now you've got a whole system operating on fear, avoidance, and passive aggression. And you—you're still wondering why no one speaks up. Why execution is so hard. Why everyone seems tired.

It's not the work. It's the weight of pretending. So, what do you do?

You drop the mask. You tell the truth. You **stop rewarding behavior that contradicts the mission**—no matter how long someone's been here, how loud they are, or how politically complex it feels.

You protect your culture more than you protect your comfort. Because once you do, your real leaders will come back to life. They'll stop holding back. They'll start showing up again.

And the people who were never built for excellence? They'll leave. Or they'll grow. But they won't set the standard anymore.

And you? You'll finally become **a leader again.**

The Slow Death of Trust

Trust doesn't collapse in a single scandal. It doesn't die in one catastrophic moment, one tweet, or one bad quarter. **Trust dies in silence.** In small, incremental decisions. In the subtle betrayals of clarity, over time, in the name of comfort.

It dies every time you reward *niceness* over honesty. Every time you sideline the truth to "keep the vibe intact." Every time you water down feedback so no one gets upset. Every time you platform underperformance in the name of "culture" or "inclusiveness" or "team chemistry." Every time you act like everything is fine—when your top people know it isn't.

And make no mistake: your best people *always* know. They notice the moment you start tolerating dysfunction. They feel the moment the standard slips. They hear the coded language in your all-hands updates—the subtle avoidance, the spin, the celebration of mediocrity dressed as "collaboration."

At first, they speak up. They try to help. They challenge. They contribute with urgency, with edge. And then… they start to slow down. They talk less in meetings—not because they have nothing to say, but because they've learned that saying it doesn't matter.

They stop raising concerns—not because they don't care, but because they've realized caring costs them political capital. They get quieter. More distant. Less emotionally present. And eventually, they quietly start updating their resumes.

Not because of a bad day. But because of **a pattern**. A pattern of protection over performance. A pattern of appeasement over accountability. A pattern of praise for the wrong people—and silence around the right ones.

And as your best quietly exit stage left, another group begins to thrive.

When the Worst People Win

Your worst performers—the ones who contribute the least and consume the most—are always watching, too. And when they see that outcomes don't matter but optics do, they adapt quickly.

They learn to perform alignment. To master emotional language. To insert themselves into process conversations and "team temperature" talks. They say things like "I just want to feel heard" and "We should revisit this collaboratively"—not because they care, but because **they've figured out how to stay in power without ever delivering**.

Now the culture flips. Your performers check out. Your manipulators plug in. And your mission starts to hemorrhage momentum, clarity, and belief—*without anyone raising their voice.* Because you didn't create a culture of trust. You created a culture of **emotional diplomacy and earned helplessness**. Where truth is seen as abrasive. Where excellence is threatening. Where silence is rewarded as professionalism.

This is the quiet funeral of trust.

Death by a Thousand Deferrals

It's not the storm that sinks the ship. It's the slow leak no one notices. Or worse—the one everyone notices, but no one has the courage to name.

You can feel it in the language of your team. In the absence of risk-taking. In the way bold ideas now arrive with disclaimers and nervous laughter. In the way energy has flattened, meetings feel like formalities, and no one is really sure what they're fighting for anymore.

This is death by a thousand deferrals. Not one decision. But hundreds. Each one a small retreat from clarity. Each one a missed opportunity to lead.

The Path to Resurrection

Want to rebuild trust? Then **stop managing optics** and start *defending what's real.* Start by acknowledging what people already know but are too exhausted to keep repeating: "Yes, we let some things slide." "Yes, we protected the wrong people." "Yes, we've made decisions that prioritized feelings over function." Then draw the new line. Hold it with consistency. Anchor it in values. And defend it with action.

Because trust doesn't come back through words. **It comes back through *visible courage.* Through *decisions that feel dangerous—but right.* Through a leadership presence that says: "We're building something real again. And I'm willing to lose comfort to protect it."**

What Real Leadership Requires

You want to rebuild trust? You want to reclaim your culture from the slow drift of mediocrity and avoidance? Then **stop coordinating and start commanding.**

This doesn't mean barking orders. It doesn't mean hierarchy for its own sake. It means leading with a presence that **shapes the room**, not reacts to it. It means creating a culture where truth doesn't have to be filtered to survive, where performance standards are sacred, and where emotional honesty doesn't get mistaken for insubordination.

Too many leaders are stuck in the role of orchestrators—forever trying to get everyone aligned, comfortable, and emotionally calibrated before making a move. That's not leadership. That's **emotional stage management**.

Leadership—real leadership—requires decisiveness, clarity, and the willingness to **break the pattern**. It means:

- **Speak hard truths with calm clarity.** Don't perform outrage. Don't soften reality into suggestion. Say what needs to be said—directly, respectfully, but without compromise. If something is broken, say so. If someone isn't delivering, say it out loud. If the culture is drifting, name it before it calcifies.
- **Confront underperformance with compassion—but without delay.** The longer you wait, the more you teach everyone that accountability is negotiable. Compassion is not an excuse for inertia. Kindness doesn't mean silence. You don't have to attack—but you do have to act.
- **End the culture of emotional tiptoeing.** Create space for hard conversations without requiring perfection in tone. Don't demand people walk on eggshells to preserve someone's comfort. If your culture can't handle tension, it can't handle growth.
- **Reward those who take risks to speak truth—even when it makes you uncomfortable.** Stop protecting your ego. Stop quietly punishing dissent because it threatened your narrative. The people who challenge you are giving you a gift. If you crush that gift, don't be surprised when no one brings you anything valuable again.

- **Stop pretending that "consensus" is more important than courage.** Consensus is a comfort drug for leaders who fear isolation. But courage is what actually builds cultures of resilience. You don't need everyone to agree—you need people to act with alignment and commitment, even if they wouldn't have made the same choice.

Real Leadership Is Sharp

Real leadership isn't soft. It's sharp. It cuts through fog. It creates edges. It defines reality. **Real leadership isn't about being liked—it's about being *respected*, *trusted*, and ultimately, *followed*.** And here's the irony: when people see that you're willing to do the hard thing for the right reason, they may not always like you—but they will trust you more than the leaders who coddled them.

Because trust is not built in the absence of discomfort—it's built in the **presence of integrity**. **Real leadership forces the system to face reality—even when it hurts.** It refuses to let emotional volatility set the standard. It doesn't bend the mission to match everyone's feelings. It doesn't dilute excellence to avoid friction. It says: "This is who we are. This is what we stand for. And this is what we will no longer tolerate." Not with arrogance. With authority. With soul.

Clarity Over Comfort

If you want to lead—not manage, not accommodate, not emotionally babysit—but *lead*… Then you must become the one who disrupts **fake harmony** before it poisons your team's capacity for growth.

Because in every organization, there comes a moment when comfort becomes **a mask**. A ritual. A sedative.

You'll see it in the all-smiles meeting where no one mentions the obvious failure. You'll feel it in the soft language carefully wrapped around every piece of feedback. You'll hear it in the echo chamber of "alignment" that's really just avoidance in disguise.

And that's when real leaders are called to **break the illusion**—not with violence, but with *precision*. You say what everyone else has been too exhausted or too scared to say: "This isn't working."

Because if no one names it, no one changes it. Because silence protects the problem, not the mission. "We've lowered the standard, and it's costing us." Because excellence doesn't slip all at once—it erodes in inches, hidden beneath smiles and soft phrasing. And every inch of compromise teaches your people that mediocrity is the new normal. Because effort without results is not excellence. Because good intentions are not a substitute for growth.

Because real leaders don't just protect people—they call them to rise. "No, we're not aligned—and that's why we need to act now." Because misalignment doesn't fix itself. Because waiting until everyone's emotionally calibrated is how innovation dies. Because speed matters—and sometimes, courage has to come before consensus. "I know this is uncomfortable. That's why it matters." Because transformation never feels safe at first. Because truth-telling often feels like betrayal in systems that have confused harmony with health. Because discomfort is a **signal**, not a sin.

These Are Not Easy Conversations

Let's be clear: These conversations will cost you. They will make people squirm. Some will question your tone. Some will accuse you of changing. Some will say you're "not the same leader you used to be."

And you know what? **They're right.** You're not. <u>You've evolved.</u> You've outgrown the emotional caretaking that leadership impostors have normalized. You've stopped believing that your job is to manage everyone's experience. You've realized that **courageous clarity is the highest form of care**.

Because when you speak hard truths with steady hands, you give your people something sacred: **The chance to grow. The chance to change. The chance to finally see what's real.** And that's the moment your team stops performing—and starts becoming.

You have a decision to make. You can keep performing leadership—for safety, for likeability, for your career. But know this: **your team already sees the truth.** They're watching what you tolerate. They're watching who you promote. They're watching whether your words are backed by action—or buried in fear.

You are not here to protect people from discomfort. You are here to protect your mission from decay. And that means tearing down the culture of politeness before it collapses under its own dishonesty.

In the Mirror

If this chapter hurts a little—**good**. That means your conscience is still alive. That means the leader buried beneath the performance, the appeasement, the politeness—the one with fire in their gut and truth in their chest—is **still trying to break through**.

Pain is a signal. And in leadership, pain is often the first honest thing you've felt in months. Because until now, you've been too busy managing narratives to notice that the mission's been bleeding out behind you.

So, before you turn the page, before you reframe this as "good insight," before you forward this to someone else—**look in the mirror.** And ask yourself:

- **Where have I tolerated what should've been confronted?** Not out of love. Out of fear. Fear of conflict. Fear of being misunderstood. Fear of breaking the "culture." But every time you made peace with dysfunction, you taught your team that performance is optional—and you betrayed your own standard.

- **Who have I protected at the cost of credibility?** Maybe they were loyal. Maybe they were loud. Maybe they just knew how to play the emotional game better than you. But deep down, you knew. You knew they were hurting the mission. You knew they were draining the culture. And you kept them. You praised them. You built systems around them. And now your best people are asking themselves why they still care as much as they do.

- **When did I last choose harmony over honesty—and what did it cost my team?** You didn't lie. You just edited the truth. Softened it. Deferred it. And in doing so, you let your team walk blind into a reality they weren't prepared for. You traded temporary emotional comfort for long-term clarity—and now you're seeing the wreckage.

This Is the Work

This is what they don't teach you in MBA programs or TED talks. This isn't about vision decks or performance reviews. This isn't about quarterly targets or town hall applause.

This is the war **for your leadership soul.** Because real leadership doesn't start on the stage. It starts alone. In silence. With a mirror. When no one's watching and no one's clapping. It starts when you admit that *you* have been part of the problem. That your fear dressed up as empathy. That your indecision wore the costume of inclusion. That your avoidance masqueraded as patience. And that your team followed you into the fog—because that's where you led them.

Now is the moment you either double down on performance…Or you rise into something *real*. So, take a breath. Stare back at your own reflection. And choose: Will I keep protecting the illusion? Or will I finally become the leader this mission actually needs?

You already know the answer. **Now go act like it.** We've exposed the system. Now we confront the self. Ready?

Let's go.

Field Manual: Cut Through the Fear

Fear doesn't always look like panic. In high-performing cultures, it often hides in plain sight: masked as coordination, disguised as empathy, dressed up as respect. But make no mistake — fear left unchecked will kill velocity, truth, and trust.

You want a clean leadership culture? You're going to have to slice through the layers of **emotional armor** your people have built to avoid confrontation. Here's how to do it:

1. Kill the Politeness Pact
Directive: No more false harmony. No more smiling while the mission dies.
Watch for:
- "We're aligned" (when no one is actually moving)
- "Let's take this offline" (to avoid open conflict)

Action:
- Ask in every meeting:

"What's not being said right now that needs to be?"
- Make tension visible. Call it out. Lead through it.

2. Burn "Nice" Language to the Ground
Directive: Emotional comfort is not a leadership value. Truth is.
Watch for:
- "Just trying to be helpful…"
- "Don't want to cause any tension…"
- "I'm not sure this is the right time…"

Action:
- Replace with direct, mission-focused language:

"Is this necessary for the mission — or just making us feel better about not deciding?"

3. Refuse to Lead for Feelings
Directive: Never sacrifice clarity for the illusion of cohesion.
Watch for:
- Leadership decisions made to avoid someone's discomfort
- People staying in roles to "keep the peace"

Action:
- Ask yourself:

"Was this decision made to move the mission — or to avoid emotional fallout?"
- Adjust. Then move.

4. Force Irreversible Decisions
Directive: Coordinated delay is still failure. Kill it.
Watch for:
- "We'll circle back."
- "Let's give it a bit more time."
- "We need buy-in first."

Action:
- In every meeting, demand:

"What irreversible move are we making today?"

o No move? No progress.

5. Promote Courage Like It's Currency
Directive: Build a system that rewards candor — not compliance.
Watch for:
- Team members who challenge groupthink
- Quiet truth-tellers who get sidelined by louder cowards

Action:
- Publicly reinforce:

"That was hard to say. But it was true. And that's leadership."

- Make truth the standard. Make courage the reward.

Final Directive-Fear doesn't just slow teams down. It makes them fake. It sterilizes innovation. It hollows out leadership from the inside. Burn it. Name it. Cut through it. **You don't build speed with more coordination. You build it with clarity, tension, and guts.** This is clean leadership. This is how the rebuild wins.

Chapter 5: The 10 Signals of a Toxic Workplace

Anna outperformed them. Outpaced them. So, they whispered about her tone. They said she was 'too aggressive,' 'unapproachable,' 'intimidating.' And slowly, her credibility bled out — not because of results, but because the culture was too weak to reward strength. This is how reputation becomes a weapon.

Most leaders don't recognize toxicity when it first shows up—because it doesn't start with chaos. It starts with a smile. It starts with silence. It starts with "Let's not make this a big deal." And before long, it becomes the air your people breathe.

By the time you're using the word "toxic," the culture is already infected. But the signs were there. They were always there. You just didn't know how to read them—or worse, you chose not to.

This chapter is the reckoning. Not the storm. The radar. If you've been wondering whether the tension in your team, the low morale, or the strategic drag is cultural… this is where we find out. Here are the ten signals that your workplace is toxic—not in theory, but in lived, destructive reality.

1. Psychological Safety Is a Myth

Toxicity doesn't begin with rage. It begins with withdrawal. The first signal that your workplace is slipping is that **people stop speaking freely**. But not just that—they stop *thinking out loud*.

The creative spark? Extinguished. The brainstorming energy? Flatlined. The challenge, the question, the uncomfortable truth? Swallowed whole.

In cultures that lack psychological safety:

- Bold suggestions are met with subtle ridicule.
- Mistakes are punished, not debriefed.
- Feedback is seen as disloyalty, not growth.

So, your people adapt. To smile through disagreement. To nod when they want to scream. To become polite, agreeable shadows of their potential. You think meetings are aligned—because no one pushes back. You think projects are greenlit—because no one voices doubt. You think your team is unified—because no one has the courage to tell you otherwise.

But here's what's really happening: **Silence has become a survival tactic.** And when silence becomes normalized, innovation dies. Learning dies. Truth dies. And your best people? They go quiet first. Not because they don't care. But because they're watching what happens when others *do*.

So, if your most courageous thinkers have gone radio silent…If your rising stars stop taking risks…If everything suddenly feels *too polite*…**Your culture isn't healthy. It's afraid.** And you don't need another retreat. You need an exorcism.

2. Communication Is Passive-Aggressive and Politically Coded

In toxic cultures, communication doesn't inform—it *manipulates*. Words aren't used to solve problems. They're used to avoid responsibility, deflect confrontation, and perform civility while *strategically slicing the air out of the room*. This is where language becomes theater—and **everyone's acting.**

- Problems aren't addressed—they're "noted for future consideration."
- Conflict isn't resolved—it's buried under buzzwords and "next steps."
- Feedback isn't honest—it's sanded down, packaged, and emailed with weaponized CCs for "visibility."

You know you're in it when:

- Emails are more about implication than information.
- "Per our last conversation" means "I'm keeping receipts."
- "Just looping you in" means "You're on record now—good luck."

This isn't communication. It's bureaucratic combat. A passive-aggressive ecosystem where clarity is dangerous and image is currency. **Truth becomes subversive. And silence becomes self-protection.** In these environments:

- People talk *about* each other, not *to* each other.
- Meetings are sanitized zones of smiling sabotage.
- Every "collaborative" thread hides a subtext of surveillance.

No one wants to be the first to speak plainly—because in this culture, plain speech is punished. So, everyone learns to **code their honesty** in layers of professionalism, to camouflage real concerns behind political optics.

You're no longer solving problems—you're interpreting signals. You're no longer driving outcomes—you're decoding tone. You're no longer running a team—you're managing a psychological Cold War. And make no mistake: this is exhausting.

When people spend more time rereading emails for subtext than they do strategizing solutions, your culture is broken. You've stopped being a company. **You've become an emotionally weaponized performance arena.**

The solution? Stop dancing. Speak plainly. Cut through the fog with direct language. Name the issue. Take the hit. Own the discomfort. Because **clarity isn't cruelty.** And in a toxic system, the truth isn't just brave—it's revolutionary.

3. Burnout Isn't Just Common—It's Normalized

In toxic cultures, burnout isn't treated like a warning sign. It's treated like a *rite of passage*. It doesn't just show up as exhaustion. It shows up as emotional resignation.

- It's the once-creative team member who no longer raises their hand—not because they don't have ideas, but because they've learned their voice costs too much.
- It's the manager who used to fight for their people—now just pushing tasks through, trying not to drown.
- It's the high performer who went from driven to detached, who nods through meetings and silently updates their résumé at night.

And the most twisted part? **Leadership calls it "resilience."** They mistake numbness for grit. They admire those who suffer in silence. They reward those who abandon their needs in service of the machine.

Meanwhile, those who *ask for boundaries*? They're branded as soft. Not a team player. Not "hungry enough." "We're all busy." "It's just a season." "We need to push through." "This is where champions are made."

No. This is where *souls are broken*. Because instead of fixing broken systems—of redesigning processes, rebalancing workloads, realigning expectations—**toxic cultures raise the ceiling.**

More deliverables. Less recovery. Higher expectations. Fewer resources. Until your best people don't quit with a bang—they quit *quietly*. They disengage. They disappear in place. They turn their passion into silence because no one protected their fire—and eventually, it burned out.

In healthy cultures, burnout is a red flag. It's investigated. It's addressed. It's treated as a system failure. **But in toxic cultures? Burnout is the benchmark.** It's the bar. The unspoken rule. The sick standard of survival that says: *If you're not running on fumes, you're not pushing hard enough.*

And that's not leadership. That's not performance. That's **institutionalized self-destruction.** So, if your people are constantly running on empty… If the phrase "it's just a busy season" has been spoken for 18 straight months… If your team praises sacrifice more than sustainability…**You haven't built a culture of excellence. You've built a machine that eats humans and calls it hustle.** And eventually, it won't just be your talent that burns out. It'll be your credibility.

4. Conflict Is Avoided at All Costs

In toxic workplaces, the mission isn't to solve problems. It's to *avoid uncomfortable moments*. Conflict isn't seen as a tool for clarity—it's treated like a threat to the illusion of "culture." So instead of confronting the real issues:

- The executive who derails meetings gets sidestepped.
- The manager who misses deadlines gets covered for.
- The team member whose passive-aggressive behavior poisons morale? Ignored. Tolerated. Enabled.

And what do we call this? "Professionalism." "Team dynamics." "Emotional intelligence." "We're just being diplomatic."

No—you're being *complicit*. You're watching dysfunction metastasize and calling it maturity. Because in these environments, the real priority isn't resolution—it's emotional anesthesia. It's about keeping things calm. Predictable. Comfortable.

So, what happens? You see the same patterns, over and over:

- People "circle back" instead of calling it out.
- Teams "check in" instead of taking a stand.
- Problems are "monitored" instead of solved.

The workplace becomes one giant rug. And everything gets swept under it. The real issues don't disappear. They fester. They sour. And what started as discomfort becomes *rot*. Eventually, the team becomes **addicted to artificial peace**.

They equate the absence of noise with the presence of health. They confuse surface harmony with real alignment. They start to believe that *avoiding conflict is the same as being collaborative.*

But here's the truth: **What's unspoken doesn't stay neutral. It becomes resentment.** And resentment—left unchecked—becomes a quiet rebellion.

You won't see it in emails. You'll feel it in hesitations. In half-efforts. In missed cues and slow execution. You'll wonder, *"Why can't we move forward?"*

Because your team is still carrying all the unsaid things they were never allowed to bring to the surface. So, let's be clear - **Avoiding conflict doesn't protect your culture. It corrodes it.** Because conflict isn't dysfunction. **Unresolved conflict is.**

In high-trust cultures, conflict is feedback. In toxic cultures, conflict is betrayal. And if your team equates honesty with danger, you've already lost alignment—you just haven't seen the consequences yet.

Real leadership isn't afraid of discomfort. It *walks into the tension, names the issue, and invites resolution.*

So, stop sweeping. Flip the rug. Face the mess. And remember: **Peace without truth isn't unity—it's quiet collapse.**

5. Trust Has Been Replaced with Control

You'll feel this one the moment you walk in. The room's quiet, but it's not calm—it's *coiled.* There's tension in the air. Not the kind that precedes a breakthrough, but the kind that signals surveillance. Because in this culture, everything is being watched—**but nothing is truly seen.**

The dashboards are endless. The metrics multiply. The KPIs breed like rabbits in a spreadsheet. Policies stack. Systems constrict. Checklists get longer—but insight disappears. Why?

Because the deeper truth is this - **Micromanagement isn't about accountability. It's about fear.** It's what leadership turns into when trust is gone but ego still needs to feel in charge. You'll see it when:

- Leaders obsess over "productivity" but can't name the emotional pulse of their team.
- Managers schedule back-to-back status meetings while ignoring the root cause of delays: fear, confusion, disengagement.
- Every step requires a signature. Every decision requires escalation. Every move must be tracked.

This isn't management. It's control theater. Because when a leader stops trusting—they stop empowering. They stop inspiring. They stop *leading.*

Instead, they monitor. They measure. They tighten the system until there's no room for breath—let alone boldness.

And the fallout? **Innovation dies.** Because no one dares to fail. No one dares to try. No one dares to stretch—because every deviation is suspect.

You cannot build a high-trust team while treating your people like threats to be contained. You can't say "we value initiative" while scrutinizing every keystroke. You can't say "we want leaders at every level" while requiring five layers of approval to move. You can't demand innovation while punishing imperfection.

Here's what control addicts don't understand- **Oversight doesn't create excellence— ownership does.** And ownership only flourishes in the soil of *trust.*

If your team is spending more time reporting what they're doing than actually doing it…If your people sound compliant but act cautiously…If your high performers are quietly disengaging while your "watch list" grows…You don't have a performance issue.

You have a fear-based leadership model with a trust deficit. And you can't solve it with another dashboard.

You solve it by backing off the throttle. By seeing your people—not just their output. By building systems that support, not suffocate. Because **what people do when you're not watching is the real test of your culture.** And if you've taught them to survive the system instead of *owning* the mission? You haven't created a team. **You've created a compliance machine.**

6. Standards Are Inconsistent and Politicized

You want to watch a culture collapse in real time? Don't fire anyone. Don't cut budgets. Just start applying standards **unevenly.**

- Hold one team to hard deadlines while another breezes by with excuses.
- Reward one person's ambition as "leadership," but label someone else's dissent as "a bad attitude."
- Protect your favorites while hiding behind HR policy for everyone else.

It won't explode. It will *erode.* Quietly. Systematically.

Because here's what most leaders forget: **Your people are always watching. And they always see.** They see who gets second chances—and who gets sacrificed. They see who can fail upward—and who gets punished for telling the truth. They see when accountability is performative—and when protection is political.

And when they realize that **outcomes don't matter as much as alliances**, they make a shift. It's not loud. It's not dramatic.

They stop playing to win. They start playing to survive. They stop bringing bold ideas— and start bringing whatever won't get them flagged. They stop raising concerns—and start perfecting the art of saying nothing. They give you just enough to appear engaged, but underneath it's **performance under protest.**

This is how mediocrity becomes the standard—not because your people can't perform, but because **they no longer believe performance is what earns respect.** In a politicized culture, trust decays. And when trust decays, effort detaches. And when effort detaches, *you can't lead anyone anywhere.*

Because now your team isn't optimizing for excellence—they're optimizing for optics. They spend more time managing perception than pursuing truth. They say yes when they mean no. They show up, nod, execute—and quietly plan their exit strategy.

You'll see it in the emails that say everything and nothing. You'll see it in the risk aversion. In the reluctance to speak plainly. In the increasing "check-ins" that are just performance rituals to keep up appearances.

So let me say this plain -- **When your standards are political, your leadership is dead on arrival.** Because you haven't built a team—you've built a court. And the only people who thrive in courts are those who've learned to bow, bluff, and betray.

7. Gossip Is the Primary Feedback Loop

In a toxic culture, when people can't speak *up*, they start speaking *sideways*. Transparency breaks down, and backchannels open wide. Private chats replace team huddles. Hallway whispers replace boardroom candor. The most honest conversations don't happen during the meeting—they happen *after* it ends, in hushed voices and safe rooms. This isn't gossip as drama.

This is gossiping as **emotional compensation.** A coping mechanism. A release valve. A survival tactic in a system where truth has been denied access to the surface.

Why does it happen? Because your people are still trying to make sense of the chaos. Still trying to find *meaning* in the madness. Still trying to figure out what's real—when your leadership communication feels like smoke and mirrors.

Gossip becomes the *underground truth.* A rogue network of clarity when the official channels are polluted with spin. And here's the brutal reality most leaders refuse to face - **When gossip becomes the only way to feel heard, your people aren't just talking behind your back—they're *voting* behind your back.**

They're voting on your credibility. They're voting on your clarity. They're voting on whether or not the truth is actually *safe* in your leadership ecosystem. And when the whispers grow louder than your comms strategy, you've already lost the narrative.

You can't fix it with another all-hands. You can't repair it with a town hall and a smile. Because gossip doesn't thrive in bad teams—it thrives in broken systems.

Where psychological safety is gone. Where feedback loops are performative. Where dissent is punished or ignored. Where vulnerability is branded as "drama" and transparency is met with silence.

If your team knows more from Slack threads, smoke breaks, and group chats than from your leadership voice, you're not leading a culture. **You're managing a rumor mill.** And every minute you ignore it, the unofficial channels become *more credible* than the official ones.

So, what do you do? You name it. You reclaim it. You build feedback systems that don't just welcome honesty—they *protect* it. Because when people trust that they'll be heard above ground, they stop digging tunnels underneath your authority.

8. High Turnover Meets Low Engagement

In a truly toxic culture, people don't storm out in rage. They *smile on their way out the door.* They write polished LinkedIn farewells. They thank the company "for the opportunity." They mention how "excited" they are for their next chapter.

But behind that corporate courtesy? Fatigue. Disillusionment. A soul-level whisper: *It wasn't worth the fight anymore.* **They didn't leave in anger. They left in quiet defeat.** Not because they were weak. But because the system had taught them that *truth was unwelcome,* and change was *unrealistic.*

They'd spoken up. They'd played the game. They'd tried. And when nothing changed, they chose peace over principle. Silence over the soul-tax of staying.

And the ones who remain? Don't mistake their stillness for loyalty. Don't mistake their presence for engagement. Because what's left behind in a culture like this isn't commitment—it's **compliance.**

- Heads down.
- Cameras off.
- Just enough to not get flagged.

They aren't dreaming. They're enduring. You ask for input—they give you pre-approved soundbites. You ask for ideas—they give you whatever won't get them assigned extra work. You ask for passion—and get a PowerPoint.

And here's the kicker-**Engagement surveys become a joke.** Not because people are cynical—because they're *smart.* They know the game. They know what happens to the brutally honest response. They've seen feedback go in and never come out.

Town halls become theater. Questions are pre-screened. Answers are rehearsed. Everyone claps—and no one believes.

And while you obsess over retention metrics? **The real damage has already been done.** Even if the bodies haven't walked out the door yet, the *souls have.*

Your best people? Already gone in spirit. Already imagining life somewhere else. Already navigating emotionally with the GPS set to *exit.*

So, let's be honest-If your culture needs *an exit interview to tell you what went wrong,* **you weren't listening when it mattered.** Because in high-trust cultures, truth is spoken *while people are still sitting at the table.*

In toxic ones, it only surfaces once their email's deactivated. And at that point? **You're not managing culture. You're reading the autopsy.**

9. Emotions Are Controlled, Not Understood

In toxic cultures, emotion isn't seen as insight. It's seen as *a threat to the brand.* You'll hear leadership praise people as - "Unshakable." "Cool-headed." "Always calm under pressure."

But what they *really* mean is - **"They never show emotion that makes *us* uncomfortable."** These environments treat emotion like a PR risk, not a signal. Like volatility, not vulnerability. Like something to be *managed*, not understood.

So instead of *coaching people through* frustration, grief, or overwhelm…They suppress it. They redirect it. Or worse—they punish it.

People learn quickly:
- Don't show disappointment.
- Don't cry—even in private.
- Don't speak with too much intensity or passion unless it's pre-approved and perfectly framed.

They stop crying in the bathroom—not because they're strong, but because they've learned that even *feeling* too much can cost them their credibility. Because in this culture:
- Tears are weakness.
- Frustration is "unprofessional."
- Honest emotion is "overreacting."

So, what do people do? They armor up. They shrink their expression. They numb out to stay employed.

And leadership? They call it *emotional intelligence, all the while they believe their emotions are intuition and magic not even remotely connected to their emotional instability.*

But let's be clear-**Emotional containment is not emotional intelligence. It's emotional exile.** And when people have to exile parts of themselves just to exist safely at work, you haven't created a high-performance culture. **You've created psychological fragility disguised as strength.**

You can't ask for creativity without making space for complexity. You can't demand resilience without honoring real emotional range. You can't preach authenticity in your values if your culture only rewards emotional silence.

So, here's your mirror, leader-If your people seem "shockingly composed" all the time…If no one ever gets visibly frustrated, passionate, or overwhelmed…If everyone seems emotionally "clean" …**That's not stability. That's suppression.**

And that's not healthy. It's lethal. Because cultures that punish emotion don't create better professionals. They create *broken ones.*

10. No One Speaks the Truth Out Loud

This is it. The **final symptom** of a culture in freefall. Not the beginning of toxicity, but the moment it becomes a **way of life**.

At this point, people aren't just frustrated—they're **resigned**. Not because they don't know what's wrong—but because they know exactly what's wrong…And they've decided it's not worth the cost to say it. Let that sink in - Everyone knows. And no one speaks.

- They know which leader is bleeding morale dry.
- They know which department hoards power and chokes collaboration.
- They know which behaviors violate the values—but keep getting rewarded anyway.

And still… **silence.** Because truth has become radioactive. And in this kind of culture, **truth-tellers don't rise—they vanish.** They get labeled as:

- "Not a team player."
- "Too intense."
- "A little too focused on the negative."

They don't get mentored—they get managed. They don't get promoted—they get isolated. And eventually, they don't get tired—they get *out*. The message becomes clear: **In this system, it's not your job to be honest. It's your job to *adjust*.**

So, what do your people do? They play the game. They start using phrases like:

- "It's above my pay grade."
- "Let's just keep our heads down."
- "Don't poke the bear."

The performance begins.

- Teams smile in meetings and scream in private.
- Direct reports say "we're good" while quietly working on their exit plans.
- Managers nod at every directive while quietly removing their fingerprints from the fallout.

You think things are calm. But underneath? A silent rebellion is growing. Because here's what toxic cultures never admit-**Truth doesn't disappear. It just goes underground.** It becomes sarcasm. It becomes gossip. It becomes apathy.

And slowly, *reality fragments.* The official story diverges from lived experience. The brand voice sounds nothing like the hallway conversations. The mission statement becomes performance art—words repeated without belief.

At this point, dysfunction isn't just present. **It's protected.** And the organization? It has ceased to be a place of progress. It has become a place of **pretending.**

You aren't managing a team—you're maintaining an illusion. You aren't building a culture—you're curating a narrative. And you aren't leading a mission—you're running a machine that punishes honesty and rewards silence.

So, let's say it plainly-**When no one speaks the truth out loud, you haven't just lost psychological safety. You've lost the *soul* of the organization.** And no rebrand can fix that. No new logo. No values refresh. No engagement survey with a QR code in the break room.

Because the truth has left the building. And until you invite it back—not politely, but *courageously*—Everything else is theater.

The Moment of Reckoning

Now we arrive at the mirror. Not the one you hang on the wall—but the one that hangs in the back of your mind. The one that doesn't care about your title, your tenure, or your quarterly performance. The one that asks the question you've been trying not to answer: **How many of these signals are alive inside your team?**

- **One?** Okay. You've got friction. Time to lead with intention.
- **Two?** The cracks are spreading. Culture repair isn't optional—it's urgent.
- **Five?** You're in dangerous territory. You're not leading a team—you're managing fallout.
- **All ten?**

Then hear this clearly-**You're not in a business anymore. You're in a *performance* of one.** You've got teams showing up, clocking in, and executing just enough to stay out of trouble. You've got leaders protecting politics, not people. You've got culture in a coma, dressed up in swag and slogans.

The metrics might still look okay. The brand might still shine. But inside? **Rot. Resentment. Resignation.**

And here's the thing that separates leaders from legacy-makers-**Will you keep pretending? Or will you confront the truth?**

Because while the signals are sobering, the *other* truth is this-**You can change it.** You don't need a reorg. You don't need a 90-day initiative. You don't need a consultant with a catchy name and a $100K slide deck. **You need a spine.**

You need *one leader*—just one—willing to stop performing and start *leading*. And if you're reading this? That leader is you.

You change the culture **one confrontation at a time.**

- One moment where you say, "We're not sweeping this under the rug."
- One meeting where you tell the truth *before* it's safe.
- One direct report you fight for, not because it's easy—but because it's *right*.

You repair trust **one broken pattern at a time.**

- One room you walk into without the mask.
- One policy you rewrite because it protects power, not people.
- One truth you let hit the air, even if it makes the room uncomfortable.

Because here's the secret: **you don't need permission to do any of it.** You don't need consensus. You don't need buy-in. You don't need someone above you to tell you "Now's the time." **You need conviction.**

And you don't need another survey. You don't need another AI-powered pulse check to confirm what your gut has been screaming for months. **You need to say the thing no one else will say. In the room where everyone else has been too afraid.**

You need to lead like truth matters more than comfort. Because it does. You need to lead like courage is contagious. Because it is. And you need to act like this isn't just your team's reckoning—**It's yours.**

Field Manual: Surviving Reputation Warfare

They can't outwork you. So, they attack your name. This is reputation warfare — the art of sabotaging outcomes through whispers, perception distortion, and strategic victimhood. If you lead with force, with clarity, with speed — they'll call you "too intense." If you demand excellence — they'll call it "intimidating." If you protect the mission — they'll accuse you of being "unapproachable."

The goal isn't to remove you. The goal is to **weaken your credibility until you remove yourself.** Here's how to fight back:

1. Own Your Narrative — Loudly and Early

Directive: Never outsource your reputation.

Watch for:
- "I heard some people feel..."
- Side comments about your "style" instead of your outcomes
- Undefined complaints about "tone," "vibe," or "approach"

Action:
- Publicly reinforce your leadership stance:

"Here's what I believe. Here's how I lead. Here's what I will never compromise."
- Anchor perception before others infect it.

2. Demand Outcome-Based Feedback

Directive: Refuse to debate feelings in the absence of facts.

Watch for:
- "She made me feel unsafe" (with no behavioral specifics)
- "He's abrasive" (despite performance metrics being high)
- Vague team "concerns" that dodge responsibility

Action:
- Ask directly:

"What specific behavior failed the mission?"
- If they can't answer, you're dealing with emotional projection — not feedback.

3. Protect Your Builders

Directive: Shield the high-performers who become easy targets when they refuse to coddle mediocrity.

Watch for:
- Quiet top performers suddenly isolated
- Rumors around those who push hard
- Resentment from emotional saboteurs

Action:
- Publicly stand beside your builders.
- Say it clearly:

"We value truth, drive, and execution — even when it's uncomfortable."

4. Counter the Whisper War

Directive: Silence is complicity. Name the game.

Watch for:

- Private slack messages slandering leadership
- "Just between us" narratives
- Passive-aggressive emotional signaling

Action:
- Bring whispers to daylight:

"If there's feedback, let's do it openly. The mission doesn't move in shadows."

- Fear thrives in ambiguity. Kill it with clarity.

5. Lead with Calm Violence

Directive: Don't yell. Don't plead. Don't shrink. Burn illusions with receipts.

Watch for:
- Attacks framed as "concern"
- Backhanded compliments
- Misrepresentation of your leadership decisions

Action:
- Respond with data, proof, and calm ferocity:

"Here's the decision. Here's the outcome. Here's the result."

- Never let false narratives outpace your documented truth.

Final Directive: Your reputation is not what they say. It's what you reinforce — through courage, through clarity, through fire. If you don't own your name, they will write it in lowercase. If you don't define your leadership, they will weaponize it against you. So, lead loud. Lead clear. And never let the whisper war win.

Chapter 6: Spotting the Saboteurs

The first time we enforced the new standard; half the room went quiet. It wasn't dramatic. There were no shouting matches. No slammed doors. Just a shift — heavy and cold — like a storm front moving through the building. We weren't asking for miracles. We weren't demanding superhuman performance. We were demanding alignment.

Truth over feelings. Action over theater. Ownership over excuses. We laid it out in blood-simple terms: *"This is the mission. These are the standards. Here's what happens if you move. Here's what happens if you don't."*

No euphemisms. No moral pleading. Just clarity — the kind that either hardens a leader or exposes a coward. And in that silence, you could see it: The calculations running behind their eyes.

Some realized they couldn't hide anymore. Some realized their excuses wouldn't work here. Some realized they had built their careers on emotional leverage — and now the currency had changed. A few walked out over the next few weeks. Some in anger. Some in quiet resignation. Some still pretending it was their choice.

And that was fine. Because the ones who stayed —They weren't staying because it was easy. They were staying because they **believed in building something cleaner than what they'd inherited**. They became the foundation. Stone by stone. Action by action. Hard conversation by hard conversation. They fought for the new culture. They defended the new standards. They carried the mission forward with their hands bloody and their hearts clear.

And that's how a clean leadership culture is born. Not by consensus. Not by inspiration. But by standing the line — and letting the fire reveal who's worth building with.

The rebuild didn't just reveal the builders. It also flushed out the saboteurs — the ones who wore the right shirts, said the right things, and played the long game of survival. Because the truth is simple: **Not every enemy carries a banner.**

Some wrap themselves in the company's values. Some mimic loyalty while quietly stalling the mission. And when you raise the standard — when you stop letting fear and comfort run your leadership **those smiling saboteurs have no choice but to show their hand.**
Not every saboteur looks like a villain. Some look like your biggest cheerleader. Some call themselves "servant leaders." Some have the company's values memorized and can quote them on demand. Some are loved by the CEO—but feared by their peers.

They're not disruptive in the traditional sense. They don't shout in meetings. They don't skip steps. Instead, they slow the machine down **one emotional manipulation at a time**.

They traffic in ambiguity. They're fluent in half-truths, delayed actions, and strategic victimhood. They position themselves as protectors—while slowly poisoning clarity, cohesion, and execution. These are the **internal saboteurs**. And in cultures that prize harmony over truth, **they thrive**.

The Hidden Cost of Unchecked Manipulation

When we think of manipulation, we often imagine **hostile, aggressive behavior**—someone overtly dominating, controlling, or undermining. But in today's high-EQ, high-performance environments, manipulation rarely looks like that. **It hides inside emotional intelligence.** These saboteurs:

- Mirror your language.
- Co-sign your values.
- Speak the language of leadership—*but use it to protect themselves, not the mission.*

And that makes them hard to see. Because they don't:

- Challenge the mission directly.
- Sabotage in front of the room.
- Openly resist direction.

Instead, they:

- Appear "on board."
- Smile through alignment.
- Champion collaboration—*while quietly unraveling it from the edges.*

The Subtle Techniques of High-EQ Saboteurs

These individuals are smart, politically skilled, and emotionally fluent. They don't confront power—they **co-opt it**. They:

- **Champion the mission in public** – then quietly stall execution behind the scenes. They'll say, "This is exactly where we need to go," but never *actually support the move* when it's time to act.
- **Agree to clarity in meetings** – only to reopen the conversation in side threads. "I know we aligned on this earlier, but I've been thinking more about it..." Suddenly the team's momentum fractures—and nobody's sure what's been decided anymore.
- **Speak empowerment** – while hoarding information. They appear collaborative but block context or slow decisions to remain *the necessary node.*
- **Use process as a weapon** – adding steps, demanding "alignment," or questioning protocol—not to improve outcomes, but to delay and destabilize.

The Hidden Damage They Cause

The manipulation doesn't hit like a bomb. It hits like a slow leak. At first, you won't even notice it. But over time, it shows up in symptoms that *look like cultural failure*—but are actually the result of **one person quietly pulling the strings.** You'll see:

1. Teams That Slow Down—Even When Priorities Are Clear

- The goals are aligned.
- The strategy is set.

- But momentum mysteriously fades. Why? Because someone's introducing friction behind the scenes. You have to look deeply to find the saboteur, but you'll find a common thread.

2. High Performers Withdraw

- Your best people stop leading visibly.
- Not because they've disengaged—but because they've learned that *every step forward will be slowed, questioned, or reversed* by the same player.

3. Meetings Become Surface-Level

- People stop speaking plainly.
- They avoid challenge.
- They leave the real talk for private conversations—because one manipulator made candor feel risky.

4. Project Delays Multiply—Blamed on "Process"

- Everyone knows what's needed.
- But somehow, *more steps* get added.
- More "alignment" is needed.
- More "concerns" surface at the last moment.

And all of it sounds reasonable. Strategic, even. But it's not strategy. **It's control through confusion.**

The Aftermath: The Fog Only Clears Once They're Gone

This is the most revealing (and heartbreaking) part. Most leaders don't realize the damage until *after* the manipulator is gone. Suddenly:

- The team accelerates.
- The tension lifts.
- Meetings become productive again.
- People speak openly.
- High performers re-engage.

And it hits you: *It wasn't the culture. It wasn't the system. It wasn't the team.* **It was one person. A skilled saboteur. A high-EQ manipulator who confused everyone—so they could stay important.**

Because in every culture, there are people who need the team *to stay broken* in order to maintain their power. And if you don't name this dynamic? If you don't design your leadership system to surface and confront it? It will steal your progress—and your clarity—while smiling the whole time.

Inside the Manipulator Playbook

Manipulators in modern leadership environments don't operate through overt aggression. They **camouflage dysfunction in emotional fluency, social strategy, and selective alignment.** They don't need a title to control the room. They need **proximity, ambiguity, and silence.** And unless leaders are trained to recognize the **subtle but consistent patterns**, the manipulator stays in play long after the damage is done. Here are the four major tactics—now fully detailed.

1. Praise as Positioning - At first, it looks like loyalty.

- Affirmation in meetings.
- "You've taught me so much" notes.

- Repeating your language and leadership mantras.
- Public endorsement of your decisions.

But it's not loyalty—it's **leverage**. **Every compliment is a coin.** And every coin is meant to be *spent* later. The real goal is **emotional IOUs**:

- Guilt immunity when they eventually cross a line.
- Political insulation when peers push back.
- The ability to reframe criticism as betrayal:

"After everything I've done to support this team, I'm shocked you'd question my commitment." They're building credit with your ego—so they can **withdraw influence** when stakes are high. And if you call them out? They play the **disappointed ally**- *"I just thought, given how aligned we've been, you'd understand..."* This is **conditional loyalty**—and it's always a trap.

2. Crisis as Control - The second move in the playbook is to **frame emotional chaos as urgent vulnerability**—especially when accountability begins to tighten. They inject manufactured or exaggerated concerns into the system, like:

- Sudden emotional outbursts when performance feedback is given.
- Retroactive "ethical" objections to strategic direction.
- Weaponized language: "unsafe," "harmful," "toxic."
- Private side conversations with HR or Legal—*not to resolve, but to escalate silently.*
- "Emergency" meetings to talk about "how the team is feeling."

What's happening here? They're shifting the narrative from performance to protection. They want to *stall strategic momentum* by forcing leadership to **tend to their emotions** instead of the mission. And because it's cloaked in "vulnerability," it's hard to challenge without looking cold. This tactic works especially well in cultures that:

- Conflate empathy with avoidance.
- Prioritize harmony over performance.
- Lack clear emotional escalation protocols.

It's not about resolving conflict. It's about using conflict to pause the game. And while leadership is trying to "hear them out," the saboteur continues rerouting control behind the scenes.

3. Projection and Victim Inversion - This is their most **psychologically sophisticated tactic** and the hardest for emotionally intelligent leaders to detect. It works like this:

- They sow division—then say *others* are being divisive.
- They breach trust—then claim *they* no longer feel safe.
- They delay deliverables—then say *they're overwhelmed and unsupported.*
- They hijack initiatives—then say *they're being excluded.*

This is **reality inversion**. It's strategic use of **emotional language to reverse roles**—so that *they* become the injured party and others are painted as the aggressors. Why does this work? Because:

- They sound emotionally fluent.
- They use just the right psychological buzzwords.
- They know that most leaders default to empathy and inclusion when conflict arises.

In emotionally sensitive cultures without strong accountability scaffolding, *feelings become facts*. And soon, the story shifts from: *"This person is obstructing progress"* To: *"This person is being mistreated while trying to help."* Unless someone names the pattern **clearly, early, and publicly**, they **win**—because they've reframed their sabotage as martyrdom.

4. Strategic Confusion - When they can't control the narrative with charm, crisis, or inversion, the manipulator falls back on one final, reliable tool: **confusion.** And it looks like incompetence—but it's *not.* They'll:
- "Misinterpret" clear instructions.
- Revisit decisions that were already agreed upon.
- Ask for clarification on processes they've executed flawlessly before.
- Miss deadlines—then claim they misunderstood what was expected.
- Delay execution by asking for "alignment" that has already happened.

The objective here is not clarity—it's **camouflage.** They know you won't push hard on someone who "just misunderstood." They rely on your *professional courtesy* to avoid appearing "too harsh." Meanwhile:
- Their peers pick up the slack.
- Deadlines slide.
- Progress stalls.

And the saboteur? **Keeps their seat—and their image intact.** This isn't a mistake. It's **defensive intelligence. It eats velocity. It drains culture. It breaks high performers. And it's happening in every organization that lacks structural accountability.**

Why Most Leaders Miss It

Let's be brutally honest. Most leaders don't miss manipulators because they're incompetent. They miss them because they're *empathetic.* Because they *want to lead well.* Because they've been told that labeling someone as "toxic" is risky—and often politically dangerous. So, they hesitate. They hesitate because:
- **They don't want to mislabel someone.**
  What if I'm wrong? What if this is just a personality clash? What if they're going through something personal?
- **They don't want to be accused of being exclusionary.**
  If I say this behavior is harmful, will someone say I'm not inclusive? That I'm judging their style, background, or communication norms?
- **They don't want to seem authoritarian.**
  If I take a firm stance, will I be viewed as controlling? Will I lose my image as a "people-first" leader?
- **They want to believe everyone means well.**
  Because most leaders operate from this core belief: *People are good. People are trying. People want to grow.*

And listen—that's *noble.* But noble doesn't mean helpful. And optimism without discernment is *naïveté in a leadership costume.* Because here's the truth-**Manipulation doesn't require malicious intent.** It only requires:
- Emotional skill

- Fear
- A need for control
- And a system that *doesn't challenge the pattern.*

What Leaders Must Understand

Manipulators thrive in ambiguity. They don't need power—they just need your *doubt.* They don't need approval—they just need your *inaction.* And they don't need to win—they just need you to *hesitate long enough for them to survive.*

So, what's the antidote? **Systems that surface behavior—not personality. Patterns— not impressions. Truth—not vibes.** You don't need to be judge and jury. You need to **build an organization where patterns can't hide**. Let's show you how.

How to Spot Manipulators—Every Time

Here's how to go beyond the gut check and actually detect saboteurs using **behavioral precision**, not emotional suspicion.

1. Look for Pattern Breakers, Not Personality Traits

Manipulators often *seem* charming, aligned, thoughtful, even humble. So, stop trying to read personality—and start tracking **inconsistency** in behavior. Ask:
- Do they agree in meetings but reopen topics later?
- Do they delay deadlines with vague confusion?
- Do they constantly ask for clarity they previously had?
- Do team members feel exhausted by interactions with them?

Character isn't what people say when they're on. It's what they do when they think no one's tracking patterns.

2. Watch for Emotional Weaponry

Saboteurs use emotions to deflect accountability. Look for:
- Sudden "hurt" feelings after performance feedback.
- Reframing of decisions as "unsafe," "harmful," or "oppressive"—*only after clarity is enforced.*
- Escalations to HR framed as "concerns," not solutions.

Emotional language isn't the problem. **Emotional redirection is.** Ask:
- Is the emotional concern paired with accountability and contribution?
- Or is it being used to pause, stall, or flip the narrative?

3. Track Contribution vs. Friction Ratio

Every team member creates a certain **ratio of value to disruption**. Some people are direct, but they move the mission. Some are emotional, but they catalyze connection.
But manipulators? They create **confusion and drag** that far outweighs their actual contribution. Track:
- How often do others clean up behind this person?
- How many projects stall when they're involved?
- How many "alignment" meetings do they initiate?

- Are their updates always polished—but never show results?

4. Ask the Team (Anonymously and Often)

Your team knows. They've already felt it. They're just waiting to see if *you're willing to name it*. Build anonymous feedback loops that ask:

- Where is clarity breaking down?
- Who consistently reopens closed loops?
- Where does conflict seem to follow one person?

Patterns don't lie. You don't need blame—you need **evidence**.

5. Make Truth a Structural Requirement

Build a system where:

- Decisions have *clear locking mechanisms*.
- Feedback is given consistently, not just in crises.
- Side conversations are logged and summarized openly.
- Cultural "pull requests" (revisiting direction) are formalized, not whispered.

Manipulators can't survive where truth is required *at every turn*.

Compassion ≠ Complicity

As a leader, it's your job to protect the mission. To guard the culture. To ensure performance *isn't derailed by personality politics*. Yes, be kind. Yes, be thoughtful. But never confuse **kindness** with **tolerance for confusion**.

Truth is the highest form of inclusion. Clarity is the most courageous form of care. And spotting manipulation isn't judgment—it's *leadership in action*.

The Unified Leadership Guide: Confronting Saboteurs with Integrity and Precision

This guide is not about witch hunts or personality clashes. It's about creating **a culture immune to manipulation**, where decisions are final, truth is visible, and the mission cannot be quietly derailed.

Saboteurs—those who gain power through ambiguity, emotional escalation, and performance theater—thrive in disjointed systems. They lose their grip the moment leaders align around **clarity, pattern recognition, and strategic unity.**

Here's your operational playbook.

I. Build Systems That Reveal Patterns, Not Personalities

You don't need to accuse individuals. You need to *uncover repeatable behaviors*.

1. Design for Decision Finality

- Declare alignment moments clearly.
- Define a rule: *"Once we align in this room, execution begins. Side channels do not reopen decisions."*
- Document all major outcomes immediately—owners, timelines, escalation paths.

Purpose: This closes the window on silent dissent disguised as "continued conversation."

2. Watch for Pattern Breaks

- Track who regularly reintroduces previously closed decisions.

- Pay attention to who constantly "needs clarity" on things they've already done.
- Look at friction patterns: *Where does execution repeatedly slow—and who is always nearby when it happens?*

Purpose: Pattern recognition keeps the conversation objective and behavior-focused—not emotional or personal.

3. Normalize Retrospectives That Name Political Drag
- Add these questions to every project or sprint retrospective:
  - *"Where did clarity break down?"*
  - *"Where did resistance show up after alignment?"*
  - *"Who added friction after decisions were finalized?"*
- Don't make it about individuals—make it about behaviors.

Purpose: Political drag can only persist when leaders are afraid to name it. This gives the team sanctioned language to surface it safely.

4. Protect High Performers from Emotional Manipulation
- Build explicit support systems for top contributors.
- Ask regularly: *"What's slowing you down that's not in your job description?"*
- Watch for signs of strategic withdrawal—not burnout. Many high performers pull back because the politics around them are exhausting.

Purpose: High performers often spot the saboteur first. Create psychological safety for them to name what others are too polite to say.

II. Confront Behavior—Not People
5. Name the Pattern, Not the Person
Saboteurs win when you make it personal. They trigger emotion. They frame themselves as victims. They flip the script. So don't get personal. Get structural.
Say:
- *"We've seen concerns raised late in the process. Moving forward, all red flags need to surface during initial planning."*
- *"I'm noticing repeated misalignment on agreed timelines. Let's revisit our commitment tracking process."*
- *"We need everyone to signal confusion before deadlines—not after."*

Purpose: This removes the saboteur's ability to redirect or emotionalize. It puts the spotlight on *systems and behaviors*—where manipulation can't survive.

III. Remove Ambiguity—Anchor Execution
6. Eliminate the Fog with Executional Anchors
Your biggest enemy isn't the saboteur—it's the **fog** they operate within. So, you eliminate it by locking down:
- **Decision Records** – Every major choice gets documented in writing.
- **Named Ownership** – Every task has one responsible person (not a team).
- **Hard Deadlines** – No fuzzy due dates. No "we'll check back."
- **Public Escalation Channels** – If someone has a concern, there's *one place* to raise it. No hallway whispering.

Purpose: You don't beat manipulation by confronting it. You make it *impossible to weaponize the system.*

IV. Lead with Empathy—but Protect Execution
7. Separate Feeling from Strategy
Saboteurs thrive on emotional escalation:
- "I feel this was unfair."
- "This felt rushed."
- "I need time to process."

You don't ignore emotions—but you don't let them override the mission.
Say:
"We'll always make space for how people feel. But we also have outcomes to deliver. What does a productive path forward look like for you?"
Purpose: This honors humanity **without surrendering clarity.** Emotion is acknowledged. Execution is *non-negotiable.*

Final Word: Leadership is Structural Courage
The most dangerous dysfunction in your culture won't be explosive—it'll be subtle. It will wear a smile. It will use the language of collaboration. It will sound helpful. But it will slow everything—until *you name it.*

When your **entire leadership team shares a unified response**, the saboteur's playbook fails. Because in a system built on:
- Clarity over charm,
- Patterns over performance,
- Structure over sentiment—

Power without responsibility has nowhere to hide.

Final Reflection: Build a Culture Where Games Can't Survive
You don't defeat manipulation by outmaneuvering the manipulator. You defeat it by building a culture where **games don't work.** That means:
- Feedback is fast.
- Truth is normalized.
- Accountability is visible.
- Emotion is honored—but not allowed to hijack execution.

And when someone tries to spin, delay, or shift the narrative? The system holds the line—even if the leader doesn't have to. Let's take a look at a specific type of saboteurs – the narcissist. Let's go.

Field Manual: Rules for the Rebuild
You survived the purge. Now you build what fear, dysfunction, and ego never could.

This isn't about making people feel safe. It's about making the truth unignorable. It's about building a culture that can survive reality without needing illusions to stay upright. Here's how you rebuild — fast, clean, and without compromise.

1. Stand Fast on First Principles
Directive: Your standards are your survival. Never negotiate them to soothe fragile feelings.
Watch for:
- Pressure to "be flexible" with core values
- Leaders trying to "soften" expectations to keep the peace

Action:
- Clarify and publish the non-negotiables.
- Repeat them until they become institutional blood, not just wall slogans.

2. Cut Early, Not Late
Directive: Rot doesn't heal. It metastasizes.
Watch for:
- Chronic emotional saboteurs asking for "one more chance"
- High-maintenance, low-performance employees creating emotional gravity wells

Action:
- Move fast.
- Cut clean.
- The team will never heal if rot is tolerated because it's inconvenient to confront.

3. Declare the Standard Publicly
Directive: Make the standard visible, undeniable, and enforced.
Watch for:
- Secret standards enforced only when someone screws up
- Favoritism or shadow policies undermining clarity

Action:
- Speak it. Post it.
- Make every team ritual reinforce it.
- If it's not lived publicly, it doesn't exist.

4. Move Despite Fear
Directive: Fear is not a signal to stop — it's a compass pointing toward what must be done.
Watch for:
- Team hesitation around truth-telling
- Leaders delaying confrontation to "wait for the right moment"

Action:
- Push into the discomfort.
- Move faster when resistance rises.
- Fear clarifies what matters most.

5. Forgive Quickly, Forget Slowly

Directive: Healing matters — but memory protects.
Watch for:
- Over-trusting those who previously betrayed trust
- Forgetting patterns of behavior that destroyed culture before

Action:
- Offer forgiveness to free your own energy.
- Maintain historical clarity to prevent repeated sabotage.
- Trust actions, not apologies.

You're not rebuilding a team. You're building an ecosystem where truth thrives and cowards starve. Clean leadership isn't a vibe. It isn't a set of slogans. It's a system of survival built through confrontation, construction, and consistency.

Stand the line. Move the mission. Defend the fire you rebuilt from the ashes. **This is leadership without apology. This is clean command. This is what the world needs — and few have the guts to build.**

Chapter 7: The Narcissist Next Door

Astrid walked into a disaster. She walked into an **ecosystem of dysfunction**, *run by insecure narcissists clinging to relevance.*

The leadership structure wasn't leading — it was **performing survival theater**. Titles meant power. Power meant image. And image was everything.

No clarity. No operational direction. Just emotional volatility and executive fragility masked as "strategic pivots."

The leaders praised each other in meetings and **trashed each other behind closed doors**. They couldn't process feedback. They equated dissent with betrayal. And the worst sin you could commit in that culture? **Making progress without them.**

That's where Astrid became dangerous. She didn't play the game. She didn't feed their egos. She didn't posture. She went to work. She understood customer service. She understood how to connect, serve, and move actual outcomes.

And that exposed the rot. Her calm execution made their chaos visible. Her clarity made their spin look foolish. Her strength made their insecurity unbearable. So, they turned on her — quietly, of course. They flooded her with tasks — not to reward excellence, but to exhaust it. They micromanaged her while ignoring their own failings.

They framed her competence as arrogance — Called her "too aggressive" in side meetings, and whispered that "she's not really a team player" while asking her to carry the load. See, narcissistic leadership **needs chaos to stay in control**. And Astrid refused to participate. She didn't argue. She didn't beg. She didn't flinch. She owned the mess. She executed anyway.

What they called "unrealistic mountains," Astrid moved like they were nothing but pebbles. And in doing so, she **broke their illusion** —The carefully protected narrative that failure was always someone else's fault. Because if one person could rise in that fire, their entire excuse matrix **imploded on contact. That's a One Percenter.** Not someone who shines on stage. Someone who **exposes the lies by building anyway**.

One Percenters like Astrid are threat vectors in ego-driven systems. Because they don't worship the structure —They operate above it. **Get enough of them**, and you don't just change performance metrics —**You change the culture's gravitational pull.**

You don't need an army to clean up a leadership disaster. You need a few Astrids — people who don't feed the dysfunction of narcissism, don't flinch under pressure, and don't need permission to do what's right.

This is how the One Percent operates: Unshakeable. Unimpressed by ego. Unstoppable under pressure. And their performance destroys the toxic leader's excuse narrative.

Not every toxic leader screams in meetings or throws things across the boardroom. Some of them laugh. Some of them charm. Some of them "mentor." Some of them build their kingdom one favor, one manipulated ally, one performative apology at a time.

This is the narcissist next door. Not the cartoon villain, but the corporate darling. Not the tyrant, but the visionary. Not the sociopath, but the "rising star." They're smart. Charismatic. Articulate. And they're **slowly hollowing out your culture from the inside.** This chapter is about them. But more importantly, it's about how to **see them**—before it's too late.

Narcissistic Leadership: Red Flags in Real Time

Narcissistic leaders don't arrive with a warning label. They arrive with compliments. They arrive with shared values. They arrive with empathy that feels real—because *they've rehearsed it.* You'll hear them quoting Brené Brown one day and gaslighting a team member the next. They don't dominate with threats. They *infiltrate* with validation. Here's how it unfolds:

1. **The Mirror Phase**-They reflect your values back to you. They say all the right things in interviews, 1:1s, and strategy sessions. They make you feel seen—not because they understand you, but because *they've studied you.*
2. **The Loyalty Trap**-You're not just a colleague—you're "one of the few who gets it." They share "how hard it's been," how others "just don't think at this level," how "you're the kind of person they've been waiting for."
3. **The Empathy Gambit**-They share vulnerabilities—but curated ones. Vulnerabilities that evoke admiration, not accountability. You feel close, but never *equal.*
4. **The Shift**-Feedback starts to bounce. Critique is rebranded as confusion. Accountability becomes a "learning opportunity"—for you. You'll notice:
   o Deflection instead of reflection.
   o Justifications wrapped in jargon.
   o Apologies that sound like PR statements: just enough remorse to reset the room.
5. **The Power Play**-They don't just seek results. They seek **credit**. They crave *optics.* They have a sixth sense for who has influence—and they orbit accordingly.
6. **The Fallout**-When something goes wrong, you'll never hear "my fault." You'll hear:
   o "I'm just surprised by how reactive everyone's being."
   o "I think there's a lot of projection happening here."
   o "The team just couldn't keep up."
   o "That's not how I experienced it."

And you'll realize-**They don't seek alignment. They seek control. They don't want feedback. They want worship.**

Why They Thrive in Modern Organizations

Narcissists are not just surviving in modern leadership cultures. **They're thriving.** Why? Because **ambiguity is their playground.**
- In cultures that value **charisma over character**, they flourish.
- In systems with **loose accountability** and **emotional labor**, they dominate.
- In performance models that reward **visibility over value**, they ascend rapidly.

They excel in:

- Flat org charts where no one really owns the outcomes.
- Environments where "feedback" is vague, inconsistent, or only goes one way.
- Cultures that confuse emotional intelligence with likability.

In other words-**They thrive in fog.** The fog of unclear expectations. The fog of constant change. The fog of leaders too afraid to call out behavior that doesn't come with a raised voice.

How to Spot the Narcissist Next Door

Here's what to watch for:
- They *broadcast* empathy, but can't tolerate dissent.
- They talk about values, but treat people as pawns.
- They over-promise, over-frame, and under-own.
- Their vulnerability always points toward applause—not growth.
- They collect influence like currency—and spend it only when it serves their brand.

And when you finally confront them? They won't explode. They'll *reframe.* They'll suggest *you misunderstood.* They'll say they're "open to feedback"—and then ghost the real conversation.

What to Do When You See It:
1. **Stop getting hypnotized by language.** Watch behavior. Consistency. Pattern. *Impact.*
2. **Ask yourself: Is this leader building systems—or building a stage?** Are they empowering others—or creating dependents?
3. **Document everything.** Narcissists are master storytellers. Protect your reality.
4. **Push for clarity.** On deliverables. On expectations. On decision rights. Narcissists lose traction in high-clarity, high-accountability systems.
5. **Don't go it alone.** They manipulate isolation. Build coalitions of clarity and courage.

The most dangerous narcissist in your organization isn't the obvious tyrant. It's the one who smiles while shifting blame. The one who "cares" while consolidating power. The one who gets promoted because they know how to *perform leadership*—but refuse to *live it.* This chapter isn't just about naming them. It's about reclaiming your culture *from* them. Because if you let them grow unchecked, you won't just lose trust. **You'll lose truth. And once truth is gone, so is your leadership.**

Divide-and-Conquer as Culture Strategy

One of the clearest—and most corrosive—signs you're dealing with narcissistic leadership is the **divide-and-conquer strategy**. But this isn't the obvious, medieval, top-down style of control most of us imagine. No, this version wears a modern suit. It cloaks itself in *strategy*, *relationship management*, even *executive presence*.

Narcissistic leaders don't build unified teams. They build **dependent tribes**. They don't want alignment. They want orbit. They're not interested in teams that think independently—they want **clusters of loyalty** competing for their approval. And here's how it plays out in real time:

The Patterns You'll See
- **Selective Elevation**

  One person gets praised relentlessly in private while others are subtly criticized. The golden child of the moment is used as a contrast— *"Why can't others just operate like [Name]?"* But make no mistake: **that golden child can be dethroned at any time.**

- **Public Undermining After Private Praise**
  You're empowered behind closed doors—then undercut in a meeting. You walk in thinking you're aligned, only to realize your credibility is being *softly questioned* in front of others. The message? *"I control how you're seen."*
- **Triangulated Conflicts**
  Instead of addressing issues directly, the narcissist drops **selective truths**, half-stories, or emotionally charged fragments with multiple parties. They never solve the tension—they *stir* it. They say things like:

"I think [Name] misunderstood your tone, but I told them you meant well." "They had concerns, but I said I'd talk to you first—it's probably nothing." Now you're paranoid, the other person's unsure, and guess who remains the intermediary? **Them. Always them.**

- **Confusion as Currency**
  Deadlines are fluid. Priorities shift. Messages conflict. Roles blur. The narcissist is always "clarifying" something—because in their world, **clarity is dangerous.**
  Why?

Because clarity leads to alignment. Alignment leads to accountability. And accountability is the *one thing they will never share.*

What It Does to the Team

Over time, the strategy doesn't just affect outcomes—it reprograms behavior:

- **Trust evaporates.**
  Colleagues become competitors for visibility and access. Every interaction becomes a game of optics and positioning.
- **People second-guess motives.**
  "Was that feedback real, or part of a setup?"
  "Should I share this, or will it be used against me later?"
- **Information gets hoarded.**
  Knowledge becomes currency. Collaboration is treated as risk. Departments silo. Teams fragment.
- **Psychological safety dies.**
  Even high performers play small—not out of incompetence, but out of *self-preservation.*

And at the center of it all? **The narcissistic leader sits untouched. Unquestioned. Indispensable.** They've positioned themselves as the **glue** holding everything together.

- "They know how to navigate the personalities."
- "They're the only one who can manage the conflict."
- "Things fall apart when they're not in the loop."

But here's the truth no one's saying out loud - **They're not the glue. They're the accelerant.** They aren't stabilizing the system. They're *strategically destabilizing it*—then inserting themselves as the solution.

The Hidden Cost: Cultural Cannibalism

This is the slow cannibalization of culture. It doesn't implode in a day—it erodes across months and quarters. You don't see it in the metrics—until it's too late. You see it in attrition that doesn't make sense. You feel it in team meetings that sound aligned but *feel off*. You see it when high-performers disengage, when talent drains, and when nobody wants to step into leadership anymore—because they've learned leadership in this system means choosing **proximity over principle**.

What to Watch For
- A single leader who always seems to be the "translator" between people.
- Patterns of team rotation—where alignment never sticks.
- People who *glow* when close to power, and *burn* the moment they stray.
- Frequent closed-door meetings followed by visible confusion.
- Praise that feels performative—always just enough to control, never enough to *empower*.

What to Do
- **Name the triangulation.** Refuse to speak *about* people—insist on speaking *with* them.
- **Drive for clarity.** Set roles, expectations, and feedback systems in stone. Ambiguity is their jungle—cut it down.
- **Break the dependency cycle.** Create structures that reward team alignment, not individual loyalty.
- **Refuse the private praise/public shame dynamic.** Force congruence between what is said in the room and outside of it.
- **Call power games what they are.** With courage. With clarity. Without waiting for consensus.

Divide-and-conquer isn't just a tactic. In the hands of a narcissistic leader, it becomes a *cultural operating system*. It doesn't just fracture relationships—it rewires behavior. And if it's not confronted directly, it will create a system where dysfunction is so baked-in, **truth sounds offensive, and trust becomes impossible. The narcissist isn't just the problem.** They've *convinced everyone they're the cure.* And that's the most dangerous lie of all.

Charisma Without Conscience: The Deadliest Brand of Leadership
In today's leadership culture—especially in the hyper-visual, hyper-performative age of social media, TED Talks, and "thought leadership" posts—we reward *polish* over principle. We elevate those who present well. We reward articulate over authentic. We mistake **charm** for **character**, and **confidence** for **conscience**.

And narcissists? They know this better than anyone. They've studied the blueprint. They've mastered the language. They've learned how to **look like a leader long before they've earned the trust to be one.**

The Performance
They know how to:
- **Perform confidence** with just the right cadence and eye contact.
- **Take the stage** and own the room, weaving vision into a magnetic narrative.

- **Cry on cue**—tears of curated vulnerability that don't cost them power but *earn them applause*.
- **Humblebrag** about past failures that conveniently position them as both warrior and sage.
- **Play both hero and victim** in their story, ensuring they are always centered.

They use mission language fluently—because they know we crave meaning. They mention "impact," "purpose," "servant leadership." But listen closely… It's *always* about them. Their journey. Their lessons. Their elevation. It's not service. It's stagecraft.

The Inner Vacuum

Here's the terrifying truth: beneath the charisma, there's no internal compass.
- No conscience.
- No integrated self.
- No capacity for real, reflective accountability.

What looks like *vision* is often **grandiosity**. What looks like *resilience* is often **emotional detachment**. What looks like *adaptability* is often **chameleon survival instinct**—adjusting only to maintain control, not alignment. They don't lead from values. They lead from **voids**. And those voids demand constant admiration. Constant reinforcement. Constant power proximity.

That's why they're never fully at rest. They need to be seen. They need to be praised. They need to be the *most*—or they feel like nothing.

Why They're So Hard to Spot

This is what makes them lethal-**They look exactly like what we've been trained to admire.** They wear the outer skin of great leadership:
- Confident, but never *self-aware*.
- Compelling, but never *accountable*.
- Adaptive, but never *integrated*.

They talk about "the team," "the culture," "the mission" …But **watch what happens when the spotlight shifts.** They re-center it. Always. Because beneath the performance, *it's never about the mission*. It's about **maintaining the illusion of their superiority**.

The Cultural Fallout

And here's what makes it devastating-They don't blow up the organization with scandal. They **reshape it in their image.**
- People stop being honest—because truth disrupts the fantasy.
- Teams stop trusting leadership—because they see who really gets protected.
- Execution slows—because clarity is replaced by drama, dysfunction, and deflection.

And somehow, the narcissist remains untouched by the fallout. Why? Because they don't fail in obvious ways. They fail *through others*. They offload consequences. They gaslight responsibility. They *infect*, then escape. They rise—**while others bleed.**

And the organization, slowly and tragically, starts to conform:
- People learn to perform instead of produce.
- Feedback becomes filtered through fear.
- Loyalty replaces effectiveness as the currency of advancement.
- And the ones who see the truth? They either leave… or go quiet.

The Call to Courage

Here's the most sobering truth of all-**If you don't see it—if you don't name it—you will become complicit in it.** Not because you're malicious. But because you've been conditioned to admire the mask. So, this is the call:

- Look deeper than performance.
- Stop rewarding charisma without conscience.
- Stop mistaking power for trustworthiness.
- Start asking *who is being built by this leader—and who is being erased*?

Because the most dangerous leaders aren't the ones who make mistakes. **They're the ones who make sure someone else always pays for them.** And until we stop confusing magnetism with integrity, we **will keep giving microphones to performers—and calling them leaders.**

What It Costs You

Unchecked narcissistic leadership is not a minor personnel issue. It is not "just a strong personality." It is not a "culture fit concern" to tiptoe around in performance reviews. It is **a slow cultural collapse** wearing the costume of competence. And the longer it goes unaddressed, the deeper the damage goes. Here's what it will cost you—not in theory, but in the daily reality of organizational erosion:

1. Your High Performers

Narcissistic leaders don't manage performance. They manage *perception*. And your best people? They're allergic to that game. They don't want to grovel for praise. They don't want to politic for promotion. They don't want to be part of a system where visibility trumps value. So, what happens? They leave.

- They disengage.
- They stop speaking up.
- They ghost opportunities.
- They polish their résumé while sitting in back-to-back meetings pretending not to notice the favoritism.

And the truly tragic part? **They don't leave because they're weak. They leave because they're strong enough to refuse the compromise.** Does that hurt? It should. They're leading themselves more than the masked leaders pretending.

2. Your Innovation Pipeline

Narcissists don't innovate—they *curate* what makes them look good. They're not building future-facing solutions. They're building *mirrors*—systems that reflect their brilliance. So, they suppress risk. They crush experimentation.

They redirect creativity toward projects they can brand with their name. Ideas are stolen, reshaped, rebranded—and repackaged as *theirs.* The team stops ideating. The flow stops flowing. Innovation flatlines. And slowly, the organization trades disruption for decoration.

3. Your Trust Equity

Trust isn't built with a vision deck. It's built over time—through consistency, integrity, and relational safety. And narcissists? They torch that bank account for fuel.

They:
- Use confidential conversations as political capital.
- Turn one-on-one coaching into emotional manipulation.
- Publicly support values they privately betray.

And your people start to feel it:
- That whiplash between what's said and what's done.
- That fatigue of always wondering *"What's the real agenda here?"*
- That erosion of belief that *anyone* is truly safe.

Eventually, **manipulation fatigue sets in.** People don't just stop trusting the narcissist. They stop trusting *leadership itself.*

4. Your Time, Energy, and Credibility

One of the most insidious dynamics of narcissistic leadership? **You will spend your time cleaning up messes they set while smiling.** They create chaos, then disappear into meetings with the executive team. They escalate conflict, then act confused when it combusts. They exploit team dynamics, then spin stories about "disengagement."

And guess who gets tasked with putting out the fires?
- *You.*
- The real leaders.
- The ones still trying to protect the mission from the narrative.

Your hours get hijacked. Your energy gets drained. And your **credibility starts to bend**, because you're forced to defend a system you know is flawed—just to keep the wheels on.

5. Your Own Clarity

This is the slow, silent cost. It creeps in. You start second-guessing your instincts. You wonder if you're overreacting. You replay conversations in your head, trying to decode tone, subtext, meaning. You start to lose the most sacred asset a leader can have-**Your inner compass.**

Because narcissistic leaders are *expert gas lighters*. They warp perception. They rewrite history mid-conversation. They make you doubt what you saw, what you felt, what you *know.* Eventually, you stop trusting your gut. And when that happens? You stop leading—you start *surviving.*

6. Your Own Reflection

This is the final cost. The one no one talks about until it's too late. Because if you stay in this system long enough, two things happen:
- You leave.
- Or you **become what you once resisted.**

You start:
- Filtering your voice.
- Playing politics.
- Prioritizing perception.
- Abandoning the uncomfortable truth to stay in good standing.

You're not leading anymore. You're navigating. You're not shaping culture. You're adapting to one that was *never aligned with your values to begin with.*

Narcissistic leaders don't just harm others—they force others to become like them or get out. And if you're not intentional—if you don't draw the line—you will lose the clearest thing a leader has-Your **reflection.**

So, let's stop pretending this is benign. Unchecked narcissistic leadership will cost you:
- Your *talent*.
- Your *trust*.
- Your *truth*.
- Your *time*.
- And eventually—**yourself.**

You can't lead a team while protecting a parasite. I have had to navigate narcissists on a deeply personal level. You can't reform them. You can't coach them. And they will destroy everything you hold dear.

The real question is – do you have the courageous clarity needed? So, call it. Name it. And start the work of rebuilding the system before it swallows you whole.

How to Spot It—Before It's Too Late

One of the most dangerous myths in leadership culture is this-**That narcissistic or toxic leaders are obvious. Loud. Arrogant. Explosive.** So, we scan for the red flags we *expect* to see:
- Yelling in meetings.
- Public shaming.
- Egotistical monologues.

And when we don't see those? We assume we're safe.

But the most dangerous narcissists **don't throw tantrums.** They **perform composure.** They weaponize likability. They hide in plain sight—with clean emails, polite tone, and a perfectly curated leadership brand.

So, stop waiting for the outburst. Stop waiting for the mask to crack. Instead... **look for the patterns.** Because behavior doesn't lie. And systems always leave a trail.

The Patterns That Reveal the Truth

Here's what you'll *actually* see when narcissistic leadership is at play:
- **People Always Unsure Where They Stand**
  Praise one day, undermined the next. Empowered in private, embarrassed in public. Narcissistic leaders love ambiguity because **certainty is a threat to their control.** They never let people feel fully secure—because insecure people are easier to manage.
- **High Turnover in One Person's Orbit**
  Great people leave. Not from the organization—but from *them*. Look at who can't keep a stable team. Look at where the emotional churn is. If the turnover is always near a single person, **you don't have a hiring problem—you have a leadership problem.**
- **Strategic Vulnerability Followed by Emotional Manipulation**
  They'll share a hardship, a confession, a "lesson learned"—but it's never unfiltered. It's *performed vulnerability*, designed to disarm. And later, when you give them honest feedback or call out a behavior? They'll reference that moment to guilt you- "I can't believe you'd say that after everything I shared with you..."

- **A Wake of Disempowered Managers**
  Mid-level leaders who stop leading. Managers who are afraid to make decisions. Directors who defer everything upward. This is what happens when a narcissistic leader subtly undermines authority beneath them—until **they're the only decision-maker who matters.**

- **Perfect Executive Presentations—But No Real Ownership**
  Slides look clean. Updates sound strategic. Optics are impeccable. But when something goes wrong? **Silence.** Or worse—**blame.** They take credit when it works and disappear when it doesn't. They don't own the system—they own the story.

- **Division Cloaked in "Collaboration"**
  Cross-functional efforts that mysteriously implode. "Alignment" meetings that leave everyone more confused. They *say* they value collaboration—but only when it centers them. The moment others lead or challenge them; the collaboration mysteriously becomes "misalignment."

- **A Brilliant Performer Who's Always 'Almost Misunderstood'**
  There's always *some reason* why they didn't get the promotion, or why the team "doesn't get them," or why the last leader didn't "see their value." They're *always* nearly the victim—never quite accountable. You'll hear- "I'm just wired differently." "They're threatened by how I think." "I care too much, and it shows up strong." **This is not self-awareness. It's narrative control.**

The Question That Follows

When you see these patterns—not once, but **consistently**—you have to ask the real question: **Is this leadership? Or is this a *performance* of leadership designed to protect one person's ego at the expense of everyone else's energy?** Because that's what it becomes. A theater of confidence. A masquerade of collaboration. A machine built to elevate one and exhaust the many. And when you reach that realization—when the dots connect and the truth is undeniable—you will face a fork in the road-**The Choice**

Protect the person—or protect the culture.

You cannot do both.

- You can protect a personality—or you can protect principles.
- You can protect a legacy—or you can protect the *lived experience* of your people.
- You can continue performing alignment—or you can *rebuild it from truth.*

There is no neutrality here. Because narcissistic leadership doesn't just *exist* in a vacuum. It shapes the entire system around it. And if you keep it protected, promoted, or tolerated… **you become its enabler.** So, ask yourself, right now:

- **What patterns am I seeing—but not naming?**
- **What truths are we working around—to avoid discomfort?**
- **And what am I willing to lose—to preserve a lie that's killing my team?**

Because if your answer is *anything other than truth*...The culture has already started to collapse.

Clean Power or Corrupt Influence?

There is a kind of leadership that doesn't need credit to be powerful. That doesn't need admiration to feel worthy. That doesn't manipulate to stay safe. That's **clean power**. That's what you're here to build. But if you let narcissistic leadership, go unchecked, you're not just tolerating toxicity—you're reinforcing a model that teaches your entire organization- "Image matters more than integrity. Charm matters more than contribution. Power matters more than truth." And once that lesson embeds itself in your culture, you'll need more than a coaching session to reverse it.

You'll need a reckoning. Because toxic culture doesn't just come from toxic people. It's built—and protected—by systems designed to **look effective without ever being accountable.** Time to light up the stage. Let's go.

In the war against narcissistic leadership, your greatest asset isn't your charisma or positional authority—it's your One Percent. These individuals don't seek validation. They seek mission clarity. They don't play the optics game. They deliver results in spite of it. But in an environment polluted by narcissists, they're the first targets of sabotage.

Why? Because the One Percent expose the fraud. Their competence triggers the narcissist's insecurity. Their quiet execution threatens the false king's illusion of control.

In a culture where applause often outranks performance, and ego eclipses execution, these clean operators—the One Percent—are treated not as assets but as threats. Unless you lead differently.

This manual isn't about managing narcissists. It's about arming yourself to protect those who can dismantle their influence: your One Percent. These are your culture disruptors. Your system fixers. The leaders who, if protected and scaled, will burn out the narcissistic rot and rebuild a mission-first environment.

Lead your One Percent. Protect them from the ego-eaters. And let execution—not ego—become your culture. Here's how you lead them. Protect them. Scale them. Enable them to disrupt the narcissists and fix your culture.

1. Know What They Look Like
Directive: Don't confuse quiet strength for compliance — or visible frustration for insubordination.
The One Percent...
- Execute without showmanship.
- Push for clarity when others want comfort.
- Ask dangerous questions that expose mediocrity.
- Trigger insecure leaders by simply performing at a higher level.

Action:
Learn to distinguish between "difficult" and "disruptive."
One is a mirror — the other is a parasite.

2. Remove the Psychological Handcuffs
Directive: Kill the policies and people that suffocate clean operators.
Watch for:
- Layered approval processes that reward delay.
- Middle managers who resent talent.
- Systems that punish initiative and reward compliance.

Action:
- Flatten what you can.
- Break bottlenecks.
- Remove any obstacle between your One Percenters and forward motion.

3. Protect Them from the Ego-Eaters-Narcissists
Directive: Saboteurs *will* target your One Percent. Expect it. Plan for it.
Watch for:
- Micromanagement disguised as "coaching"
- Peers undermining them in side channels

- Emotional bait traps to trigger public conflict

Action:
- Intervene publicly when sabotage is covert.
- Say it out loud:

"They're here because they move the mission. If you can't match their clarity — learn from it, don't attack it."

4. Give Them Space to Scale Culture

Directive: Don't just use them. *Multiply them.*

Watch for:
- Quiet One Percenters mentoring behind the scenes
- New hires gravitating toward them
- Culture shifts forming around their behaviors

Action:
- Assign them systems-level responsibilities.
- Invite them into strategy.
- Let them design processes — not just execute them.

5. Build the One Percent Standard into the Fabric

Directive: If the One Percent are your future, build everything around their energy.

Action:
- Build your hiring rubric to find them.
- Craft onboarding around their behavioral DNA.
- Write performance frameworks that punish emotional sabotage and reward clean execution.

If you want more Astrids —**stop designing systems that protect the people who tried to bury her.**

The One Percent don't need you to clear the path. They just need you to stop protecting the people laying bricks in front of them. If you build with them —You will build something unbreakable. If you defend them —You will lead something worthy. **This is clean culture. This is clarity under fire. This is the future — and it only takes a few who want to stand in the sun and win.**

Part II: The Inner War — Shadow Work and the Anatomy of Fear

You can win the room and still lose your soul. You can hit the numbers, crush the metrics, get the applause—and still walk out of that building knowing, deep down, you're leading from fear. Not conviction. Not clarity. Fear.

This section isn't about others. It's about you. Not the LinkedIn version. Not the "strategic leader" in the offsite slideshow. The real you—the one behind the mask. **This is the inner war.**

Every leader fights it. Most just lose quietly. This part of the book is a descent into the psychological trenches where performance dies and authenticity is born. Where ego gets cracked, and shadow work begins.

Here's what you'll face:

- **Your own blind spots**—the ones you punish others for, but protect in yourself.
- **The unconscious sabotage**—that gut-level avoidance you call "strategy."
- **The inflated ego**—posing as confidence but rooted in fear of being exposed.
- **The metrics you trust**—until they betray you in a crisis.
- **The culture you "empowered"**—that now runs wild without direction.

You'll meet fear not as a feeling—but as a system. A hidden operating manual you didn't know you were running. And you'll confront your shadow—not just as a Jungian metaphor, but as a living force shaping every decision you make when no one's watching.

This isn't inspiration. This is interrogation.

Are you leading…or are you protecting an identity you've outgrown? Because real leadership starts when the mask cracks. Not when the audience cheers—but when the war inside gets named, faced, and finally integrated.

This section breaks open the shell. And if you let it—it'll give you your power back.

Chapter 8: The Labyrinth of Unchecked Emotions and Intuition

I thought Bob was a rock star. He prioritized everything I asked. Delivered in crisp time frames. Never missed a beat in our one-on-ones. If I needed something done fast—he was already typing before I finished the sentence.

On paper, he was perfect. In the meetings, he was polished. To me, he was gold.

But outside the boardroom? Bob was a black hole. What I didn't see—what I chose not to validate—was the reality the rest of the organization was drowning in.

Cross-functional requests to Bob's department were ignored or delayed for weeks. High-urgency operational handoffs sat untouched because they hadn't come *"from me."* Entire workflows collapsed in slow motion because one man learned to make me the sun—and let the rest of the system orbit in chaos.

And shame on me—for not having the right metrics and monitoring in place to see it. But that wasn't the worst part. The worst part was that *everyone else saw it.*

The rank and file knew exactly what was happening. They watched Bob fast-track everything I asked for while their requests sat dead in a queue. They saw the two-tier system—and they assumed I did too.

So, every day I let it continue, I wasn't just letting performance slip. I was letting trust erode. They didn't think I missed it. They thought I condoned it. And that destroyed something far more fragile than a workflow: belief.

Belief that leadership sees the truth. Belief that fairness matters. Belief that we're all on the same team.

I had dozens of warning signs. Frontline staff were raising quiet flags—nothing dramatic, just consistent signals that something wasn't lining up. They weren't pointing fingers. They were asking for help. But I didn't listen.

Because Bob made *me* feel effective. He made *me* feel seen. He told *me* what I wanted to hear. And that was the problem.

Bob had mastered the game of managing up. He knew how to deliver when I was watching and delay when I wasn't. And I allowed it—because I didn't have the systems in place to catch the grift. That's on me.

We'll dig deeper into the cost of poor KPI design and visibility in an upcoming chapter. We will also connect perceptions and unchecked emotions to the shadow.

But for now—know this…I trusted my gut—and I was wrong. I didn't validate. I didn't measure. I didn't check. And we paid for it—with speed, with trust, and with culture.

The Mirage of Perception

Leadership doesn't happen in a vacuum. It happens inside our heads long before it ever lands in a meeting room. And that's where it gets dangerous. Because what feels true—what feels *certain*—can be nothing more than a mirage. Emotion feels immediate. Data feels distant. We are biologically hardwired to trust what's visceral. The tone of someone's voice, the urgency in their eyes, the fact that they always respond quickly when we reach out. These create emotional impressions, not factual clarity. They create the illusion of alignment, competency, or urgency—but impressions aren't infrastructure.

And impressions without validation? They become decision-making cancer. Bob made *me* feel effective. That was the trap. He was responsive to me. He reflected my values in our conversations. He performed well—*when I was watching*. But performance in proximity isn't performance in the system. And I let that false sense of control and connection override the reality others were living every day.

The uncomfortable truth is this: leaders often default to instinct because it *feels* like leadership. Quick. Decisive. Sharp. But leadership isn't about what feels fast—it's about what proves durable.

Instinct makes us feel powerful. But it's only as strong as the system beneath it. And when that system is built on partial truths, filtered narratives, and secondhand status reports, we're not making decisions—we're guessing at scale. We're flying through a storm with painted-over instruments, telling ourselves the sky is still clear.

Cognitive Biases in Leadership Decisions

We love to believe we're rational. But the higher we go in an organization, the more we operate through layers of abstraction—and those layers get filled not with facts, but with filtered interpretations. Let's talk about the common biases that distort executive perception:

Confirmation Bias-We seek evidence to support what we already believe. I thought Bob was solid. So, every time he delivered for me, it confirmed that belief. Meanwhile, every complaint or delay coming from others? That just "wasn't his fault"—because I had already decided he was competent. I saw what I wanted to see.

Recency Bias-We overweight recent interactions. If Bob had a rough Q1 but crushed a project for me last week, I unconsciously reset my evaluation. That's how failing performance becomes normalized. We forget the trend because the last interaction felt great. Emotion rewrites memory.

Projection Bias-We assume others operate like us. If I'm fast, responsive, and mission-first, I assume others are too—especially if they say the right things. But shared language doesn't mean shared execution. It just means someone learned how to speak "boss fluently."

Halo Effect-We let competence in one area paint over weaknesses in others. Bob was amazing in crisis communication—but that masked the operational mess he left behind. I let one strength create a false image of wholeness.

Authority Echo-As a senior leader, your views are echoed back to you. No one wants to tell the emperor he's not wearing clothes—especially if you've already labeled someone a top performer. Your belief becomes gospel. Your perception becomes prophecy. That echo chamber? It's not alignment. It's obedience in disguise.

When you lead from unvalidated perception, you're not steering a team. You're navigating a dream. And every decision you make in that dream can create real damage in the waking world. You approve strategy built on faulty assumptions. You defend the wrong people. You alienate the right ones. You miss the erosion happening right beneath your feet.

And here's the quiet tragedy: the people closest to the truth—the frontline staff, the team leads, the cross-functional partners—they're watching it unfold. They see the disconnect. And with every day that passes, they don't just lose faith in that one mid-level manager. They lose faith in *you*. Because if you're still praising the person who's hurting them, you must be one of two things: either oblivious—or complicit.

Emotions Are Real—But They're Not Truth

Let's get something straight: emotions matter. They're not weakness. They're not noise. They're not irrational detours on the path to logic. In fact, they're often the first signal that something beneath the surface is shifting.

But emotions are *indicators*, not *instructors*. They're like a fire alarm: designed to get your attention, not tell you where the flames are or what caused them. If you hear the alarm and start smashing windows without locating the fire—you cause more damage than the fire ever would have.

The same goes for leadership. You feel frustration? It's a signal. You feel anxiety? It's a signal. You feel suspicion, anger, guilt, resentment? All signals.

But if you act on those feelings without interpreting them—without validating them against reality—you're not leading. You're reacting. You're projecting. You're managing shadows and calling it strategy.

Emotions as Indicators, Not Instructors

Carl Jung once said that emotions are the messengers of the unconscious. They arise when something inside us—something old, wounded, unresolved—is being touched by the present moment. They can point to deep truth. But they can also be echoes of trauma, archetypes, or internalized fear masquerading as urgency.

In leadership, this gets dangerously amplified. Because your unexamined emotions don't just affect you—they become part of the operating system for everyone beneath you.

A leader who feels betrayed—without confirming facts—starts tightening control. A leader who feels disrespected—without understanding context—starts punishing loyalty. A leader who feels threatened—without vetting reality—starts replacing high-performers with compliant underachievers.

All because a feeling was misread as a fact. Emotions are incredibly valuable—but only when held up to the mirror. Feel them? Yes. Honor them? Absolutely. But *obey* them blindly? That's how companies die.

The Leadership Hallucination

When you confuse perception with reality, you're no longer leading people—you're managing ghosts. You think you're responding to a trend—but it's just the echo of one loud voice. You think you're rewarding performance—but you're really feeding your need to feel appreciated. You think you're protecting the team—but you're shielding your own ego from confrontation.

This is what I call the *Leadership Hallucination*—when your internal narrative becomes more powerful than the evidence in front of you. And here's the worst part: people can't tell the difference. When a leader starts reacting emotionally, they assume it's strategic. They assume it's intentional. They assume it's real.

So, when you lead from unvalidated emotion, you inadvertently weaponize your psyche. You become a puppet of your projections—punishing people who aren't guilty, elevating those who play to your insecurities, and slowly, invisibly, corrupting the very culture you're trying to protect.

You stop solving problems. You start defending phantoms. You manage a grudge instead of a team. You escalate suspicion instead of accountability. You turn your organization into a stage—and your emotions write the script.

This is why emotional literacy isn't optional for leaders—it's survival.

You have to know what's yours and what's theirs. You have to discern between a real threat and a triggered fear. You have to do the inner work—or your shadow will do the outer damage.

Because if you don't lead through clarity, you lead through distortion. And when you lead through distortion, the people who see clearly will leave first. The ones who stay? They'll learn to manipulate your emotions—and run the show behind your back.

That's not leadership. That's illusion. And illusions, when trusted too long, become disasters.

The Externalization Trap: Turning Emotion into Culture Contagion

Some leaders confuse visibility with vulnerability. They think narrating their emotional state in real time is a form of authenticity. That "processing out loud" is a modern, open style of leadership. But let's call it what it really is—*leakage.*

And when leaders leak emotions instead of containing and processing them properly, they don't create transparency. They create confusion. Fear. Reactive behaviors. A culture constantly checking the emotional weather forecast instead of executing with clarity.

When you process out loud—you poison the room. Leadership is a burden. That's not cynicism—it's structural. When you speak, people react. When you shift emotionally, the whole organization tilts. So, when a leader "processes out loud"—especially in frustration, anxiety, or wounded pride—they are *outsourcing emotional labor* onto the team.

You might think you're just being honest. But to your people, it feels like instability. They can't tell the difference between a cathartic moment and a strategic shift. They don't know if they're supposed to solve the feeling or just survive it. So instead of performance, they focus on interpretation. Instead of pushing forward, they freeze.

Every meeting becomes a psychological chessboard:

- "Is she mad?"
- "What's this really about?"
- "Do we shift strategy now—or wait for the next mood swing?"

This isn't empowerment. Its confusion disguised as authenticity.

There's a subtle but deadly distinction between leading with emotional intelligence and leading through emotional exposure. If your team spends more time decoding *you* than decoding the problem, they're no longer operating. They're adapting—to your unresolved inner world. And that creates dangerous consequences:

- **Hyper-vigilance:** Staff Walk on eggshells, trying to avoid triggering your reactions.
- **Performance masking:** Team members shift into performance mode, saying what you want to hear to manage your mood—not to surface truth.
- **Downward delegation of emotional labor:** Instead of owning your internal state, you implicitly ask others to carry it.

When you're emotionally erratic, the organization becomes emotionally rigid—overcorrecting, under-communicating, and slowly calcifying into a culture of fear and stagnation.

And here's the worst part: *They think you know.* They think the way you behave is intentional. That the silence, the sarcasm, the sharp tone or quiet frustration is part of some larger, tactical choice. They don't see a leader struggling. They see a leader judging. And that judgment reshapes the culture more than any memo or mission statement ever could.

Emotional Leakage = Cultural Chaos

You cannot build a psychologically safe culture if the emotional climate is unpredictable. Every unresolved feeling you unload into the organization becomes a ripple:

- A sigh in a meeting becomes a warning sign.
- A raised voice becomes an unspoken threat.
- A passive-aggressive comment becomes gospel truth.

Over time, these ripples become currents—and those currents reshape the culture. Not through policy, but through tone. Through tension. Through the unspoken belief that everyone needs to "manage up" emotionally just to get through the week.

That's not culture. That's climate instability. And it's not leadership. It's undisciplined projection in a suit. Let's be clear: vulnerability is powerful when wielded with *precision*. When you share a lesson from pain *after* doing the internal work. When you reveal your growth edge— not your raw nerve. But vulnerability without boundaries is not courage.

It's collapse. It turns the leader's internal chaos into a cultural condition. And if left unchecked, it infects everything—from performance reviews to team trust to executive cohesion.

The cost of unfiltered emotion in leadership in chaos disguised as strategy. In this situation:

- **High performers leave** because they crave clarity and get caught in drama.
- **Mediocre performers stay** because they've learned how to navigate moods, not metrics.
- **Culture becomes crisis-based**—responding to how the leader feels instead of what the organization needs.

Discipline in leadership isn't about emotional suppression. It's about emotional sovereignty. You can feel deeply—but lead cleanly. You can process—but not project. You can struggle—but you must *own* it, not export it.

Otherwise, your emotions don't just move through the room. They *become* the room. And no culture can scale inside a storm.

The Balance: Intuition + Intelligence + Calm Clarity

Great leaders don't eliminate emotion. They *alchemize* it. They don't dismiss data. They *demand* it. And they don't wear calm like a mask. They *embody* it—so their teams don't have to compensate for their chaos.

True leadership isn't a pendulum swinging between instinct and over analysis. It's the disciplined integration of all three faculties:

- *Intuition* to sense.
- *Intelligence* to validate.
- *Clarity* to act—without panic, noise, or self-serving drama.

Let's break it down.

Thinking or Feeling Doesn't Make It True

Leadership invites intensity. Tough calls. Broken processes. Conflicted stakeholders. Flares of betrayal or fatigue. It's easy to confuse the *volume* of your thoughts or feelings with the *validity* of them.

But here's the truth: just because something burns in your gut, doesn't mean it belongs in the room. Not every insight needs to be spoken in real time. Not every emotion is a call to action. Not every hunch is a commandment.

Wisdom is knowing the difference. It's the restraint to sit with a spike of anger—and *not* weaponize it in the next meeting. It's the ability to distinguish between intuition and anxiety, between pattern recognition and projection. It's the maturity to say, "I feel something here—but I need more signal before I speak." That's not hesitation. That's *precision*.

Leaders who haven't learned to sit with intensity will offload it onto others and call it action. But real leaders understand the difference between *momentum* and *reverberation*—between what's needed and what's just loud.

Clarity Without Calm Is Just Force

Clarity alone is not enough. You can know exactly what needs to be done. You can have the right diagnosis, the right plan, the right metrics. But if you deliver it with volatility, resentment, or panic—you turn truth into trauma.

Calm isn't apathy. It's *authority*. It's what anchors a team when the winds are ripping at the sails. Because here's the reality: your tone *is* the organization's tempo. If you lead from chaos, they will scramble. If you lead from pressure, they will hide. If you lead from steadiness, they will *execute*.

Calm doesn't mean emotionless. It means emotionally governed. It means your presence reduces ambiguity, not amplifies it. It means the team can focus on performance, not on guessing whether you're about to erupt.

When calm and clarity combine, leadership stops being reactive and starts being *rhythmic*. It becomes predictable in the best way—anchored, consistent, and trustworthy.

Shadow Integration: When Your Archetypes Are Running the Show

Here's the psychological undercurrent most leaders never see coming: Your instincts might not be instincts. They might be *archetypes*—unconscious patterns shaped by wounds, defense mechanisms, or unmet needs.

Let's call it what it is: you might think you're being strategic…but it's the Warrior in you seeking a fight. Or is it…the Orphan in you reacting to perceived betrayal. Or is it…the Ruler in you grasping for control when your relevance feels threatened.

If you haven't done your inner work, your leadership isn't grounded—it's *puppeted* by your shadows. And those shadows? They don't care about organizational strategy. They want vindication. Validation. Victory. Or vengeance.

That's why real leadership work includes the *inner audit*:

- Where did that urgency come from?
- Why did I feel personally triggered by that pushback?
- What part of me is getting activated here—and does it serve the mission or just soothe the ego?

When you integrate your shadows, you stop making the organization your therapist. You stop mislabeling emotional baggage as strategic priority. You stop punishing people who remind you of your past. You stop turning fear into policy.

Because until your inner world is managed, your leadership is a projection—not a practice. **Balance isn't perfection. It's awareness.** The awareness to feel—but not fall. To think—but not assume. To speak—but only when your words *serve*, not *spill*.

And when you find that balance—of intuition, intelligence, and calm clarity—you stop reacting like a threatened leader. You start *leading* like a whole one.

The Discipline of Validation

Intuition might light the path, but only validation makes it walkable. In the trenches of leadership, instinct often fires first. And in crisis, that rapid inner signal can be invaluable—it's a form of pattern recognition trained through experience. But here's the trap: experience isn't evidence. And intuition isn't infallible.

If all you're doing is acting on gut impulses without validating them against data, behavior, and external reality, then you're not practicing leadership. You're gambling—with people's careers, reputations, trust, and sometimes the very survival of the organization.

This is why real leadership demands *discipline*—the kind that slows the ego and sharpens the lens. It requires a framework for moving from emotion to execution without dragging everyone through your personal fog of war.

From Gut Feeling to Measured Hypothesis

Emotion is not the enemy—but it must be interrogated. When something feels "off," it may be. But that's where the leader must begin *investigation*, not execution. Let's walk through the discipline:

1. Frame the Perception as a Testable Belief

This is the move from *reactivity* to *reflection*. If the thought is "Marketing is stonewalling Operations," don't run into battle with that sword drawn. Reframe it: "It seems like the Marketing team may not be processing Ops requests on time. I need to test if this is systemic or isolated—and if it's intentional, procedural, or capacity-related." This simple shift protects your credibility. It also protects the team from being ambushed by a mood disguised as a mandate. You turn emotional fog into a functional hypothesis. And from there—you can test, not attack.

2. Seek Contradictory Evidence

Here's the gut-check: If you can't find a single piece of evidence that contradicts your perception, you're not investigating. You're reinforcing. Confirmation bias is the silent killer of good judgment. And leaders who don't resist it end up constructing decisions to defend their ego—not solve the problem. So, when you think, *"Bob is playing favorites,"* look for:
- Timelines where Bob prioritized others.
- Metrics showing balance or inconsistency.
- Staff who disagree with the narrative you're building.

If you're only gathering evidence that supports your suspicion, you're not validating—you're scripting a drama for which you've already written the ending.

3. Invite Neutral Observation Before Acting

Find someone who doesn't need to agree with you to keep their job. Invite them into the situation. Show them your data. Explain your hypothesis. And then ask: *What am I missing?*

They may see your blind spot. They may point to something structural, cultural, or historical that reframes the issue. And that reframing may be the key to solving the real problem—not just the one your instincts are fixated on. Because leadership inside a distortion field is indistinguishable from dictatorship. And if you've surrounded yourself with people who mirror your assumptions, you've built an echo chamber—not a team.

Leadership Is Not a Feeling—It's a Skill

Let's confront the illusion: just because you feel something deeply does *not* make it right. Or actionable. Or strategic. Emotional intensity is not the same as insight. And if that intensity becomes your steering wheel, you'll drive your organization right off a cliff—with conviction. Real leadership is less about certainty and more about process. You don't *feel* your way through high-stakes environments—you *build* your way through them. Brick by brick. Metric by metric. Loop by loop. Decision by decision.

- You build clarity through *feedback loops*—not just applause.
- You build foresight through *patterns*—not reactions.
- You build culture through *consistency*—not charismatic bursts of emotion.
- And you build trust by *validating* before you *act*—not just "going with your gut" and hoping people understand later.

If it's all emotion or intuition, you're not leading. **You're *stabbing in the dark with an emotional sales pitch*—and asking your stakeholders to cosign the chaos.** That's not strategy. That's theatrical desperation.

And while your energy may feel compelling, your results will erode. Because sooner or later, emotion without validation creates:

- Initiatives that implode.
- Morale that collapses.
- Teams that guess, hedge, and withhold.
- And cultures where nobody says what's real—because reality no longer matters to the boss.

This is the discipline: Feel deeply. Think clearly. Validate relentlessly. And when you do, you transform your instinct from impulse into insight—from unprocessed fear into informed action. You stop being the emotional center of the storm. You become the compass in the chaos.

And that's the difference between a leader who reacts to the fire— —and one who builds the architecture to prevent it.

Data as a Mirror, not a Weapon

Let's make this brutally clear: **Data is not dangerous. But how leaders use it can be.** Metrics don't lie. But people under fear do. In the hands of an insecure or reactive leader, data becomes an instrument of judgment—a way to spotlight failure, consolidate control, or create performance theater that looks clean but hides decay.

In those environments, metrics don't drive truth. They drive distortion. They don't promote improvement. They promote survival. And that, right there, is how culture quietly begins to rot—one KPI at a time.

Using Metrics to Reflect, Not Just Punish

There's a profound difference between using data as a *reflection* and using it as a *weapon*. One invites growth. The other provokes fear. **A reflective data culture asks:** "What does this tell us about our system?" "Where are we misaligned?" "What do these patterns mean about our process, our load, our leadership?"

But a punitive data culture asks: "Who dropped the ball?" "Why didn't you hit your number?" "How do we make sure this never happens again?" That second voice? It may sound like accountability. But it's actually fear in disguise. Fear of uncertainty. Fear of imperfection. Fear of vulnerability at the top—projected downward as punishment. And here's what happens next, every time:

- **Teams start performing to the metrics, not the mission.**
- **Dashboards look pristine, but friction is exploding behind the scenes.**
- **High performers burn out from hiding their real struggles.**
- **Low performers learn how to look good without actually delivering.**

Because when the metrics become a magnifying glass, people start hiding under the rug.

The Psychological Cost of Weaponized Metrics

Let's talk about the human fallout. When you weaponize data, you create a climate where:

- Honesty becomes a liability.
- Metrics are manipulated to avoid scrutiny.
- Learning loops collapse under defensive silence.
- Everyone becomes more interested in *looking safe* than *being effective*.

In this world, dashboards become the enemy of progress. Because no one trusts the data to help them—only to hurt them.

And the real tragedy? You lose *signal fidelity*—the very thing data was supposed to give you. You lose the capacity to diagnose breakdowns early. You become a pilot flying by instrument—except your dashboard lies to protect itself.

How Real Leaders Use Data

Real leaders use data as a mirror, not a magnifying glass. They don't zoom in to assign blame. They zoom *out* to see what's missing from the system. They ask questions that widen the frame:

- "What's the pattern across functions—not just this team?"
- "Where's the friction that's not being verbalized?"
- "If this is our outcome, what assumptions upstream are flawed?"

They treat data like a *conversation starter*, not a courtroom exhibit. Because they know leadership isn't about who's right. It's about what's true—and how we get better from it. Real leaders build data cultures where:

- Vulnerability is rewarded with support, not scrutiny.
- Misses become diagnostics, not death sentences.
- KPIs are anchors for alignment, not ammunition for shame.

When Data Becomes a Culture-Shaping Force

When data is used as a mirror:

- Teams start surfacing issues early—because it's safe to do so.
- High performers thrive—not just from recognition, but from meaningful feedback.

- Underperformers get clarity—not just pressure.
- Leaders can *see the system*—not just the symptom.

And more importantly: **People trust the dashboard.** They trust the process. They trust that telling the truth won't get them punished—it will get the problem solved. That's the kind of trust that turns metrics into momentum. That's when data becomes not just a management tool—but a leadership multiplier.

The Ultimate Test for Data in Leadership

Ask yourself this: "Does my team see data as a way to get better—or a way to get burned?" If it's the latter, your metrics aren't helping. They're hiding. They're hurting. They're shaping a culture of deception where no one tells you what's really going on—until it's too late.

So, use data wisely. Use it with humility. Use it to reveal reality—not reinforce narratives.

Use it to foster safety—not fear. Because if data is a mirror, it will show you what's broken—so you can build again. But if data is a weapon, you'll just keep swinging—until there's no one left to follow.

The Cost of Unvalidated Leadership

Leadership without validation is not just a missed opportunity. It's an *active threat* to your culture, your systems, and your legacy. When you lead without verifying, measure without listening, or decide without interrogating your instincts, you don't just lose alignment. You create chaos that wears a name tag and draws a paycheck.

You don't see the damage at first—because performance still happens. People still show up. Deadlines still get met. But behind the scenes, beneath the dashboards and smiles, the foundation is cracking.

Why? Because unchecked instincts eventually become unquestioned norms. And when perception becomes the only filter for truth, the whole organization starts reacting to shadows instead of signal. Here's what that costs you.

Organizational Amnesia: The System That Keeps Forgetting Itself

When leadership decisions are made emotionally—without validation, without data, without reflection—you train the entire system to forget.
- You forget *why* a decision was made.
- You forget *what* the actual problem was.
- You forget *who* flagged the risk in the first place.

Reactivity erases memory. It deletes context. It overrides patterns. It resets the logic every time a new emotion enters the room. And when that happens, the same problems come back—louder, more expensive, and more entangled.

You don't just lose efficiency. You lose *institutional intelligence*. Every meeting becomes a form of organizational déjà vu: "Didn't we already try this?" "Didn't we already flag that?" "Didn't someone raise this issue six months ago?"

Yes, they did. But no one remembered. Because no one built the loop. No one captured the learning. No one validated the emotion, so the action dissolved into fog. You're not just leading from instinct—you're condemning the team to relive the same pain under different PowerPoints.

Cultural Erosion: When Fear Replaces Evidence

Let's speak plainly: In an organization led by unvalidated emotion, fear becomes the language. And drama becomes the currency. People don't solve problems. They posture. They don't surface truth. They signal safety. They don't ask hard questions. They align with moods.

Because if decisions are based on how the boss feels, not what the data shows, then performance is no longer predictable. It becomes political. High performers start leaving—not because they're fragile, but because they refuse to waste their clarity in a fog machine. They see what's coming: that results don't matter as much as emotional compliance. That insight gets ignored unless it flatters the right people. That asking for accountability is seen as defiance. So, they go. Quietly. Quickly.

And the ones who stay? They learn the rules of emotional survival. They become performers in a psychological drama. Masters of optics. Experts in energy management. Not builders—navigators. Because in a culture ruled by reactivity, survival isn't based on contribution. It's based on staying out of the emotional crosshairs.

When Drama Becomes Strategy

In this kind of ecosystem:
- The loudest voice wins.
- The most reactive person dictates direction.
- Feedback loops collapse into gossip.
- Strategic planning gets hijacked by emotional favoritism.

And here's the kicker: the organization *thinks* it's moving fast. Because there's always motion. Always fire. Always urgency.

But motion without validation is *just spinning*. And fire without direction is *just destruction*. You're not leading transformation. You're fueling drama and calling it "agility."

The True Cost: You Break What You Were Trusted to Build

When validation disappears, so does credibility. And eventually—*so do you*. Because leadership without validation burns through trust, people, and capital at an unsustainable rate. It's leadership as spectacle, not stewardship. It's a performance—until the curtain drops and the consequences are all that remain.

So, ask yourself:
- Are we solving root problems—or replaying old ones with better branding?
- Are we building a culture of feedback—or one of fear?
- Are our KPIs reflections of reality—or props for performance?

Because if you're not validating your leadership, then everything beneath you is just performing. And performers don't build empires. They just keep the lights on until the audience leaves.

Courage Doesn't Panic, It Validates

Leadership today doesn't suffer from a lack of passion. It suffers from a lack of *process*. There's no shortage of emotion. Or urgency. Or charisma. But there is a critical shortage of *validation*—the ability to test what you feel against what's real before you unleash it on the people who depend on your clarity.

And let's be real: we've glorified a form of emotional leadership that *looks* like courage but is really just adrenaline in a blazer. It's not courage to trust your gut and act recklessly. It's not brave to make bold calls based solely on instinct. It's not noble to lead through intuition alone. That's not leadership. That's ego in a hurry.

Real Courage Doesn't Need Applause. It Needs Process. The leader who pauses before reacting—the one who frames the feeling, checks the data, listens to dissent, and waits to see the full picture—isn't being indecisive. They're being *dangerously effective*.

Because they understand what most performative leaders don't: **Courage isn't loud. It's disciplined.** It's the quiet strength to say: "Something feels off—but let's test it before we torch the team." "This might be urgent—but I won't act until I understand." "I trust my gut—but I don't worship it." That's the kind of courage that doesn't just win moments—it builds legacies. Because fire-starting leaders may light the room up—but anchor leaders hold the damn structure when everything shakes.

The Leader Who Validates Before They Escalate Becomes the Anchor—Not the Accelerant

Here's the test: In the heat of tension—when systems fail, tempers rise, politics flare—are *you* the one calming the room, or fanning the flames? Are you pulling the team toward facts? Or pushing them deeper into narrative? Are you helping them *focus*? Or are they just trying to survive your storm?

Anchors don't avoid emotion. They honor it—but they *contain* it. They validate, then decide. They measure, then move. They don't act from fear. They act from *functional awareness*. And in doing so, they become the rarest kind of leader—*the one everyone else can orient around* when things fall apart. Not because they're always right. But because they're grounded, clear, and *earned* their authority through discipline—not emotional theater.

So, here's your mirror: If your team is afraid to tell you the truth…If your systems can't survive without your adrenaline…If your instincts are louder than your insight…Then you're not leading. You're reacting. You're performing. You're burning down the culture—and calling it leadership.

Real leaders don't just *feel* the fire. They *know* when to hold it—and when to wield it. Because courage doesn't panic. **It validates.**

Field Manual: Mastering The Emotional Labyrinth

Leadership isn't about suppressing emotion—it's about mastering its role. In the labyrinth of unchecked emotions and untested intuition, many leaders lose themselves, confusing urgency with clarity, and instinct with wisdom. This manual isn't designed to help you feel better. It's designed to help you lead better.

Every decision you make ripples outward. If your emotions dictate those decisions, your culture inherits your confusion. If your gut drives your strategy without validation, you're not intuitive—you're reckless.

This field manual arms you with tools to:
- Identify when emotions are shaping decisions covertly.
- Convert intuition from reaction to hypothesis.
- Build systems that balance emotion, intelligence, and calm clarity.
- Prevent your inner turbulence from becoming organizational chaos.

Leadership isn't a feeling. It's a skill. This manual is your guide to map the emotional labyrinth.

1. Operational Premise: Leadership Is Not a Feeling

Unchecked emotion isn't leadership fuel—it's leadership sabotage. Emotional energy may drive short-term action, but it clouds judgment and distorts perception over time. Leaders often mistake emotional certainty for operational clarity. Intuition, though valuable, can be laced with subconscious biases and unresolved fears.

Command Decision: Treat emotions as inputs, not imperatives. Emotions reveal where to investigate, not where to act. Always validate your instinct with hard data or corroborating evidence before making strategic moves.

2. Identifying Emotional Leakage

No leader contains their internal state perfectly. Like a breach in a submarine hull, your suppressed emotions seep into your team's ecosystem, subtly altering its operational tone.

Why it matters:

Your team mirrors you far more than you think. If your frustration, urgency, or insecurity leaks out:
- Decisions accelerate prematurely.
- Projects pivot emotionally, not strategically.
- Organizational trust erodes as the team senses inconsistency.

Tactical Move: Assign a trusted observer, someone empowered to speak hard truths—to monitor and report your emotional shifts weekly. Treat emotional containment as seriously as cybersecurity monitoring.

3. The Externalization Trap

When emotion shapes your perception of reality, it doesn't just affect you, it infects your culture. Leaders broadcast their internal state. If you act on unexamined feelings, your people will inherit your uncertainty, anxiety, or false confidence.

Why it matters:

Unchecked emotions spread organizational confusion. What begins as your stress response ends as your culture.

Action Steps to Contain the Spread:
- **Pre-decision ritual:** Force yourself to articulate your current emotional state before acting. Identify whether that feeling is shaping your conclusions.

- **Calm Checkpoints:** Empower your team to detect your emotional escalation and pause discussions. This creates operational guardrails against emotional decisions.
- **Post-decision logging:** Reflect whether key decisions were rooted in data or feelings masquerading as logic.

4. Reprogramming Intuition: From Gut Feelings to Hypotheses

Your gut reaction is not wrong—it's simply raw data from your subconscious. Treating gut instinct as gospel turns it from helpful pattern recognition into dangerous cognitive bias.

Why it matters:

The untested gut can lead leaders into overconfidence, repeating past failures disguised as bold moves.

Three-Step Intuition Calibration:

1. **Capture the Instinct:** Write your immediate conclusion as soon as it arises.
2. **Translate to Hypothesis:** Reframe your instinct as a testable assumption.
3. **Test the Hypothesis:** Before acting, seek data to challenge—not confirm—your instinct.

Field Command: Your gut is your early warning sensor. It should guide questions, not answers.

5. Balance Framework: Intuition + Intelligence + Calm Clarity

Effective leadership requires dynamic balance between:

- **Intuition:** Subconscious pattern recognition (raw but fast).
- **Intelligence:** Data and analysis (slow but precise).
- **Calm Clarity:** Emotional detachment to prevent narrative bias.

Why it matters:

Overweighting any one element creates failure modes:

- Intuition alone: Emotional hijacking.
- Intelligence alone: Analysis paralysis.
- Calm Clarity alone: Inaction disguised as strategic patience.

Command Protocol: If in major decisions, any one element becomes dominant (exceeding 75% of decision weight), pause and rebalance your approach.

6. Command Tools: Data Over Drama

Crises make leaders prone to narrative-thinking: they act based on the story they're telling themselves, not the facts.

Why it matters:

Data may be slow. But drama is deceptive. In critical decisions, systemize objectivity.

Action Tools:

- Conduct pre-mortems before decisions, anticipating what could fail and why.
- Monitor team morale and cultural indicators as rigorously as financial KPIs.
- After major events, hold separate debriefs: one for operational performance, one for emotional impact. Mixing the two distorts analysis.

Leadership Mandate: Never let today's adrenaline decide tomorrow's mission path.

7. Crisis Response Protocol: Courage Doesn't Panic, It Validates

In crisis, most leaders confuse movement with leadership. Momentum is mistaken for control. The real task is resisting emotional hijack.

Crisis Protocol:

- **Stop:** When your instinct says "act now," force a pause.
- **Validate:** Use your decision ritual to name your emotion and check your data.
- **Act:** Only proceed when your emotional signal is treated as advisory, not authoritative.

Why it matters:

Panic in leaders masquerades as courage. Distinguishing between the two determines whether your team survives the storm or sinks in it.

8. Weekly Shadow Audit

Unchecked, your emotional state evolves into your leadership style. Prevent your unconscious from becoming your operational doctrine.

Each Week, Audit Yourself:

- Did my emotions act as instructor, or as indicator?
- Where did I act on intuition without hypothesis testing?
- Did my emotional state shape team energy, for better or worse?

Why it matters:

Without structured reflection, emotional leadership becomes normalized—until the fallout is too large to hide.

Core Doctrine: Emotion is part of leadership. But leading with emotion is optional—and often fatal.

Lead as Architect, Not as Reactor

Leaders architect systems. Systems outlast moods. Systems survive storms. Calm clarity isn't passive—it's the bedrock of decisive, measured leadership in chaos. **Remember:** If your gut, data, or calm clarity falter, your system—not your state—should guide you. Build the system now, so it holds when your emotions inevitably crack.

Chapter 9: Operational Illusion – How False Metrics and Misplaced Trust Destroy Execution

"The truth is not what you want it to be. It is what it is and you must bend to its power or live a lie."
—Miyamoto Musashi

We thought we were crushing it. Dashboards were green. KPIs were "on track." Mid-levels were presenting with confidence, and the room was full of nods and strategy jargon that made us feel like we were winning.

But we weren't. Revenue wasn't climbing. Customer issues weren't shrinking. Operational velocity was stalling. And worst of all—*nobody could explain why*.

We hadn't built a high-performing team—we'd inherited a theater. And that theater was being orchestrated by the top leader.

Jill stood center stage, casting vision with polished charm, telling us things were "in flight" and "so close" you could feel it. She showed up every two to four weeks like a hopeful magician checking to see if the rabbit had finally appeared in the hat, throwing glitter around like it was pixie dust.

No data. No timelines. No listening. Just feelings—because they were "powerful." Because "the energy felt right."

Behind her dazzling updates were PowerPoints that looked like momentum but weren't. Slack threads echoing team wins that never materialized into throughput. Happy talk in meetings as if morale could compensate for missed milestones and blocked KPIs.

And downstairs? The operations floor was on life support. Requests backed up for days, sometimes weeks and months. Wait times tripled. Cross-functional integrations choked like a clogged artery. Support, fulfillment, tech, revenue ops—they all sent the same message: "We're stuck. Again."

But Jill didn't see it. Or didn't want to. Because acknowledging the dysfunction would have meant confronting the reality that the magic wand wasn't working.

She claimed to have done her shadow work. Said she was healing. But every time we tried to bring up real signals—actual breakdown points in the system—if it threatened one of her "favorites," the mask slipped. The hurt little girl returned. And instead of solving, she stonewalled.

It wasn't leadership. It was obstruction—dressed as empowerment. Jill wasn't building a team. She was curating a story. And we all bought it for too long.

Why?

Because we wanted to believe the story. Because the alternative—that we were being led by emotion, not strategy—was harder to swallow. Because challenging her meant facing the dysfunction head-on, without the protection of fantasy.

But at some point, every illusion runs out of stage. And we were bleeding behind the curtain.

Why?

Because we didn't build KPIs that *measured what mattered*. We didn't track **decision-to-execution velocity**. We didn't measure **interdepartmental response times** or **support load throughput**. We didn't monitor **task handoff friction across revenue-critical workflows**.

We had the wrong data. Focused on the wrong direction. And worst of all—we liked how it looked. So, we stopped asking how it worked. We were eating our own BS and drinking our own Kool-Aid. And we kept refilling the glass.

The wake-up call never rang. Because we didn't create a system that *could* send one. And when it finally did—it wasn't a call. It was a collapse.

Revenue didn't just plateau. It plummeted. Customers started walking. Frontline teams started whispering. And the house of metrics we built came crashing down with one question: "If everything looks green—why are we still bleeding?"

We didn't have an answer. Because we never asked the right questions. And that's when we realized: **Hope isn't a system. Trust isn't a metric. And leadership without operational visibility is just confidence wrapped in blindfolds. This is the lie Musashi warned us about.**

The Illusion of Alignment

In operations—whether you're leading a cyber incident, managing a supply chain, or running a service pipeline—the most dangerous moment isn't the breach, the breakdown, or the missed milestone. It's the illusion that everything's fine.

It's the dead calm before the storm, where complacency dresses itself in the uniform of competence. Where people confuse motion with momentum. Where silence is mistaken for stability.

I've watched it unfold again and again. The war drums start banging, and suddenly, the room is full of blank stares. Eyes widen. Voices crack. Decision trees evaporate.
Why?

Because their systems were never tested. Their processes were theater. Their people were busy—but not battle-ready. And we—at the top—confused proximity and busyness with performance. We measured effort, not impact.

But let me take it one level deeper—if you think "operations" only applies to the department labeled "Operations," you're a clown in a suit.
Operations is a system, not a silo.

If Finance misses a reimbursement window that halts a shipment—you're down. If HR delays a critical hire—your delivery chain breaks. If Facilities neglects a hardware refresh—the uptime you banked on vanishes.

Every function that *feeds* your ability to deliver is part of your operational stack. If you're not measuring their turn times, responsiveness, and execution rhythm, then you are leading with blinders on. You are *willfully* ignorant of your system dependencies. And you deserve every bit of legacy you will be remembered for – failure.

And here's the punchline: just because you *think* it doesn't impact operations—doesn't mean it doesn't.

This isn't philosophy. It's physics. So, if you're not tracking the performance of those interdependent domains as rigorously as you track frontline delivery, you're not a leader. You're a liability in a lanyard.

And that's on us. Because real leadership doesn't just manage the obvious. It anticipates the invisible. It integrates the peripheral. It holds every link in the chain accountable—or it accepts the break when the chain snaps.

Wake up. Lead better. Or step aside for someone who will.

Mid-Level Confidence ≠ Operational Competence

Let's say it clearly: **confidence is not competence**. Especially in the mid-level strata of your organization, where the politics are tight, the visibility is limited, and the performance theater is fully booked.

You have people speaking in slide decks and acronym soups. They walk into meetings with rehearsed updates and talking points designed not to inform—but to *pacify*. You ask how things are going, and they nod, smile, and say:
"We're on track." "The team's adapting." "We've addressed the issue."
But when you peel back one layer—just one question deep—you find a system held together by hope, habit, and heroic effort at the frontline. No process. No resiliency. No plan.
Ask them:
- "Describe your FIFO logic under a service surge."
- "What's your response protocol when request volume doubles?"
- "Which metrics tell you when your function is about to fail?"

If they can't answer with precision, they are not leading. They are *narrating*. And narration under pressure is worthless. Because when crisis hits, the narrative doesn't matter—*execution does*.

And you can't fake execution. This is when Musashi's comment on how you must bend to the power of truth or live a lie comes home to roost. Truth doesn't give a damn about your ego, your theater or your fragile reputation. It is going to hit you like a sledgehammer if you ignore it for long periods to sell your lie to look cool. Do you really want to wait for that blow or do something about it?

The Delegation Delusion

This one hurt, because it's so pervasive in senior leadership-**We think that delegation equals resolution.** We hand a task, a function, or an initiative to someone we believe is "solid," and then we mentally check it off the list. We think: "They've got it." "They're sharp." "They said it's handled."

What we forget is that *trust without inspection is not leadership*. It's fantasy. If you haven't validated:
- Their process,
- Their decision logic,
- Their failure modes,
- Their downstream impacts…
…then you're not delegating. You're abandoning.

And when it blows up—which it will—you'll have no operational root to trace. Just smoke, excuses, and a calendar full of follow-ups that never fix anything. If you have people in critical positions regularly missing deadlines or creating chaos without action from you, you need the sledgehammer of truth.

The Fog of War Test

You want to know who's actually running operations? Don't look at how they present. Look at how they respond to chaos. **Create a fog-of-war simulation.** Take away the ideal conditions. Strip out the stability. Ask:

- "Your top three staff leave or are out on a surprise medical. What breaks first?"
- "Your queue doubles overnight. What gets dropped?"
- "You have a breach, an outage, and a public escalation. What's your playbook?"

If they stumble, deflect, or give you philosophical fluff—they're not operational. They're theatrical. Because real operators don't theorize under pressure—they deploy. They've walked the terrain. They know the edge cases. They understand where the system cracks and who owns the glue.

And if they can't describe those things in detail, they are not ready. Not for crisis. Not for scale. Not for leadership. And why the hell are you still betting on someone not ready?

False Alignment Is a Leadership Mirage

Here's what no one tells you in executive school: **Your most dangerous leaders are not the ones who make noise. They're the ones who make you feel safe.** Because safety without proof breeds delusion. And when those leaders sell you calm—but can't explain the chaos they're supposed to manage—you inherit their blind spot.

You let the performance seduce you. You start believing your own narrative. You stop testing, validating, and digging. And in that moment, you're not leading anymore. You're a spectator—cheering for a story that's quietly falling apart.

Alignment isn't agreement. It's verifiable, resilient execution under pressure.

If you don't know how your leaders operate in crisis, if you've never stress-tested their systems, if you've confused composure for competence—**You're not aligned. You're in danger.**

When systems fail, it's rarely the technology that breaks first. **It's the people. The assumptions. The blind spots. The hidden fragilities you didn't know existed—until everything was on fire.**

We like to think that operational failure comes from catastrophic events—cyberattacks, server outages, global supply shocks. But more often, it starts with something smaller and more dangerous: *Uninspected expectations.*

And here's the truth—**most operations aren't built for stress.** They're built for performance reviews. For status updates. For optics. We confuse activity with readiness. We confuse green KPIs with system health. And we assume that because it *hasn't* failed, it *won't*. That assumption is the loaded gun under your desk.

What Breaks First in a Real Crisis?

It's not your tech stack. It's your process stack. It's people. **It's the gaps between roles. The ambiguity between silos. The protocols no one reviewed in a year. The escalations no one rehearsed.**

Your systems aren't fragile because of complexity. They're fragile because no one validated how they behave under load.

- You assumed every team knew how to handle double volume.
- You assumed "accountability" meant readiness.
- You assumed people would *speak up* when they felt overwhelmed.

And assumptions, in operations, are operational *suicide*. Because what really breaks first isn't the software. It's the human procedures you never stress-tested.

Symptoms of an Uninspected System

You don't need a crisis to diagnose fragility. The signs are already there—*if you're willing to look.*

Here's what you'll see: **KPIs That Are Green, But Culture Is Red** Everyone's metrics look great. But morale is dropping. Turnover is rising. Tension simmers just below the surface. This isn't misalignment. It's *mutiny in slow motion.* ***Green dashboards with red culture mean you've built a reporting system that rewards performance theater and ignores human cost.***

Leaders argue over what's happening because no one has visibility. There's no shared dashboard. No operational telemetry. Just hunches, anecdotes, and emotional narratives in conflict. When perceptions become policy and feelings become strategy, you're not managing performance. You're refereeing internal politics.

No Measurement of Decision-to-Execution Velocity Between Teams

This is the silent killer. If one department sends a request and it vanishes into another team's black hole, your operation is already breaking—*you just haven't paid the invoice yet.* No one is tracking how long it takes for a decision to turn into action. No one is monitoring how long it takes for interdepartmental requests to get answered. No one is surfacing where the delay lives—so *everyone* suffers in silence.

And when leadership tries to drive accountability? The team that's been waiting in silence thinks: "Now you care?" "Now you want results?" You've lost the moral authority to hold anyone accountable—because you never held *the system* accountable. This isn't inefficiency. It's **cultural demolition**.

When operational muscle memory replaces strategic awareness, you have automation without intelligence. People follow SOPs like rituals. They complete steps. But they don't know what those steps *create*. They don't know the *why*—only the *what*. That's how systems keep moving even as they decay.

You think you're getting work done. But what you're really doing is *rehearsing irrelevance*.

Here's the final symptom—and it's deadly. Everything works… until it doesn't. Your protocols collapse the moment complexity enters the room:
- Escalation paths vanish in ambiguity.
- Capacity thresholds crack under silence.
- Ownership dissolves in blame-shifting and bureaucracy.

And the worst part? **You thought you were ready.** Because you had the SOP. You had the metrics. You had the illusion. But not the truth.

Fragile systems aren't obvious until they're overwhelmed. But the warnings are always there.
- In the delays that go unspoken.
- In the feedback you dismissed as complaining.
- In the frontline burnout you labeled "attitude."

You didn't build a resilient operation. You built a stage. And now that the curtain's on fire, you're wondering why no one knows where the exits are.

This is the anatomy of failure. Not dramatic. Not cinematic. Just quiet, daily erosion disguised as progress. And if you don't dig into the system now— If you don't trace the friction, test the stress points, demand real cross-functional telemetry— You're not leading operations. **You're managing the countdown to collapse.**

Real Leadership Audits the Machine

Leadership isn't a title. It's a *diagnostic function.* If you're not auditing your operation, then you're not leading it. You're watching it perform—and hoping it doesn't explode on your watch. Real leadership doesn't wait for failure to start asking questions. It inspects. It validates. It tests for friction—*before the fire.* And that starts with a shift in mindset:

Too many executives walk their organizations like royalty—checking optics, listening to surface narratives, and getting filtered answers designed to preserve perception.

But real leaders? They move like *mechanics.* They don't need to know how to write the code—but they know where the latency lives. They don't need to build the pipeline—but they damn well understand what flows through it and where the choke points are. They ask:

- "Where does this system fail under load?"
- "What happens when volume spikes?"
- "Who owns the moment of failure?"
- "What's the real contingency if our golden path breaks?"

And here's the acid test: **If complaints are coming in about turnaround times, customer impacts, or execution delays—and you can't validate if they're real—you've already lost operational visibility.** But worse? **If you *know* you don't have visibility and you're not fixing it—then you're no longer just unaware.**

You're complicit in failure as you practice Kabuki theater. You're more focused on *looking effective* than *becoming aware.* You're curating an illusion instead of confronting the culture you've allowed to grow under your negligence. And that's not leadership. That's *cowardice in a tailored suit.*

Test the System Before the Market Does

Waiting for real-world stress to expose your system's weakness isn't brave. It's lazy. It's irresponsible. And it costs far more than you realize. The market *will* stress your operation eventually. The question is whether you'll uncover the fault lines before it does—or *after* you've lost the customer, the reputation, or the revenue.

Here's how real leaders test the machine:
- **Simulate Stress**
- Run pressure scenarios. Not theoretical. Real load simulations.
  What happens if your volume triples?
  If two critical systems fail simultaneously?
  If a partner system underperforms for 48 hours?
- *If your team doesn't know, your system is not ready.*
- **Walk the Floor**

- Get out of your executive echo chamber.
  Walk into the workflow.
  Shadow the people doing the work—not the ones summarizing it.
- Watch the delays.
  Feel the friction.
  See the inconsistencies no report will ever show you.

Operational truth isn't in the slide deck. It's in the hallway tension you pretend not to notice.

Cross-check reports with reality. You trust your metrics? Good. Now *validate* them. Compare your dashboards to ticket logs, customer complaints, throughput rates, manual workarounds. Ask: "Does the data say it's fast, but the customers say it's broken?" "Are we green on paper but red in the inbox?" That's not an ops issue. That's a *leadership hallucination*—and it's on you.

Ask your junior staff what hurts. The truth lives closer to the ground. Frontline staff don't have time for performance theater. They live in the friction. They see the choke points. They adapt to the chaos you think is under control. Ask them:
- "What slows you down the most?"
- "What do you wish leadership understood?"
- "What's the most absurd workaround you've had to build?"

If that makes you uncomfortable—*good*. That discomfort is where your actual strategy begins.

You're not a real leader until you're willing to go where the pain lives.

You're not leading a system until you know what breaks it. You're not building culture until you understand how it suffers. You're not operationally competent until you can explain, diagnose, and adjust the machine under stress.

And if you're not doing that? You're not leading the company. You're just hosting the show.

Your mid-level isn't telling you the truth. You keep asking yourself, *"Why didn't anyone say anything?"* Why didn't anyone raise the alarm earlier? Why didn't someone tell you the workflow was broken, the team was overwhelmed, or the plan wasn't working?

Let me give it to you straight: **Because they either didn't know, or they were afraid to admit they did.** And that's not just a personnel issue. It's a *leadership systems failure*—built on flawed assumptions, flawed promotions, and flawed feedback loops.

They Don't Know What They Don't Know

Let's start with the uncomfortable truth: **Many mid-level leaders weren't promoted for clarity. They were promoted for loyalty.** They were consistent. Friendly. Politically safe. They responded quickly. Agreed in meetings. Didn't rock the boat. They made leadership feel *comfortable*—and comfort got mistaken for capability.

But now?

Now they're in charge of a system they've never had to build. They've never managed operational complexity under real pressure. They've never designed FIFO request handling under load. They've never run a simulation. They've never been accountable for execution *at scale*.

So, when the storm comes, they don't pivot—they *perform*. They rehearse the lingo. Quote the SOP. Build a narrative. Because that's what they think leadership wants. And if you—the senior leader—don't dig, don't test, don't press for specifics?

Your silence becomes their strategy.

Because to them, *no questions mean everything's fine*. And when the top stops validating, the middle stops growing. They manage perceptions—not outcomes.

Fear of Looking Incompetent

The second layer is psychological. And it runs deep. Even if your mid-levels sense the problems—even if they feel the inefficiencies, the lag, the systemic delays—they often won't tell you.

Why?

Because they're terrified of looking incompetent. They believe:

- Admitting a broken system makes them look like a failure.
- Surfacing a capacity issue gets them labeled "not ready."
- Asking for clarity shows weakness.

So, they nod when they should challenge. They smile when they should dig. They rush to "fix" surface issues instead of diagnosing root causes. You ask, *"How's the project tracking?"* They say, *"We're on it."* But what they really mean is, *"We're improvising and hoping it works out before you notice."*

And this is where the cultural infection spreads: They train their teams to do the same. Silence becomes policy. Impression management replaces operational truth.

Here's the hard truth you have to swallow: If you've built a culture were looking good is more important than telling the truth, if you've promoted based on loyalty instead of tested clarity, if your leaders aren't stress-tested before they're empowered—Then mid-level silence isn't a mystery. It's a *mirror*.

And what it's showing you is not incompetence.

It's the *reflection of your leadership architecture*. **You cannot fix what they won't say. You cannot grow what they don't see. And you cannot lead what you refuse to inspect.** The problem isn't just that mid-levels aren't telling you the truth.

The real problem? **They think you don't want it.**

KPI Theater: When Metrics Lie

There's a special kind of rot that forms in mature organizations—the kind with shiny dashboards, executive briefings, and meetings full of graphs that tell you everything is "on track."

But the phones are ringing off the hook. Customers are pissed. Your operators are underwater. And somehow, *all the metrics are green.* That's not alignment.

That's **KPI theater.**

It's one of the greatest lies in modern leadership: "We're performing great—just look at the numbers." But when those numbers haven't been validated, cross-checked, or tied to actual operational behavior—they're not metrics.

They're *props* in a leadership performance.

- They hide delays in customer response under "average handling time."
- They bury systemic friction under "volume completed."
- They smooth out operational collapse under "tickets closed."

You think you've built a data-driven culture. What you've actually built is *a theater of false assurance*. And the worst part? **You feel good.** Because nothing burns as bright as self-deception dressed up in metrics. This is the perfect example of Musashi's living the lie.

What Real KPIs Must Do
Real metrics don't flatter—they expose. They don't entertain—they warn. They don't soothe—they prepare.
If your KPIs don't do the following, they are part of the lie:

-Reveal Capacity Thresholds
You should know *exactly* when the system starts to crack.
- At what volume do response times degrade?
- At what load do errors spike?
- What team size is required to maintain velocity?

If you can't answer that, you're not managing capacity—you're hoping it holds.

-Show Burn Rate of Operational Time
Every function burns time like fuel. But do you know *how much*?
- How many hours are consumed responding to cross-functional requests?
- How long does it take to close a revenue-impacting task across three departments?
- What's the real cost—in time and human energy—of your SOPs?

If there are no metrics to show this, your org isn't managing time—it's bleeding it. **No burn rate visibility = dead man walking.**

-Predict Failure Points
Good KPIs act like seismic monitors—they shake before the quake. They show early stress. They highlight imbalance. They surface procedural drag *before* it becomes public failure. If your metrics only show the aftermath, they're not KPIs. They're tombstones.

-Illuminate Velocity, Not Just Volume
Volume is easy to count. It makes you feel productive. But *velocity* is what builds trust.
How fast do decisions become actions? How quickly does an escalation close? How long does it take to go from "we need to" to "we delivered"? Velocity measures flow, not flattery.

-Questions That Cut Through the Noise
Want to find out if your metrics are telling the truth or selling a lie? Ask questions no dashboard can dodge:
- **"What happens if this team loses 20% capacity tomorrow?"**
  If the answer is vague, your risk model is a fairy tale.
- **"Who owns the triage decision when we're overloaded?"**
  If no one knows, then no one's leading.

- **"How long before a degradation in performance shows in the data?"**
  If it's days or weeks, your feedback loop is broken—and by the time you know, it's too late.

These aren't just operational questions. They're **truth tests.** And if your leaders can't answer them with clarity and confidence, you're not running a high-performing org. You're managing a myth.

KPIs are not for show. They are for survival. If your metrics can't survive pressure, they can't protect your business. If they don't reveal pain, they'll never direct growth. And if they only make you feel safe, they are quietly killing your capacity to lead.

The question is: Are you willing to stop performing—and start seeing?

Know the Battle Plan—And the Battlefield

Most leaders know *the strategy*. Fewer know *the system*. And only a rare few understand *the terrain they're actually fighting on.*

The rest? They're giving commands from the hilltop—watching the smoke rise from operations they never truly understood. By the time they realize what's burning, it's too late to do anything but blame and react.

Let's kill a myth right now: **Leadership isn't about "being in the room."** It's not about receiving reports. It's not about having a seat at the table. And it's definitely not about projecting confidence in meetings.

Leadership is penetration. It means *knowing the pulse* of your operation—not just the PowerPoint. It means you can walk through any department you're accountable for and:
- Diagram their workflows.
- Name their current constraints.
- Anticipate what happens when their lead analyst burns out.
- Predict where friction will surface when load doubles.

Because if you can't? You're not leading the function. You're just *sponsoring it*. You're overseeing a surface-level illusion—and when that illusion breaks, so does your credibility.

Leaders who focus on optics will always be blindsided. Not because they're stupid. But because they're *detached*. And in leadership, detachment isn't neutral. **Its negligence dressed as strategic distance.**

Every system breaks somewhere first. But if you don't understand the terrain, you won't see it. You'll find out only *after*:
- Customers are complaining.
- Revenue is stalling.
- Morale is cracking.
- The team is improvising disaster recovery in silence.

If you need an email, a meeting, or a fire alarm to know something's wrong—**you're already late**.

You need to be close enough to operations to *feel* the friction before the fire. How? By being *present with purpose*, not just proximity. **Knowing the battle plan isn't enough if you've never walked the battlefield.**

"Inspect what you expect" is not just a tactical mantra. It's the spine of real leadership. But inspection isn't passive. It's not a status update. It's not reading dashboards on the weekend and calling that insight.

Inspection is invasive. Personal. Unapologetically curious. You should:

- Walk the handoff between Sales and Fulfillment.
- Trace the lifecycle of a Tier 1 incident from intake to closure.
- Sit in on backlogged request queues to hear the chaos no chart will show you.
- Ask the hard question: *"Where are we pretending this works, but it really doesn't?"*

Because if you don't inspect it, it's decaying. And if you don't understand it, it's breaking somewhere you can't see.

High-performing teams don't rise because you trust them. They rise because you *know them.* You've seen the process. You've questioned the constraints. You've tested the thresholds. You've validated the capability—not assumed it. And when something breaks, they don't panic. Because they've *seen you in the fire.*

The "battle plan" is theory. It's the roadmap, the org chart, the playbook. But the battlefield? That's the lived reality:

- Where processes break under pressure.
- Where cross-functional latency ruins customer experience.
- Where no one knows who owns the final mile.
- Where data looks clean, but velocity is dead.

And if you haven't walked the terrain, you're leading from hallucination.

Know where the hills are. Know where the choke points live. Know where the mines are buried—because they're going to blow up under someone's feet. And if it's yours, it's on you.

You can't lead what you don't touch. You can't audit what you don't understand. You can't command what you never questioned.

This isn't about micromanaging. It's about *situational dominance*—earned through presence, clarity, and relentless validation. So, ask yourself:
"Do I know the system—or just the story I've been told about it?"

If you don't know the difference, then you don't know the battlefield. And if you don't know the battlefield? You don't know your war.

Final Reflection: Stop Hoping They're Right—Make Sure They Are

"If you haven't tested the system under pressure, you don't have a system. You have a story—and stories don't survive the truth of reality." Hope is not a leadership strategy. Trust is not an operational framework. And confidence—without confirmation—is the road to ruin.

You keep telling yourself they've got it. That they know what they're doing. That if something was really wrong, someone would speak up.

But here's the thing: **If you haven't *made sure*—it's still on you.**

That hope you're clinging to? That assumption that silence equals strength? It's a gamble. And worse—*it's a gamble you're placing on other people's backs.* Because if your mid-levels are guessing, improvising, or curating your reality for optics…If your teams are overwhelmed and under-instrumented…If your KPIs are green and your culture is red…

Then every day you don't validate is another day you're choosing the story over the system.

Stories feel good. Systems survive pressure. Stories are what people build when they're trying to protect the illusion of readiness. They sound great in meetings. They look great on slides. They're digestible, inspiring, and often completely divorced from friction.

But systems?

Systems tell the truth. Systems surface capacity. Systems reveal where things lag, break, and fail. Systems bring feedback—*even when it hurts*. And they never lie, if you've built them to speak without fear.

You can no longer afford to "trust" your operation. You must *know* it. Break it. Stress it. Inspect it. And only when it holds—*under fire*—can you call it ready.

Until then, everything you're building is fragile. You're not scaling success. You're stretching a story until it snaps.

The battlefield of reality will test your systems whether you do or not. The only question is—will you find the weakness in simulation, or in disaster?

So, stop waiting. Stop hoping. Stop pretending your silence is safety. Make the call. Walk the floor. Audit the flow. Ask the hard questions. Validate the system. And when you find the friction—own it.

Because leaders don't leave it to chance. They break it to make it stronger. And if that's not what you're doing…You're not leading. You're narrating.

Field Manual: Functional Integrity Checklist

You say your operation works. Good. Now prove it. Not with charts. Not with performance theater. With inspection. Interrogation. Execution under pressure. This checklist is your no-BS guide to finding the weak links before they break. Use it like a surgeon, not a spectator.

-Audit FIFO or Job Processing Queues — Can the Lead Describe Request Prioritization

Ask the lead, *"How do you triage requests when everything hits at once?"* If they give you a vague answer— "we just handle the urgent ones first"—you've found your first point of failure. You're not looking for speed. You're looking for:

- Defined logic.
- Documented process.
- Clear delegation.
- Failover procedures.

And let's make something crystal clear: **Anyone who delays requests simply to meet deadlines for leadership visibility, while jamming or ignoring cross-functional dependencies—isn't a leader.**

They're your biggest liability.

If they manage up but defer everything else, they're not part of your operational system—they're quietly poisoning it. **Delaying delivery that breaks someone else's workflow is not time management. It's performance sabotage.** If they can't articulate how work flows under fire—and ensure other teams don't pay for their visibility—you've got theater, not throughput.
Operational integrity starts with truth-telling around friction. And if they can't speak to that—they're not ready.

-Walk Through KPI Source Data — Who Owns Accuracy?

Every KPI has a root. A source. A process behind it. Don't trust the roll-up chart—dig into the guts. Ask:

- "Where does this data come from?"
- "Who inputs it?"
- "Who validates its accuracy before it hits the dashboard?"

If ownership is fuzzy, shared, or "automatic"—you have a façade, not a metric.
No clarity = No credibility. No credibility = No control. Metrics are only as strong as the process that feeds them. If you wouldn't bet your reputation on the integrity of that data, it's not a KPI—it's a mirage.

-Identify Pressure Scenarios — How Will Each Function Respond Under Stress?

Pick a load test. Any load test.

- System goes down for 6 hours.
- Request volume doubles overnight.
- 20% of staff go offline mid-cycle.

Now ask: *"What breaks first?"* *"What gets triaged?"* *"Who owns the fallback?"* If the room stares back at you, stunned, you just uncovered a silent vulnerability.

No pressure protocols = no operational resilience.

If they haven't rehearsed failure, they won't survive it. You're not leading a team—you're hoping a storm never comes.

-Interview Junior Team Members — What Are They Afraid to Tell Leadership?

They know. The entry-level, boots-on-the-ground, real operators—*they know where the bodies are buried.* They've seen the workarounds. They've been told to "just fix it." They carry the weight of unspoken dysfunction. Ask them:
- "What's broken that no one will say out loud?"
- "What do you wish leadership understood?"
- "What's the worst part of your day—and why hasn't it been fixed?"

Their answers will either confirm your culture is transparent—or indict it as toxic. **Truth doesn't live in the boardroom. It lives at the edge of the workflow. Go there. Listen. And then act.**

-Demand Operational Clarity from Mid-Levels — If They Can't Teach It, They Don't Own It

You want to know if your mid-levels are leading or performing? Make them teach.
Sit down. Say: "Walk me through your department's critical functions. Show me how requests move through your system. Explain what happens when volume spikes. Teach me how you recover from failure."

If they stumble, stall, or abstract—it's theater. If they teach with clarity, walk the flow, and show stress-tested logic—*that's ownership.*

If they can't teach it, they don't own it. And if they don't own it, you've got a ghost in your org chart where there should be a commander.

Run this checklist monthly. Quarterly. After every incident.

Make it part of your leadership cadence. Because the moment you stop inspecting, the drift begins. The illusion creeps back in. And soon, you're trusting systems that are quietly rotting beneath the dashboard. **Lead with clarity. Inspect without apology. Audit like your credibility depends on it—because it does.**

This isn't micromanagement. This is the difference between commanders and curators. Only one of them survives when the battlefield gets real.

Chapter 10: When "Empowerment" Becomes Abdication

Cameron was the best network manager I'd ever seen. Global telecoms called him directly when things went sideways.

He didn't just know the infrastructure — he *saw it*, like a chessboard. He was brilliant. Rare. And for a while, **he made us bulletproof**.

Then it changed.

Personal issues hit. The performance eroded. He stopped showing up—sometimes physically, sometimes mentally. Projects missed. Signals dropped. Teams stressed.

And I didn't act.

Not because I didn't see it. But because I was **afraid**. Afraid to lose the brilliance. Afraid I'd never find someone like him again. Afraid of what the team would face without that firepower.

I told myself it was loyalty. I told myself he just needed time. But the truth was darker —**I was being led by fear.** The team saw it. They watched me bend around the problem. They watched accountability fracture. They watched me protect a ghost because of what he used to be.

Then one day it hit. Like a blunt instrument across the skull: *You can have a genius on your team, but if he doesn't show up —you're multiplying by zero.*

No matter how gifted Cameron was, **zero times anything is still zero.** That realization changed me. I stopped calculating around potential. I started calculating around mission goals delivery on a daily basis.

And that day, I let him go. Not with anger. Not with spite. But with the clarity I should've had months earlier.

And when I did? We hired someone less gifted — but rock solid. Steady. Reliable. Consistent. Never missed a day and produced. Instead of zero, we were back to positive numbers.

That's when I saw it — my own Shadow. The fear of losing rare brilliance had made me weak. Had made me indecisive. Had made me someone I swore I'd never become: A leader who *knew* the truth… but wouldn't move.

That's what fear does. It doesn't scream. It whispers rationalizations. And it makes you build systems around your anxiety instead of your mission.

I thought I was protecting the team by holding on. But the truth? I was protecting myself from loss. And it was costing everyone.

Letting Cameron go didn't just confront my fear of loss. It confronted a lie I had been telling myself —**that I was "empowering" him by giving him time.** But it wasn't empowerment.

It was avoidance.

I wasn't offering autonomy. I was outsourcing leadership because I didn't want to make the hard call. I wrapped my fear in a noble word and called it wisdom.

And that's what we do, isn't it? We dress our discomfort in virtue. We hide behind phrases like *"Let them lead"*, *"Give them space"*, or *"They need to own it"* — all while silently praying, we won't have to be the one to say, *"This isn't working."*

And here's the truth: **Sometimes what we call empowerment… is just fear wearing a nice suit.**

Empowerment is one of the most overused—and most misunderstood—words in leadership today. We love to say it. We put it in mission statements, slide decks, leadership workshops. We talk about empowering our teams, our managers, our people. We say we want ownership. Autonomy. Initiative.

But let's tell the truth: **sometimes empowerment is just cowardice with a nice vocabulary.** Sometimes, "empowerment" is the lie we tell ourselves when we're too afraid to lead.

In this chapter, we're not talking about tyrants or narcissists. We're talking about the good leaders. The kind ones. The "servant leaders." The emotionally intelligent, hyper-collaborative, well-meaning people who—without realizing it—are creating just as much chaos as the toxic ones.

Why? Because they've confused empowerment with abdication.

They think they're trusting the team. But they're actually avoiding conflict. They think they're creating space. But they're actually **failing to provide structure**. They think they're being humble. But they're actually **shirking responsibility**.

And the cost? Execution failure. Organizational drift. And a team that quietly loses faith.

The Chaos of Kindness

They don't yell. They don't manipulate. They don't demand attention.

In fact, they're usually the most *liked* person in the room. Well-spoken. Well-meaning. Emotionally intelligent. They *facilitate* beautifully. They *defer* generously. They *listen* carefully.

But here's the problem: **They never *decide*.** These leaders are the architects of soft confusion. The high priests of "collaborative chaos." The smiling mirror who reflects every voice… but never speaks with finality.

And it feels good—at first. Because these leaders are "safe." They don't challenge too hard. They trust you. They believe in your potential. They say all the right things:

- "I trust your judgment."
- "Let's see what the group comes up with."
- "I don't want to get in the way."
- "You've got this—just let me know how I can support."
- "What do *you* think is best?"

It sounds like empowerment. But it *functions* like abandonment. Because when the road gets hard—when decisions are ambiguous, emotional, or unpopular—**these leaders disappear.** Not physically. Not in title. But *spiritually*.

They disappear into consensus. They disappear into vagueness. They disappear behind the language of collaboration, using emotional deference to mask psychological avoidance.

They form committees for collaboration to avoid owning decisions they're putting off due to cowardice and/or narrative exposure.

This is not trust. This is not delegation. This is **emotional outsourcing disguised as empowerment.**

What It Actually Creates

What does this soft leadership chaos look like on the ground?

- **Endless decision loops.** Every question becomes another meeting. Every meeting ends with "Let's revisit next week."
- **Overstretched teams.** People are "empowered" to take on roles, scopes, and decisions they were *never actually equipped* to handle—then held silently responsible for the fallout.
- **Execution fatigue.** When clarity never comes, teams slow down—not from laziness, but from confusion. They aren't sure where they're headed. They aren't sure what matters. And they aren't sure *who's in charge.*
- **Feedback becomes foggy.** No one wants to critique the kind leader. So, accountability gets filtered through "growth mindset" language that *never lands.*
- **Trust erosion.** Not because the leader is mean. But because they *aren't present* when it counts. People start thinking:

"You say you support me, but where were you when I needed backup?" "You trust me—but are you just afraid to step in?"

What's Really Happening?

At the root of this isn't malice. It's not incompetence. It's *fear.*

- Fear of being "too authoritative."
- Fear of making the wrong call.
- Fear of disappointing someone.
- Fear of emotional discomfort.

So instead of leading, these leaders defer. They *abdicate* with elegance. They trade *command* for *comfort.* They've confused:

- **Humility with passivity.**
- **Support with surrender.**
- **Empowerment with escape.**

They believe they're "creating space." But they're actually abandoning the throne of responsibility.

And here's the paradox: **In trying not to dominate, they destabilize. In trying to protect the team, they undermine it.** Because empowerment without structure is chaos. Autonomy without clarity is anxiety. **And kindness without courage is not leadership—it's** *emotional outsourcing.*

What Real Empowerment Looks Like

True empowerment **requires boundaries**.

- It says, "You own this—but I've got your back if you fall."
- It says, "You have autonomy—but I will draw the line when direction is unclear."
- It says, "Your voice matters—but I will make the hard call when the team can't align."

Real empowerment feels both freeing and grounded. It expands trust *without withdrawing guidance*. It builds capacity *without abandoning clarity*. Because leadership isn't just about listening. It's about **deciding.** And it's about owning the emotional weight of that decision—even when it's unpopular.

Kindness is Not a Strategy

Kindness is a *posture*. But **clarity is a responsibility**. Empathy matters—but it cannot carry the culture alone. A well-meaning leader who avoids conflict is still *avoiding leadership.*

So, if your team is drifting…If your top performers seem confused…If people praise you to your face but disengage behind the scenes…It may not be because you're not "empowering" enough.

It may be because you're not *leading* enough. And that doesn't make you bad. It makes you ready—for the next level.

Lead. Own. Decide. And stand.

Even if it means stepping out of the circle of comfort. Because empowerment without direction is abandonment in disguise. And your people were not built to wander. They were built to *follow someone worth trusting.*

Make sure that someone is you.

Disempowered Executive Syndrome (DES)

No, **DES** isn't a clinical diagnosis. But it *should* be an organizational one. Because it doesn't just happen to bad leaders or broken teams. It happens to **high-performing, well-intentioned executives** who genuinely want to build empowered, collaborative cultures. And yet… they end up overwhelmed, emotionally spent, and surrounded by teams that don't seem to move unless pushed.

It starts with good intentions. It ends in organizational paralysis. DES is subtle. It doesn't begin with dysfunction. It begins with *fear of dysfunction*—and a well-meaning overcorrection. It begins with:

- A desire to avoid micromanagement.
- A commitment to psychological safety.
- A promise to be the "anti-boss."

But instead of building systems that balance autonomy with clarity…These leaders build systems that slowly **remove themselves from power**—not in principle, but in practice. And that's when the symptoms start to show.

The DES Pattern: What It Looks Like in Real Time

You'll know you're witnessing Disempowered Executive Syndrome when:

- **Leaders Stop Enforcing Standards—To Be Liked**
  Standards exist on paper, but no one enforces them when tension rises. Because holding the line feels "too harsh." So, leaders retreat into likability—and the team drifts into entropy.
- **Vision Becomes a Group Exercise—With No Final Voice**
  Everyone is invited to "shape the vision," but no one is willing to own it. Decisions are diluted. Strategy becomes crowdsourced. And the organization becomes a boat with five rudders—and no captain.

- **Managers Are Told to Take Initiative—But Without Authority**
  They're encouraged to "own the outcomes," but blocked from reallocating resources, saying no to toxic behaviors, or adjusting timelines. They're empowered in word—but not in structure.
- **Freedom Is Given Without Boundaries—Then Punished After Failure**
  Teams are told to "be bold," but when bold decisions go wrong, leaders swoop in with retroactive corrections. So, the message becomes clear:
  You're free… until we don't like the results.
- **Ownership Is So Distributed That No One Can Actually Move**
  Everyone is "responsible," but no one owns. Tasks overlap. Decisions stall. Momentum dies in the name of "shared accountability." And you have to get the buy in of the least productive and least valuable player in the organization, which just never happens.
  And perhaps the **most destructive pattern of all**:
- **Hard Decisions Are Delegated Down—While Consequences Stay at the Top**
  When things get tough, executives delegate authority—but not risk. Managers are asked to "figure it out," but when it fails? **The weight comes crashing back down on the executive's desk.**

Why It's So Destructive

DES doesn't look toxic from the outside. There's no yelling. There's no micromanagement. There are no public power plays. That's what makes it so dangerous—it hides behind **culture-positive language**:
- "We want to empower our people."
- "We trust the team to figure it out."
- "We're building a flat structure."

But the reality? The system lacks *clarity, courage, and cohesion.* Here's what happens next:
- **Same issues, quarter after quarter.** Because nobody owns the root problems—and no one's empowered to enforce change.
- **High performers burn out.** They carry the load, navigate the ambiguity, fix what's broken—without authority, recognition, or protection. Eventually, they leave or emotionally disengage.
- **Feedback loops fracture.** Everyone "wants transparency," but nobody feels safe naming the real problem. So, the hard truth dies in hallway whispers and after-hours vent sessions.
- **And executives start asking questions that should haunt them:**
  - "Why won't anyone just step up?"
  - "Why does everything end up on my desk anyway?"
  - "Why do I feel like I'm still carrying all of it?"

Because you are. Not because you're a control freak. Not because your people are incompetent. But because you *never replaced authority with alignment.* You removed your voice without building structure. You built freedom without fences. You mistook collaboration for clarity.

The Real Diagnosis: Clarity Without Courage Is Just Confusion

Here's the truth leaders in DES don't want to face: **Empowerment without anchoring is a lie.** People don't need empty phrases. They need:
- **Boundaries.**
- **Structure.**
- **Clear roles.**
- **Real authority.**
- **Protected decision space.**

Empowerment is not: "Let me know how I can support." It's: "Here's the outcome I need. You have the freedom and the protection to go make it happen. I will back you, even if it gets messy. And I will not disappear when things get hard."

Take the Power Back—Then Share It Right

If you've been shouldering too much, and still feel like you're carrying it all—this is your wake-up call. **DES doesn't mean you're weak.** It means you've avoided your own authority. Now's the time to fix it. Not by yanking back control. But by **rebuilding clarity with courage.**
- Say the hard truths.
- Reclaim your right to lead.
- Set standards that stick.
- Empower people with real ownership—not just borrowed pressure.

Because if everyone's confused and no one is moving…It's not a team problem. It's a *leadership clarity* problem. Fix that—and watch your culture rise again.

Empowerment Without Boundaries Is Sabotage

Too often, organizations mistake *empowerment* for simply "getting out of the way." But *real empowerment* doesn't leave people alone—it *equips* them. It doesn't just give people freedom—it gives them *form.*

Here's what it actually takes to empower someone in a meaningful, sustainable way:

1. Clarity of Outcome-Before anything else, people need to know what success *looks like.* Not just vague aspirations. Not just "run with it" energy. Real empowerment starts with a crystal-clear *destination.*
- What are we trying to achieve?
- By when?
- What's the non-negotiable?
- What would "wild success" look like—and what does failure mean?

Without this clarity, "empowerment" becomes **chaos in business casual.** You didn't unleash creativity—you unleashed *cognitive load.*

2. Defined Authority and Limits-Next, empowered people need to know where their decision space *begins* and where it *ends.* This includes:
- Budget thresholds.
- Approval boundaries.
- Resource access.
- The power to say no, to re-scope, or to pivot when reality hits.

Giving someone responsibility without decision rights is not empowerment—it's a **set-up.** And it sends a dangerous message: "We'll call it yours, but you'll still have to ask permission to act." That's not delegation. That's a **political booby trap.**

3. Access to Truth and Support-You can't empower someone to lead in the dark.
- Do they have access to the *real* data?
- Do they know the back-channel dynamics that will shape perception?
- Are they getting air cover from leadership when the stakes rise?
- Do they know who's in their corner—and who isn't?

Empowerment without visibility is emotional entrapment. You didn't empower them. You sent them into battle blind—then asked why they lost.

What It's Not: The Lies We Tell Ourselves

Let's dismantle the soft lies that keep circulating in "progressive" leadership environments— often with the best intentions, but devastating outcomes:

- **Giving someone a title without decision rights?** That's not empowerment. That's *a setup for failure.* It says: *"You're accountable for the outcomes, but we still control your options."*
- **Letting a team decide "how they want to work" without performance anchors?** That's not autonomy. That's *a fog machine.* Collaboration doesn't mean direction lessness. You gave them ambiguity and called it innovation.
- **Asking a burned-out manager to 'run with it' after five others bailed?** That's not trust. That's *trauma transfer.* You didn't empower them—you offloaded the emotional weight you didn't want to carry.

And then, when it all unravels?
- When the deadline is missed…
- When the conflict explodes…
- When the best people start quietly slipping out the side door…

These same leaders shrug and say: "I don't understand. I *thought* I was empowering them."

Let's be honest: **No, you weren't empowering. You were disappearing. You were avoiding.**
You were hiding behind empathy and collaboration instead of making the hard calls. You gave them the wheel—but never the map. You handed off responsibility—but kept all the risk. You praised initiative—but refused to protect it when the bullets flew.

The Courage to Truly Empower

Here's what real empowerment demands from *you* as a leader:
- **Courage to clarify—even when people resist definition.**
- **Willingness to define ownership, even when it costs you control.**
- **Emotional maturity to stay present when they struggle, not just when they shine.**

Because empowerment isn't a word you use in a keynote. It's a **contract**. A promise that says: "You own this. And I will not leave you to drown in it. I will walk with you, I will advocate for you, and I will back you—even when the system shakes." That's not delegation. That's not abdication. That's **leadership with a spine.**

The Cost of Abdication

We throw around the word "empowerment" like it's a universal good. But empowerment without structure? Without clarity? Without ownership? It doesn't just cause confusion—it *costs* you everything. Let's break it down.

1. It Costs You Credibility-You may think your team doesn't notice—but they do. They notice when you:

- Smile through meetings where you should be setting direction.
- Ask *them* to "take the lead" on decisions you were hired to make.
- Facilitate conversations instead of drawing boundaries.
- Retreat behind phrases like "I trust the team" when pressure mounts.

They feel it. They feel it when the emotional weight of ambiguity lands in their lap. They feel it when they're told they're "Empowered"—but no one steps in to back them when they act. They feel it when there's a leadership vacuum, and they're silently expected to fill it *without authority or protection.* And when your team sees the gap between **what you say** and **what you do**—your credibility takes the hit. You may still be liked. You may still be admired. **But you will not be *trusted*.** And once you lose credibility, the erosion of influence is not far behind.

2. It Costs You Talent-Let's set the record straight: **High performers don't crave freedom. They crave *structure with room to stretch*.** They don't want:

- A blank canvas with no expectations.
- Authority without protection.
- The illusion of ownership with none of the tools to lead effectively.

They want:

- A *mission* they can believe in.
- *Clear lanes* so they can go fast.
- *Boundaries* they can push against, not fall through.
- A *leader* who will hold the line when pressure, politics, or chaos strikes.

So, when you give them free reign without real guidance, or when you disappear into "support mode" at the first sign of complexity, here's what happens:

- They don't feel empowered. They feel *set up*.
- They don't feel trusted. They feel *abandoned*.
- They don't rise. They *retreat*—either into another job or into emotional detachment.

And the most dangerous talent loss is the quiet kind: When your best people are still on payroll—but they've *already left in spirit*.

3. It Costs You Execution-This is where the organizational body starts to break down. With no clear ownership, what begins as collaboration quickly devolves into chaos:

- **Projects stall.**
  Everyone's "collaborating," but no one is driving. Timelines blur. Dependencies tangle. And critical tasks get lost in the fog.
- **Strategy dilutes.**
  What began as a clear initiative now has 14 owners, 9 Slack threads, 3 redundant meetings, and no momentum.

- **Accountability vaporizes.**
  When everyone's responsible, no one is. Action items become suggestions. Deadlines become decorations. People feel busy—but nothing moves.

  And eventually, the most tragic symptom appears: **People stop moving.** Not because they're lazy. Not because they don't care. But because they *don't know what they're allowed to do anymore.* They've been "empowered" so many times without direction, feedback, or backup that they start asking themselves:
  - "Am I stepping on someone else's toes?"
  - "Will I get in trouble if I take initiative?"
  - "What happens if I make the wrong call?"

And when questions like that go unanswered? **Initiative dies. Momentum dies. Execution dies.**

Brutal Truth: Empowerment Without Leadership is Betrayal

So, let's stop pretending that empowerment is always the noble choice. Because when done poorly, it's not noble—it's **neglect.** It's a leadership shell game that makes you feel generous while making your team feel lost.

If you're empowering people without clarity, without boundaries, without support— you're not giving them freedom. You're handing them **emotional liability** without organizational protection.

And when the wheels come off? You'll hear the same tired refrain: "I don't get it. I thought I was empowering them." Let me say it plain: No, you weren't empowering. You were *avoiding.* You were hiding behind empathy instead of exercising authority. You were outsourcing responsibility to people who needed *a leader,* not a cheerleader.

What Real Empowerment Requires

Let's strip away the slogans and speak plainly: **Empowerment is not a hands-off philosophy. It's a leadership *discipline*.** You don't empower teams by stepping away. You empower them by showing up—with backbone, with vision, with *clarity*.
Because true empowerment doesn't mean letting people "figure it out." It means building the structure, safety, and standards that allow them to *thrive* while they do. So, what does real empowerment demand? Let's get specific.

1. Define the Mission—With Clarity and Conviction
Empowerment without a clearly defined mission is just chaos in a costume. It's not enough to say: "We want innovation," or "We're trying to be more agile."
You must define:
- The *what* (clear goals and deliverables),
- The *why* (strategic alignment with vision and values), and
- The *what you will and will not tolerate* (cultural guardrails and behavioral standards).

Empowerment begins with anchoring. Your team can only steer if they know the coordinates—and what cliffs to avoid. Without this, you're not empowering. You're *abandoning direction* and calling it flexibility.

2. Give Real Authority—Not Just Responsibility

Nothing erodes morale faster than the illusion of ownership. When you tell someone, "This is yours," but require them to seek permission for every meaningful decision—you've handed them stress, not power. Empowerment means:

- The authority to choose.
- The authority to shape.
- The authority to say no.

Not just tasks to complete, but *decisions to make that actually impact the mission.* **Responsibility without authority is a trap. Empowerment without control is a lie.**

3. Be Present When It's Hard

This is where false empowerment collapses. When tension shows up—misalignment, interpersonal conflict, failed initiatives—many leaders retreat into silence or deference. They say: "I trust the team." "Let them work it out." **When teams haven't been able to work it out over days, weeks or months, sending them back again is not empowerment. That's** *evasion. Its cowardice in a high-performance mask of lunacy.* Empowered leaders stay *in it.*

- Not to micromanage.
- Not to control.
- But to **co-regulate, guide, protect, and reinforce boundaries** when things get hot.

You can't empower people to lead *if you vanish the moment leadership is required.*

4. Back Them Publicly, Correct Them Privately

True empowerment doesn't mean turning a blind eye to failure. It means creating an environment where **people can stretch without fearing public exposure**. That means:

- If they stumble in public, you defend them.
- If they miss the mark, you coach them quietly and directly.
- If they overstep, you correct without shaming.

Because when your team knows you'll stand with them even when it's messy? They stop hedging. They stop playing it safe. They start *owning the mission.* **You can't build courage in others if they're worried, you'll fold under pressure.**

5. Hold the Line—Starting with Yourself

Empowerment doesn't work in cultures where standards flex based on convenience. You don't just hold the line with underperformers. You:

- **Hold it with yourself.**
- You model consistency.
- You show up prepared.
- You admit mistakes.
- You say the hard thing first.
- You never ask for resilience you aren't willing to embody.

Because people don't follow ideas. They follow integrity. **Empowerment without leadership modeling is empty. It asks others to take risks you won't.**

Your Team Doesn't Need More Freedom—They Need More *Trustworthy Leadership*

We've romanticized the idea that teams are crying out for more space, more freedom, more flexibility. But the truth? **They don't need more space. They need more leaders who can be trusted with it.** They're not looking for a passive supporter. They're looking for:

- A protector of clarity.
- A consistent presence.
- A voice of truth when things get murky.
- A leader who doesn't disappear in the name of empowerment.

So don't just cheer them on. **Lead them. Back them. Anchor them. Own the hard parts. And watch them rise with a strength they didn't know they had—because you helped them build it.**

Are You Empowering, or Avoiding?

Let's ask the uncomfortable question: ***Are you empowering your team—or are you avoiding your role?*** Are you giving them space to grow—or space to **take the fall** for your inability to lead? Are you holding them capable—or are you *transferring accountability* because you don't want to make the tough call?

Empowerment without clarity is chaos. Empowerment without presence is abandonment. Empowerment without courage is **a façade**. And if you're not careful, the people you claim to be empowering will stop trusting you altogether—not because you were cruel, but because you were never *truly there*.

Field Manual: Diagnosing and Disarming Fear-Based Leadership
Fear isn't always panic. In leadership, fear wears masks. It shows up dressed as strategy, empathy, and collaboration. It sounds like: *"They just need more time." "Now's not the right moment." "I trust them to figure it out."*

But underneath, it's fear whispering: *"I don't want to be the one who pulls the trigger."*

If you're not conscious of your fear, it will lead your team for you —**and it won't lead them anywhere clean.** Here's how to spot it, break it, and move with fire.

1. Fear as "Strategic Delay"
Directive: Kill the illusion of patience when it's just fear to act.
Watch for:
- Endless reassessment
- "Waiting for the right data"
- Pushing decisions into "later quarters"

Counter:
- Ask: *"If we had to move today, what would we do?"*
- Then ask: *"What's stopping us?"*
  If the answer is discomfort — move anyway.

2. Fear Disguised as Empowerment
Directive: Empowerment without accountability is abdication.
Watch for:
- Delegating decisions just to avoid being the bad guy
- Giving "autonomy" when what's needed is confrontation
- Allowing confusion to fester under the banner of trust

Counter:
- Say it out loud: *"Here's what I expect. Here's when I'll step in."*
- Don't hide boundaries behind buzzwords. Make them real.

3. Fear as Niceness
Directive: Don't weaponize kindness to avoid truth.
Watch for:
- Smiling through sabotage
- Coaching people who clearly don't want to grow
- Withholding feedback to "keep the peace"

Counter:
- Ask: *"Is this kindness protecting them — or protecting me from discomfort?"*
- Kindness without clarity is betrayal. Lead clean.

4. Fear as Talent Worship
Directive: Never let brilliance blind you to decay.
Watch for:
- Making exceptions for high-performers who hurt the culture
- Avoiding tough calls because "we'll never replace them"
- Justifying their dysfunction with past results

Counter:

- Ask: *"If they don't show up fully, what are we multiplying by?"*
- Genius that doesn't show up still equals zero. Do the math.

5. Fear in the Body
Directive: Trust the twitch.
Watch for:
- Physical hesitation before a confrontation
- Shallow breathing before a critical conversation
- Tight jaw, sweaty palms, increased verbosity when challenged

Counter:
- Breathe. Center. Own it.
- Say to yourself:

"This discomfort is my signal.   This is where the truth lives.   This is where I move."

Final Directive:

If you don't confront the fear that leads you —you will build an organization that avoids truth to protect your ego. Fear that isn't faced becomes policy. It becomes culture. It becomes decay. **Face it. Name it. Burn it.**

And when you do —You'll lead without compromise, without theater, and without apology. That's clean command. That's clarity in the fire. That's leadership that can't be bought, bullied, or broken.

Chapter 11: The Death of Heroic Leadership

Let me tell you about Jack. Jack was an executive. He preached ownership. He said all the right things. Perfect posture. Perfect slides. Perfect theater.

He performed accountability the way seasoned actors hit their marks—emphatic, eloquent, and utterly empty. His voice dripped with investment. His eyes sparkled with mission alignment. Every word landed like it had been rehearsed for months. But two things exposed his.

First—he couldn't hit a goal to save his life. Neither could his team. Quarter after quarter, performance metrics slid off the map like oil on glass. But instead of facing the data, Jack weaponized the shadows. He didn't point fingers in public. That would have required courage. Instead, he hosted quiet little blame rituals behind closed doors. Whispers. Private meetings. No witnesses.

Until the mask slipped.

It was the fifth straight quarter of missed goals. A board meeting. High-stakes. Serious players in the room—seasoned operators with global portfolios. The conversation turned surgical. Revenue shortfalls. Growth bottlenecks. Questions he couldn't dodge.

And then it happened. Jack put his hand over his heart, took a theatrical breath, and said: "I'm just so proud of how hard my team has worked to try and hit the goal."

There it was.

The leadership equivalent of a three-foot zit on his forehead. He thought it was a display of emotional intelligence. The board saw it for what it was: the final tells. A performance. A script. A justification for failure wrapped in the language of empathy.

The murmurs started before the meeting ended. Polite, at first. Then blunt: "You don't get points for effort at this level." "Results are not optional." "Pride in failure isn't leadership. It's delusion."

Jack sipped his water, nodded solemnly, still thinking he'd nailed it. The longer he sat there, the more he mixed up his special brand of Kool-Aid, drinking it feverishly with the hope everyone would want a glass. The more he drank without everyone else, he thought he was convincing everyone.

He hadn't. He'd exposed himself—and his entire charade of "shared accountability."

Because here's the brutal truth: "I'm proud we tried" is not the language of leadership. It's the language of failure in a suit. So, stop the play at heroics We see through it. And we're done applauding.

Jack's story isn't rare. It's a case study in what happens when **performance masquerades as leadership**—when emotion replaces execution and theater replaces truth. And it all hinges on one word: **accountability**.

Accountability. It's one of the most overused words in leadership—right up there with "alignment," "ownership," and "culture." Every executive swears by it. Every mission statement promises it. Every strategy deck builds it in. But walk into the average organization, and you'll quickly see:

What we call accountability is often just performance in disguise. We've created systems where people appear busy, appear aligned, appear productive—but in reality? They're managing optics. They're hedging blame. They're doing just enough to not get called out—but never enough to actually move the mission forward.

This isn't accountability. It's **accountability theater**. And it's not just a problem of performance—it's a **cultural lie** that protects the wrong people and punishes the right ones.

Performance Without Ownership

At first glance, everything looks healthy.

- KPIs are being tracked in beautiful dashboards.
- Tasks are logged and color-coded in the project management software.
- Deadlines are discussed in meetings.
- Status updates are flowing in Slack threads.
- Everyone is "looped in," copied, cc'd, or tagged.

It looks like *movement*. It smells like *momentum*. It *feels* like accountability. Until something goes wrong.

- The launch misses its window.
- The numbers don't land.
- The deliverable stalls out in a sea of "next steps."

And suddenly, all that visibility? All those bullet points and check-ins? **They vanish into a fog of well-rehearsed excuses.**

- Everyone has a story.
- Everyone has a reason.
- Everyone has a Google Doc, a spreadsheet, a thread that proves: *"I tried."*

That's when it hits you: **This wasn't accountability. It was activity masquerading as ownership. Being busy does not equal productivity. Busy means busy. Productivity means productivity.** You had:

- Effort—but not outcome.
- Involvement—but not investment.
- Participation—but not *presence with power*.

Why This Happens: The Culture of Covered Bases

Modern work culture has trained us to avoid blame at all costs. So, we document. We update. We speak the language of contribution. But **contribution without consequence** is not ownership. In this system:

- Accountability is *distributed so widely* that no one is clearly in charge.
- Everyone "did their part"—but no one owned the whole.
- Everyone was *engaged*—but no one was *responsible*.

This is how **accountability theater** thrives. It's a system designed to protect perception, not pursue progress.

The Symptoms You'll See

In a performance-without-ownership environment, the warning signs are everywhere:

- **Meetings are filled with updates—but no hard calls.**
  Information is shared. Nothing is decided. Deadlines shift like sand.
- **Everyone's "in the loop," but no one has the wheel.**
  Everyone's consulted. No one's committed. Every decision dies in a group chat.
- **When the project fails, everyone talks about process—not responsibility.**
  "We had a communication issue." "The timeline slipped." "There was some confusion about who was doing what." **The real issue is never named: Nobody actually *owned* it.**

The Difference: Ownership vs. Participation

Here's how to spot the difference between real accountability and its theatrical twin:

Participation	Ownership
"I was involved."	"I'm responsible."
"We ran into blockers."	"I didn't remove the blockers."
"I flagged the risk."	"I built a plan to solve it."
"I updated leadership."	"I made the call."
"I did my part."	"I own the outcome—whatever it is."

In real accountability, someone says: **"If this fails, it's on me. If it succeeds, I'll bring the team with me."**

The Consequence of False Accountability

When accountability is simulated instead of practiced:

- **Projects stall.**
- **Culture deteriorates.**
- **Trust fractures.**
- **High performers burn out—while low-accountability contributors hide in the fog.**
  And leadership begins asking questions like:
- "Why does no one step up?"
- "Why do I always end up cleaning the mess?"
- "Why is everything moving, but nothing *finishing*?"
  Because you've built a system where being visible is safer than being *accountable*.

Where the loudest contributor is rewarded over the *quiet finisher.*

The Structure of Illusion

How do high-functioning teams end up drowning in chaos? How do high-trust cultures devolve into high-conflict environments where no one seems to lead—and no one seems to deliver? It starts innocently enough—with **good intentions.** We say things like:

- "We don't want to micromanage."
- "We want to empower people to lead."
- "We trust the team."

And that's a beautiful foundation—until **clarity is sacrificed at the altar of comfort.** So, we start making changes:

- We flatten hierarchies to "remove barriers."
- We form cross-functional pods to "increase agility."
- We decentralize decision-making to "encourage autonomy."
- We adopt flexible metrics to "focus on innovation."

But in the process...**We forget to assign ownership.**

When Everyone is Involved—But No One is Accountable

In the absence of clear roles, decision rights, and outcome anchors, teams drift. Fast.

- Nobody knows who's leading the initiative.
- Everybody contributes, but nobody directs.
- Discussions multiply, but decisions stall.

The intent was trust. The impact? **Performance theater.** Everyone learns the same lesson: **"If I don't protect myself, I'm exposed."** So, they start *gaming the system.* Not out of malice—but **as a survival strategy.**

The Anatomy of Defensive Performance

When people are held accountable for results, they can't truly control, they shift from ownership to *optics management.* Here's what it looks like:

- **They manage up**: Constantly informing stakeholders of what they're doing to avoid downstream blame.
- **They CC executives**: Not for collaboration—but as insurance. Every email becomes a receipt.
- **They narrate their effort in real-time**: "Just wanted to update you on what I'm doing…" becomes a daily refrain. Visibility replaces progress.
- **They polish the appearance**:
  - The meetings are long.
  - The decks are immaculate.
  - The language is collaborative and compliant.

But the actual *results*? Sloppy. Late. Disconnected. And somehow—**nobody's fault.**

Why It Feels Safe to Perform—and Dangerous to Own

When teams exist in a structure of illusion:

- **Truth becomes dangerous.**
  Because naming the real problem risks being labeled "negative," "not a team player," or "lacking political awareness."
- **Ownership becomes risky.**
  Because taking full responsibility might mean taking full blame.

- **Accountability becomes transactional.**
  People deliver just enough to show effort—but avoid stepping far enough into ownership to be held responsible if it fails.
  So, what do you get?
- Culture built on defense, not delivery.
- Teams performing contribution, not pushing for clarity.
- Leaders surrounded by *activity—but starving for progress.*

The Slow Collapse: Why It Breaks Execution

This kind of culture doesn't explode. It erodes. One project stalls. Then another. Innovation slows. Turnover creeps in. Meetings multiply. Decisions blur. And trust? It gets replaced by politics. People stop asking:

- "How do we win?"

They start asking:

- "How do I protect myself from losing?"

And at that point? You're not managing a team. You're *curating a performance.* A structure built to *look like* leadership—but engineered to *avoid real consequences.*

Narcissistic Systems: Where Truth Gets Punished

The most dangerous environments are the ones where **honesty gets you hurt**. Where saying, *"We missed this because I didn't prioritize it,"* makes you a target. Where saying, *"This person isn't a good fit,"* gets you labeled toxic. Where saying, *"We need to call this what it is— failure,"* gets you pushed out of the room.

In these systems, you're expected to take accountability—but only if it makes leadership look good. Truth is allowed—but only if it's convenient. Ownership is celebrated—but only when it protects the narrative.

This is how narcissistic cultures work. They don't reward performance. They reward loyalty. They don't protect the truth. They protect **the image**.

And if your honesty threatens that image? You become the problem. I've seen high performers get destroyed for telling the truth. And I've seen professional illusionists get promoted for spinning failure into "learning opportunities."

In systems like this, **accountability is not distributed—it is weaponized**.

The Cost of the Illusion

What does it cost? Everything. You lose the trust of your best people—the ones who care more about results than recognition. You burn out your top contributors—because they're too busy compensating for the failures of those who "narrate effort" without impact. You confuse the system—because everyone starts managing optics instead of outcomes. And eventually, **you lose your edge.**

You stop making decisions fast. You stop innovating boldly. You stop telling the truth— because truth creates friction, and friction is no longer tolerated. In the end, the organization becomes like a glossy presentation with no data behind it: *beautiful, articulate, hollow.*

What Real Accountability Looks Like

We've seen what happens when accountability is confused with performance. We've seen what it costs—credibility, talent, execution, and trust. So now it's time to **rebuild it.** But not with platitudes. With **principles.**

Because real accountability isn't about blame—it's about **ownership with structure.** And it isn't about fear—it's about **alignment with courage.** Here's how to make it real.

1. Clarity of Ownership This is the foundation. *One person owns the outcome.* Not the meetings. Not the process. Not the updates. **The outcome.** That means:

- Their name is on it.
- They have the *authority* to make real decisions.
- They have the *resources* to lead execution.
- They're not managing by consensus—they're *driving to closure.*

It doesn't mean they're doing it alone. It means they're accountable for seeing it through.

Ownership = Name on the Line + Power to Act.

No shared ambiguity. No vague team assignments. No fuzzy "alignment." If everyone owns it, *no one* does.

2. Radical Truth-Telling You can't build accountability in a culture of fear. Real accountability thrives where **truth is spoken without punishment.** It's the ability for a team or a leader to say:

- "We missed the target."
- "This decision was wrong."
- "This process broke down."
- "This is on me."

Without:

- Getting scapegoated.
- Losing influence.
- Being quietly pushed out of visibility.

In high-accountability cultures, **failure becomes feedback.** In low-accountability cultures, **failure becomes a firing line.** This is why so many avoid ownership—they've seen what happens to the last person who tried. So, you must:

- Normalize real post-mortems.
- Reward those who name breakdowns first.
- Create psychological safety *and* performance expectations.

Because without truth, there can be no real accountability. Only performance and survival.

3. Shared Consequences This is where most systems fall apart. In accountability theater, consequences flow one way: *down.* The team misses a goal? Middle management absorbs the heat. High performers scramble. And executives ask, "Why didn't you speak up?" But in real accountability? **Leaders share the cost.** Not just the credit.

When the system breaks:

- Leaders inspect *their* design, not just the team's execution.
- They own *why* someone failed under their direction.
- They say, "We missed this—and here's what I'll change about how I lead."

Accountability doesn't mean handing pressure to the people below you.

It means standing beside them, and sometimes in front of them—**especially when it costs something.**

Let's Be Clear: Accountability ≠ Cruelty

This isn't about public takedowns. It's not about sharp words, pressure-posturing, or leadership bravado. **Accountability isn't cruelty. It's integrity—with teeth.** It's not a whip—it's a *promise*. The promise that:

- *"We don't fake ownership here."*
- *"We don't vanish when it gets messy."*
- *"We hold the line because the mission matters more than our comfort."*

You're not shaming people—you're **protecting meaning.** You're not looking for perfection—you're building trust through *consistent truth*. And when something breaks? You don't pass it off. You say:

"This matters. We don't drop it. And if we do? We own it."

Building a Culture of Real Accountability: 3 Rituals That Work

If you want to turn this philosophy into action, start with these three daily practices:

1. Name the Owner in Every Meeting

- For every deliverable or decision: ask, "Who owns this?"
- Not who's helping. Not who's tracking.

Who owns the outcome?

2. Start Every Project with an Ownership Contract

- Define the outcome, decision rights, authority, and support needed.
- Align on: *"What does success look like—and who is ultimately responsible?"*

3. End Every Initiative with a Retrospective That Asks:

- What worked?
- What didn't?
- What was *owned well*—and what was *avoided*?
- And most importantly: What did we learn that changes how we lead next time?

The Myth Ends Here

You can't build a culture of accountability by demanding it from others while avoiding it yourself. You can't call your team to courage while hiding in optics. You can't praise ownership while letting narcissists run your culture like a courtroom. If you want real accountability, it starts in the mirror.

What do you protect more—**truth or comfort**? What do you reward more—**results or performance theater**? What do you model—**clean ownership or defensive storytelling**? Because your culture isn't what you say.

It's what you tolerate. It's what you reward. It's what you embody—*especially when the numbers aren't great and the politics get hot.* This is your line in the sand.

Field Manual: Walking It Alone
**You've confronted the rot. You've rebuilt from the fire. You've faced the shadow —
and you're still standing.** Now comes the hardest part:
Walking clean... in a world that still rewards performance, passivity, and political survival.
This field manual is for **you** — the clean leader. Not the loudest. Not the most liked.
But the one who **refuses to lie** to protect comfort – a truth operative with courageous clarity.
Here's how to lead when you're the last one holding the line.

1. Expect the Silence
Directive: Don't confuse quiet with failure.
Watch for:
- Teammates pulling back after accountability rises
- Leaders above you "checking out" when you raise the standard
- The absence of affirmation after you tell the truth

Counter:
- Trust the silence.
- You just shifted the gravity. People are recalibrating.
- Keep moving.

2. Anchor to the Mission, Not the Applause
Directive: Don't lead for validation. Lead for outcome.
Watch for:
- The urge to "soften" messaging for optics
- Leadership peers rewarding theater over truth
- The temptation to prove your worth through emotional appeal

Counter:
- Write the mission where you can see it.
- Ask daily: *"What's the one move today that moves the mission?"*
- Do that. Repeat.

3. Build Without Permission
Directive: Lead like the culture already exists — even when it doesn't.
Watch for:
- Organizational hesitation
- Slow adopters waiting for approval
- Peers stalling with "we're not there yet"

Counter:
- Move anyway.
- Be the proof of concept.
- Culture changes when someone lives the future out loud.

4. Guard Your Fire
Directive: Your clarity is fuel — protect it.
Watch for:
- Exhaustion disguised as empathy
- Saboteurs returning in new packaging

- Old fear patterns whispering in new language

Counter:
- Get quiet often.
- Re-read your own battle scars.
- Surround yourself with builders — not survivors.

5. Live the Clean Leader Code

Directive: Let your actions write the legacy.

The Clean Leader...
- Chooses clarity over comfort
- Speaks truth without venom
- Cuts rot without apology
- Moves when others rationalize
- Walks alone without losing purpose

Code to live by:

"I will not lie to keep the peace.
I will not shrink to avoid blame.
I will not perform.
I will build.
I will move.
I will lead clean."

Final Directive

Leadership is lonely by design. But clarity makes the solitude worth it. You're not here to be liked. You're here to build what others are too scared to start. So, move. Quietly. Deliberately. Without apology. **Because you are the standard now. Because you are the line. Because you are the clean leader.**

Chapter 12: The Pillars of True Leadership (From Reflection to Execution)

It was my idea. I pitched it. Fought for it. Burned hours convincing the board, the execs, the team. I believed in it—not just logically, but viscerally. Strategy meetings turned into war rooms. Timelines were tight, resources tighter. But this was the hill I said we'd take.

Then the numbers came in. Soft KPIs. Quiet resistance. A sense in the room that no one wanted to say it, but everyone knew: **we were losing**.

The most brutal feedback didn't come in words. It came in the silence after I asked for updates. The downcast eyes. The careful optimism. That's when I realized: we were spending more energy justifying the direction than fixing the results.

My ego wanted to double down. Make excuses. Blame execution. Rewrite the narrative.

But the mission whispered something else. *"Kill your favorite idea before it kills your credibility."* So, I did.

In front of the team, I said it plainly: "This isn't working. I led us here. I own it. We're pivoting—effective immediately."

I watched the tension drain from their shoulders. Not because the pressure was gone, but because the performance was. And the room shifted—from cautious loyalty to real alignment.

They didn't cheer. They didn't need to.

Because the good ones—*the ones who help you win*—respect truth more than pride. They don't need you to be perfect. ***They need you to be honest.***

That moment didn't make me weaker. It made me real. And real leaders build momentum from broken ideas—because **the mission is always worth more than the mask.** That day taught me something they don't put in leadership books.

You don't earn trust by being right all the time—you earn it by being *honest* when it counts. When the data turns against your pride. When your name is tied to the strategy that's failing. When you're the one who brought the team into the fire—and still have the courage to lead them out.

Leadership isn't about never falling. It's about how fast you get up, how clean you make the pivot, and how loud you signal that **the mission comes before your ego**.

And that's when I learned the truth: Leadership without execution is performance. Leadership without structure is sentiment. Leadership without truth is sabotage—no matter how inspirational it sounds.

That's the line I crossed. Not from failure to success—but from illusion to clarity. From image to impact. And that's where this next chapter begins.

There comes a point in every real leader's journey when burning the illusions is no longer enough. It's not enough to call out narcissism. It's not enough to reject performance theater. It's not enough to admit where we've failed to lead.

Eventually, you must **step forward and define what leadership actually looks like.** Not the version you post about. Not the version your mentors admired. But the kind that's forged in the crucible of reflection and proven in the discipline of execution.

Leadership is not a mood. It is a structure. It's not a performance. It's a posture. It's not something you do when it's convenient—it's who you must become when the pressure is highest and the cost is real. And it all starts here.

Integrity Is Not Optional

Leadership isn't about having the loudest voice or the brightest spotlight. **It's about holding the weight of responsibility with consistency, conviction, and courage.** It's about aligning your *intentions, decisions, and behaviors* to a principle higher than ego, comfort, or popularity.

In real leadership, that principle is **the mission**—the reason your organization exists. Every decision must be anchored in one sacred question: **"What is best for the principal—the mission, the organization, the people we serve?"**

When leaders forget this—when decisions become about protecting relationships, reputations, or their own egos and narratives—they don't just lose clarity. **They forfeit integrity.** And once you lose that, the entire structure starts to crack.

Here are the non-negotiable **pillars** of true leadership—rooted in reflection, proven in execution.

1. Integrity: The Backbone of Everything Let's get this straight: **Integrity is not a branding word.** It's not a tagline for your company values. It's not a leadership buzzword. It's not "aspirational." It's the *non-negotiable standard* on which all real leadership is built. Without it?

- Communication becomes manipulation.
- Empathy becomes a mask.
- Vision becomes a vanity project.

You can look emotionally intelligent. You can sound empowering. You can feel inspiring. But without integrity, it's just ego *managing outcomes.* **Integrity in action means:**

- You tell the truth—**even when it costs you** politically, emotionally, or relationally.
- You enforce the standard—**even when it's inconvenient** or uncomfortable.
- You own the failure—**even when others contributed.**
- You *refuse* to let relationships become excuses.
- Your team never has to guess where you stand—**because your actions match your words.**

In the absence of integrity, **everything is theater.** In the presence of integrity, **everything has a spine.** This doesn't mean perfection. It means *congruence.* It means *alignment.* When you say one thing and permit another, **you don't just fracture trust. You fracture your identity as a leader.**

2. Decision-Making Anchored in Principle, Not Politics Leadership decisions are *not about how you feel.* They are not about:

- Who you like.
- Who you're afraid of disappointing.
- Who helped you get where you are.

- Or who might push back.

Decisions must be anchored in what is best for the principal—the organization, its mission, and the people it serves. If you can't separate personal emotions, allegiances, or favoritism from your judgment? **You don't have integrity. You have cronyism.**

And if that's the case? **Step down. Give up the chair. Get out of the way. You're nothing but a clown in a mask pretending to be a leader on a theater stage.**

Because leadership is not a reward. It's a *sacrifice.* And the moment you use that power to serve your own comfort instead of the mission? **You become the rot you were supposed to guard against.**

3. Clear Standards and Relentless Congruence True leadership draws a line—and **lives on it**.
- You say what matters.
- You enforce what matters.
- You live what matters.

There's no softening the standard when it gets hard. There's no selectively applying values when someone close to you violates them. There's no **"let's see how this plays out"** when integrity is breached. **Because your people don't need more inspiration.**

They need consistency they can believe in. Not charisma. Not charm. **Congruence.**
They need to know:
- You'll tell the truth even if it costs you the deal.
- You'll hold the line even if your favorite person crosses it.
- You'll name dysfunction even if it breaks the illusion of "alignment."

Because **leadership without consequences is performance. And performance without principle is poison.**

4. The Courage to Execute—Not Just Reflect It's not enough to have good values. It's not enough to say the right thing in private. To write the beautiful memo. To journal about your convictions. **Reflection without execution is just self-flattery.**
The final pillar of true leadership is courage in motion.
- Saying what needs to be said—**publicly.**
- Correcting what needs to be corrected—**immediately.**
- Protecting what matters—**consistently.**
- Walking into tension—**without flinching.**

Because in the end, real leadership is not about being right. It's about *being responsible* for creating the conditions where people can trust, move, and grow.

The Chair Is Not Yours—It's Borrowed

If you're sitting in a seat of leadership, remember: **That chair belongs to the mission—not to you.** You are there to steward it. Not dominate it. And the day you use it to protect your own reputation, relationships, or preferences?

You're no longer a leader. You're an actor guarding your stage. So, hold the line. Lead with integrity. Make decisions that honor the mission.

And if you can't? Have the courage to walk away so someone else can. Because in leadership, the only legacy that lasts is **the one built on truth.**

Transparency as Structure, Not Vulnerability Performance

In many modern workplaces, we've swung the pendulum from stiff, hierarchical secrecy to emotional oversharing—often without understanding the difference between **strategic transparency** and **vulnerability theater**.

Real transparency is not an emotional performance. It's a system of structured clarity that ensures *everyone knows what's true, what matters, and what's being done.*

What Transparency *Is Not*

- **It's not emotional dumping.** Saying "I'm overwhelmed too" without providing stability or direction doesn't create trust—it creates anxiety. You're not leading. You're leaking.

- **It's not oversharing personal feelings to seem relatable.** There's a growing trend of leaders sharing personal stories, struggles, and insecurities to appear authentic. But when done without purpose, this becomes a *vulnerability performance*—one that centers the leader's need for connection instead of the team's need for clarity.

- **It's not naming the problem and walking away.** Transparency isn't just saying, "Here's what's wrong." If you stop there, you've created panic, not alignment. Transparency requires *follow-through.*

What Real Transparency *Is*

Transparency is about creating *shared understanding through disciplined clarity.* It's about building trust through *structure, not spectacle.* **Transparency is not a vibe. It's an operational value.**

When done well:

- **People know where the ship is headed.** Vision is communicated clearly and repeatedly. Priorities are known. Goals are not just aspirational—they're visible.

- **People know what's broken and what's being done.** You don't hide dysfunction. You name it, explain its impact, and lay out what's being done to address it.

- **Decisions are explained.** Not every choice will be popular—but it should *never* be mysterious. When people understand the "why" behind decisions, even tough calls earn respect.

- **The story is consistent.** What people hear in the hallway matches what's said at the town hall. The private Slack matches the public roadmap. You're not managing perception—you're aligning people to truth.

- **Context is shared, not hoarded.** Leaders don't use information as currency to maintain power. They use it as *oxygen*—fueling clarity, trust, and coordinated action across teams.

- **Ambiguity is removed—not used as a shield.** Vague language, passive voice, or evasive timelines are not signs of diplomacy. They're signs of fear. Transparent leaders are precise. Not harsh—but *unflinchingly clear.*

Why This Matters

Without structured transparency:

- Teams waste energy trying to *decode* what's really going on.
- Rumors become more trusted than leadership statements.
- Morale drops, not from bad news—but from **confusion and inconsistency.**
- Psychological safety erodes because people don't know what's real.

But when transparency is built into the structure? **Truth becomes the default. Trust becomes the norm. Alignment becomes natural.** People stop managing perception and start *managing the mission.*

How to Build Structural Transparency

1. **Use consistent messaging across all leadership layers.** If your executive team says one thing but department heads are spinning another, you've got a cultural fracture. Fix it.
2. **Create a "Decision Communication Protocol."** For every major decision:
   - What was decided?
   - Why was it decided?
   - Who made the call?
   - What's next?
3. **Replace "open-door" policies with scheduled truth sessions.** Don't just *say* you're transparent—*design systems* that surface truth regularly and without fear.
4. **Develop a clarity contract.** A leader's job is not just to inspire. It's to ensure *no one has to decode the truth.* Build that expectation into your leadership DNA.

Precision Over Performance

Real transparency doesn't need applause. It creates alignment. It's not about being liked. It's about being *understood.* It's not about "being real." It's about **removing friction between people and the truth.**

So, stop trying to look transparent. Be *clear. Be consistent. Be brave. And most of all—be real without needing to be dramatic.* Because in a world drowning in noise, *the rarest leadership trait is clarity that doesn't flinch.*

Respect Is the Currency of Culture

Respect is not about being nice. It's not about agreement. It's not about making people feel comfortable at the expense of truth. **Respect is what builds trust, performance, and unity in a culture where standards matter.** You don't lead with respect by lowering expectations. You lead with respect by **believing people are capable of rising to them.** Because here's the truth: **What you reinforce is what you really respect. What you tolerate is what your culture becomes.** Let's break it down.

You Respect Your Team When You Set the Standard—and Stand in It

Respect is demonstrated *through clarity and courage*, not compliments and avoidance. You respect your team when you:

- **Speak truthfully** – even when it's hard, inconvenient, or unpopular.
- **Give feedback cleanly** – no hedging, no sugarcoating, no delay.
- **Listen without defensiveness** – showing your team that *your ego isn't the center of the room.*
- **Confront directly, not emotionally** – not to punish, but to course-correct with precision.
- **Hold them to a higher bar** – because you *believe in them enough to expect more.*

You don't respect people by lowering the bar. You respect them by calling them to *be more than they're currently showing up as.* Soft leadership doesn't make people feel safe. It makes high performers feel alone—and low performers feel unchecked.

You Respect the Mission When You Protect Its Integrity

Mission integrity matters more than personal comfort or political optics. You respect the mission when you:

- **Say no to scope creep** – because distraction is dilution.
- **Protect the culture from ego contamination** – refusing to let high performers become untouchable toxins.
- **Let go of "indispensable" people who quietly destroy morale** – because no skill is worth cultural sabotage.

Loyalty to talent must never outweigh loyalty to the *team*.

And respect means being willing to *lose a contributor to protect the collective.*
That's not cold. That's leadership.

You Respect Yourself When You Refuse to Shrink or Perform

Leadership is not martyrdom. It's not silence. It's not muting yourself to preserve fake harmony. You respect yourself when you:

- **Don't shrink to be accepted** – even if the room is uncomfortable with your clarity.
- **Don't hide your voice in the name of harmony** – because alignment requires *honest tension.*
- **Don't perform empathy at the expense of effectiveness** – because empathy isn't permissiveness.

Self-respect is the *engine* behind courageous leadership. If you betray yourself to please others, you teach everyone around you to *disrespect your voice.*

Respect Isn't Sameness—It's Equity

Let's be real: **Treating everyone the same is not respect. It's cowardice.** True respect means:

- Recognizing when someone needs to be challenged—*not coddled.*
- Calling out high-performers when they drift—*not excusing them because of their track record.*
- Holding the line *especially* when the person crossing it is close to you.

Equity isn't about favoritism. It's about fairness based on what's at stake. Your top performers need feedback *just as much* as your struggling ones. And if you let certain people get away with more—because of proximity, influence, or fear—you've told the team exactly what (and who) you truly respect.

Respect Is a Leadership Mirror

Respect isn't a strategy. It's not a poster in the hallway. It's not something you demand. **It's something you model. And something you measure—in what you *reinforce and protect*.** So, if you want:

- A respected team,
- A respected culture,
- A respected mission…

Then stop avoiding discomfort. **Say the hard thing. Make the unpopular call. Protect the line. Be the leader whose actions are congruent with their principles.** Because in leadership, the real question isn't "Do they like me?" It's: **"Can they count on me to protect what matters—when it matters most?"** That's respect. And that's the currency of cultures that don't just survive—but *thrive.*

Shared Accountability: The Death of Isolationism

Leadership today isn't about one person with all the answers. It's about building **systems of trust, clarity, and distributed ownership.** The myth of the heroic leader was forged in a different era:

- When information was scarce.
- When hierarchy was absolute.
- When charisma could replace clarity.

That era is over. Today's leadership environment is:

- Networked, not vertical.
- Transparent, not controlled.
- Fast, complex, and emotionally intelligent.

No single person can lead effectively without a system behind them. So, when you cling to the heroic model?

- You suffocate your team's autonomy.
- You slow down execution.
- You exhaust yourself trying to carry weight that should be *shared.*

And worse—you create a culture of **disempowered dependency**.

Modern Leadership is Shared Accountability

This is the shift: From **centralized command** to **mutual ownership.** From "I'll take care of it" to *"We move this forward—together."* Shared accountability isn't just a buzzword. It's **structural.** It looks like:

1. Authority is Distributed

- Everyone knows their lane.
- Decision rights are clearly defined.
- Leaders empower—not just assign.

This doesn't mean chaos. It means *clarity with autonomy.*

2. Ownership is Explicit

- Every initiative, deliverable, and outcome has a name.
- Not a team. Not a task force. A *name.*
- That person has the tools, power, and backing to lead it.

If failure happens and it's unclear who owns it? That's a leadership *design* problem.

3. Credit is Shared

- Success doesn't belong to the most visible contributor.
- Praise goes to the system, not just the speaker.
- Leaders lift others up—and step back from the spotlight.

In healthy cultures, the best leaders **deflect credit and absorb heat.**

4. Mistakes Are Admitted—At the Top

- Loudly. Without caveats.
- Without "but I was misinformed."
- Without "my intent was good."

When leaders admit failure first, they create a **psychological permission slip** for honesty to flow. Your vulnerability *sets the tone* for organizational courage.

Your Team Sees Everything

Don't forget. **Nothing is hidden.**

- If someone on your team fails quietly and you explain it away in public? Your team sees it—and you lose credibility.
- If someone at your level undermines strategy and you say nothing? Your team sees that too—and you lose trust.

Every moment of silent complicity erodes the very culture you claim to lead. Because in today's transparent, emotionally attuned organizations, your silence *speaks louder than your values slide.*

Accountability is a Web, not a Wall

Think of your leadership culture not as a chain of command, but as **a web of integrity.**

- It connects across functions.
- It holds pressure in every direction.
- And when one strand is weak—or one leader dodges responsibility—the *whole structure shudders.*

Healthy leadership ecosystems are:
- **Mutual** – Everyone is both accountable *and* supported.
- **Open** – Anyone can speak truth to power without retribution.
- **Responsive** – When something breaks, people respond—not with blame, but with *ownership.*

You Want to Model Real Leadership? Start Here.

Stop looking for someone to go first. *You* go first. Say: "That was mine. I missed that. I'll fix it—and here's how." No caveats. No redirects. No PR-spin. Because **true leadership is not demonstrated in how you explain away problems.** It's shown in how you *own them.*

And shared accountability means this: **You never hold someone to a standard you're not holding yourself too first.** That's the death of the heroic leader. But it's the *birth* of something better: A leadership culture where power is shared, truth is spoken, and progress belongs to *all of us.*

Vision: From Abstraction to Execution

Vision is not a vibe. It's not a paragraph on a slide. It's not what you say in your quarterly video message. Vision is **a repeated, embodied call to movement.** It tells your team:

- Where we're going.
- Why it matters.
- What it demands from all of us.
- What we're willing to sacrifice to get there.

Too many leaders mistake passion for vision. But vision without execution is just romanticism. And vision without feedback is tyranny.

Real vision adapts. It listens. It holds firm on values and flexible on method. It isn't just inspirational—it's **operational**.

If your team can't articulate your vision without checking the website, it's not a vision. It's branding. If they don't know how their role contributes to it, it's not a direction—it's decoration.

Vision must be lived to be believed. And that starts with how you show up when things get hard.

From Inner Clarity to Outer Command

These are the pillars: Integrity. Transparency. Respect. Shared accountability. Vision. But these are not virtues. They are **structures**—to be enforced, not just admired.

And they must begin with **you**. You cannot preach integrity and weaponize ambiguity. You cannot demand respect while protecting dysfunction. You cannot promote vision while hiding from execution. You cannot build trust if you won't hold the weight of accountability on your own shoulders first.

This chapter is the hinge. Before this, we diagnosed the sickness. Now, we build the body that can withstand the fire. Your reflection is done. Now we lead.

Field Manual: Building the Pillars of Real Leadership

This is where the work begins. No slides. No summits. No slogans. Just you, the mission, and the mirror. The five pillars aren't theories—they're decisions you make daily. Below is your leadership trench map. Use it.

PILLAR 1: INTEGRITY IS THE OPERATING SYSTEM

Mission Question: What *internal contradiction* am I tolerating?

Field Actions:

- Identify one area where your actions betray your values.
- Kill the loophole. Align or cut.
- Say it out loud in front of your team: *"We're fixing this. I was wrong to let it slide."*

Stop saying integrity is a value if it's never tested.

PILLAR 2: DECISIONS > POLITICS

Mission Question: Am I making the right call—or the one that avoids conflict?

Field Actions:

- For every major decision this week, write down:
  - What's the right call?
  - What's the politically safe call?
- Choose the one that moves the mission. Not the one that saves face.

If you keep punting clarity, your team will start kicking your credibility.

PILLAR 3: ACCOUNTABILITY IS A WEB

Mission Question: Who holds me accountable *without fear of consequence*?

Field Actions:

- Establish a personal accountability partner. Title doesn't matter—integrity does.
- Give them the green light: *"If I drift, you hit the brakes."*
- Set monthly reviews where *they* speak first. You just listen.

If you have all the answers and no one challenges you, you're already lost.

PILLAR 4: VISION = CLARITY + EXECUTION

Mission Question: Is our vision *an artifact on a slide deck—or a behavior on the floor*?

Field Actions:

- Ask your team: *"What does our vision require from you this week?"* (If they can't answer—*that's on you.*)
- Define one visible behavior per team that embodies your core values.
- Start measuring *behavior* as much as output.

A vision without behavioral clarity is corporate poetry. Beautiful. Useless.

PILLAR 5: SELF-REFLECTION THAT CONFRONTS, NOT CUDDLES

Mission Question: Where is my ego still pretending to be "strategy"?

Field Actions:

- Journal these three prompts weekly:
  1. What decision am I avoiding?
  2. Where did I protect image over outcome?
  3. Who needed truth—but got diplomacy?

- Set a timer. Answer honestly. Then act.

You don't need another self-care day. You need a reckoning.

Final Directive: Execute Or Evaporate

You don't become a leader by inheriting a title. You *prove* it—by executing under pressure with zero applause. Burn the scripts. Confront your patterns. Build the damn thing for real. Because if you're not building something true— You're just cosplaying a leader in a culture that's dying for the real thing. Now let's focus on something to move faster and evaluate the ability to do so.

Chapter 13: The Shadow in the C-Suite

Peter was an executive. Respected. Polished. Commanding.

He walked into rooms like a preacher entering a revival tent — quoting God, the Devil, and destiny in the same breath.

And at first, people followed. He had presence. He had fire. He could stir the room with one sentence and silence it with a glance.

But underneath the cadence, something darker moved. Peter didn't hire leaders. He hired worshipers. If you made him feel like the smartest man in the room, you were safe. If you challenged him — even gently — you were already bleeding and didn't know it yet.

He spoke of service. He spoke of God. He spoke of vision and values.

But behind closed doors, Peter shoved knives into his peers with a grin. He undercut initiatives that weren't his. He stalled good ideas because they came from someone else. He turned every strategic conversation into a mirror — and demanded the reflection bow back in admiration.

The problem wasn't Peter's ambition. The problem was his possession. He wasn't leading a company. He was feeding a demon — his ego — and it demanded constant worship.

It was the reverse Midas touch: Everything golden he touched turned to rust in real time. Talent withered under him. Trust eroded. Culture died behind smiles and all-hands meetings filled with empty praise and private fear.

And God forbid you told him the truth. He'd call it betrayal. He'd label you toxic. He'd pray over you with one hand and fire you with the other.

Because Peter didn't want truth. He wanted affirmation. And in his world, disagreement was blasphemy.

This is what happens when the Shadow runs the boardroom. This is what it looks like when power becomes a pulpit — and the unconscious demands a congregation.

Peter isn't an outlier. He's not rare. He's the inevitable result of **unchecked ego and unexamined fear** sitting in a seat of power.

You don't need to be malicious to become dangerous. You just need to be unconscious. And that's the trap: **Most leaders never see the damage they cause—because they've never seen the parts of themselves causing it.**

What ran Peter wasn't strategy. It was shame, fear, projection, and a need to control his image at all costs. That's not executive dysfunction.

That's the Shadow, operating in a tailored suit. And unless you're willing to confront that force in yourself—you're already losing battles you don't even know you're in.

Most leadership books talk about vision, strategy, and influence. But very few are willing to confront the single most powerful force shaping your leadership effectiveness:

Your unconscious. It doesn't wear a badge. It doesn't show up in org charts. And it sure as hell doesn't introduce itself in meetings. But it's there—guiding decisions, distorting perceptions, hijacking feedback, and scripting reactions before your conscious mind even knows what's happening.

This is the chapter where we stop pretending that leadership is purely logical. Because it's not. It's deeply psychological. And if you're not aware of what's lurking beneath your own ego—**you are leading in the dark.**

The Most Dangerous Leader Is the One Who Can't See Himself

There's a specific kind of organizational damage that doesn't come from bad strategy or poor market fit—it comes from **self-unaware leadership**. And it's the most corrosive kind. Because unlike incompetence, which is easy to spot, **ego-fueled blindness** wears a mask. It performs. It presents. It plays the part perfectly.

These leaders enter the room with impeccable posture, sharp language, and an executive presence that checks every box on the surface. But beneath that polish? There's a roiling, unintegrated mess—**fear, inadequacy, control addiction, imposter panic, trauma wounds still leaking into every interaction**.

They haven't done their inner work. And so, their leadership becomes a projection—an unconscious theater where everyone else is forced to act out their unresolved story.

They make impulsive decisions—**not rooted in data, not grounded in discernment— but based on raw projection**. If someone challenges them, they see betrayal. If someone shines too brightly, they see a threat. If someone disagrees, they see insubordination. Because in truth, **they're not managing people—they're managing *symbols* of their own shadow.**

They lash out at team members who unknowingly reflect the parts of themselves they've buried:

- The ambitious one? Too risky.
- The emotionally honest one? Too sensitive.
- The confident one? Arrogant.
- The truth-teller? "Toxic."

They don't see these people as mirrors. They see them as enemies. And so, **they weaken the courageous** and **elevate the compliant**—not because they intend to destroy culture, but because their psyche requires emotional safety more than their mission requires progress.

They overcorrect with bravado when their authority is threatened.

You'll see it in the language shift. In the power plays. In the sudden policy changes designed to assert dominance. They don't ask, *"What does the organization need?"* They ask, *"How do I maintain control?"*

And they surround themselves with flatterers—those who reflect back a curated image of power, competence, and control. Not because they trust these people. But because **they fear the reflection of anything real**.

The Shadow at the Helm

This is not a performance issue. This is **a Jungian catastrophe**. When a leader refuses to do the internal work—when they avoid looking at the insecure, anxious, angry, or ashamed parts of themselves—they don't remove those forces from the system. **They inject them into the**

culture. Every fear becomes policy. Every insecurity becomes process. Every wound becomes an unspoken rule that others must navigate.

And here's the terrifying part: they believe they're doing it for the organization. "I'm being decisive." "I'm setting high standards." "I'm protecting the brand." "I'm shaping culture."

No. **You're serving your ego.** You're protecting your false self. You're making the entire company bow to the altar of your unhealed trauma.

And the scariest part? **You don't even know it.** You think you're building. But you're actually repeating. Repeating old survival patterns, old scripts, old defenses—now dressed in leadership language and wrapped in corporate strategy.

The Only Way Out

The only thing more dangerous than a leader with power… is a leader with power who has never looked in the mirror. Because that mirror is the portal. Not to perfection—but to **integration**.

Until you've confronted your fear of being irrelevant, you'll micromanage everyone around you. Until you've dealt with your own inadequacy, you'll constantly undercut those who shine. Until you've named your deep hunger to feel significant, you'll build kingdoms that collapse under the weight of your ego.

So, if any of this lands—even a little—don't dismiss it. Don't rationalize it. Don't call it "strong leadership" or "executive presence." Call it what it is: **a shadow running your company from the inside out.**

And ask yourself: "What part of me have I avoided so long that now my people are carrying the cost of my denial?"

Because that is the line. That is where leadership ends and damage begins.
And it's also where redemption starts.

The Jungian Lens: Projection, Ego Inflation, and Shadow Avoidance

Carl Jung didn't write business books. But he wrote what every leader needs to understand. He said: "Until you make the unconscious conscious, it will direct your life—and you will call it fate."

In leadership, that unconscious doesn't just direct your life—it **directs your team**, **shapes your policies**, and **builds your culture**. It becomes the invisible architect of **every system, ritual, value statement, and 'strategic decision'** you swear is data-driven.

Unconscious leadership doesn't show up with evil intentions—it shows up in boardrooms, offsites, Slack messages, and hiring decisions. It shows up as "alignment challenges," "personality conflicts," or "cultural friction." But underneath?

It's projection. It's ego inflation. It's shadow avoidance—playing out in real time, in real teams, with real consequences. Let's name the mechanics behind the mask.

Projection

Projection is when you unconsciously attribute your own disowned traits, fears, or emotions onto someone else. It feels real. It feels *true*. That's what makes it so dangerous. Because when you're projecting, you're not seeing the person in front of you—you're reacting to an unexamined part of *yourself*.

- That manager you label "untrustworthy"?
  Might be triggering your own fear of losing control—because you don't trust your own capacity to lead without dominating.

- That ambitious team member who "needs to be humbled"?
  Might be reflecting your buried shame about underperforming at their age, or your fear that they're the version of you that never got the opportunity you wanted.
- That colleague you say "lacks strategic thinking"?
  Might be someone who's not playing the politics you've mastered—and threatens your intellectual identity because they're moving faster than your playbook allows.

Projection disguises itself as rational critique. It comes dressed in feedback, in "fit" language, in culture code. And yet, what's really happening is this: **You're fighting a part of yourself you haven't learned to face.** And in the process, you distort reality for your team.

Ego Inflation

Ego inflation happens when your leadership identity becomes fused with your self-worth. You stop being *a* leader, and start being *The Leader*—a brand, a symbol, a persona that must be maintained at all costs. When that happens:

- Feedback becomes a threat to your identity, not a gift for your growth.
- Delegation feels like dilution—because if someone else shines, what's left of *you*?
- Visibility becomes your dopamine, and you chase it like a drug—speaking more than you listen, posting more than you build.
- Failure becomes intolerable, so you bury it. You spin it. You "reframe the learnings."

You say all the right things: "We value transparency." "We promote ownership." "We want to be challenged." But here's what your behavior actually says:

- You sabotage rising talent because they move faster than your narrative.
- You hide behind "team decisions" because you fear personal accountability.
- You value growth—as long as no one grows **past you**.

This is the quiet implosion of self-aware leadership. Inflated egos don't scale organizations. **They hollow them out from the top down.**

Shadow Avoidance

The shadow is the part of you you've rejected. Suppressed. Disowned. It's the parts you were told not to show as a kid. The shame you swallowed in adolescence. The pain you never made peace with as an adult. It holds your **envy**, your **rage**, your **need for validation**, your **fear of failure**, and your **terror of being unseen or unworthy**.

Most leaders will say, "I've done my work." They haven't. They've intellectualized their story. They've read the books. They've gone to therapy. But they haven't **felt** the parts of themselves that still sabotage their clarity.

And the shadow? It doesn't care what you *say*. And it reaches up through the body of your soul with its unseen hand and works you like a puppet who thinks it's a boy with free will and logic. It shows up in how you lead.

- You become obsessed with performance because somewhere, deep down, you still feel worthless without achievement.
- You dominate meetings because silence feels like rejection.
- You micromanage because your wounded inner child still believes, *"If I don't control everything, I'll be abandoned."*

The shadow doesn't stay inside. **It leaks.** It leaks into your hiring decisions. Into how you structure power. Into who you mentor—and who you ghost. Into how you build systems—and what behaviors you silently excuse. You think you're being strategic. But you're just being unconscious—with a budget and a title.

The Jungian Warning for Every Leader

Until you face your shadow, **your organization will keep paying its price.** It will show up in retention. In misalignment. In cultural fragility. In whisper networks. In good people quietly leaving and mediocre ones rising.

And you'll call it fate. Or burnout. Or "the cost of growth." But it's not.

It's **you**—unintegrated, unexamined, unready. And the moment you face it? The moment you look inward with the same intensity you look outward for innovation? That's the moment you stop leading from fear and start leading from wholeness.

The Unconscious Forces Shaping Leadership Failure

Let's stop pretending that leadership failure is always tactical. It's not just about missed KPIs. It's not just about flawed strategy or poor timing. It's not about lack of funding, resource gaps, or a competitive market. Those are symptoms.

The root cause? **It's often psychological. Deeply. Invisibly. Relentlessly.** Behind every failed transformation, every cultural collapse, every exodus of talent—you'll usually find a leader driven not by vision, but by *unconscious fear, ego, and shadow.*

Let's stop spinning the story. Let's name what's *actually* happening:

- A merger fails—not because the financials didn't make sense, but because the CEO couldn't stand to share power. The threat of losing status, identity, or narrative control disguised itself as "strategic concerns."
- A reorg implodes—not because of poor design, but because of simmering ego rivalries between department heads. Hidden agendas torpedoed execution, and the leadership team lacked the emotional maturity to own it.
- A promising VP exits—not because they "weren't a fit," but because they were *too much of a mirror.* Too clear. Too sharp. Too willing to speak the truth—and the C-suite couldn't stomach the discomfort of being seen.

This is what we don't talk about. That **unconscious dynamics—not data—are what sink most leadership decisions.**

What's Actually Driving It?

The real failure isn't operational. It's emotional. Psychological. Existential. It's leaders running billion-dollar companies while still driven by childhood wounds and adolescent insecurities—except now, they have a budget and a title to protect them.

It's the fear of irrelevance that causes senior execs to hoard decisions, bottleneck innovation, and kill off emerging leaders who think faster than they do. It's the unspoken need to be the smartest person in every room, so meetings become performances instead of problem-solving spaces—and your actual thinkers go quiet.

It's the quiet terror of being wrong. Not just wrong tactically—but wrong in identity. Because if you've built your worth around *always being right*, then admitting failure feels like death. So instead, you spin. You delay. You blame. You control.

This is how unconscious fear becomes **a culture killer**.

Image Protection ≠ Leadership

You cannot build a resilient team around a leader who is protecting their image more than they're pursuing their own growth. You cannot develop adaptive strategy when your decision-making is secretly tethered to a need for validation. You cannot demand courage from your people if you're unwilling to face your own ego, fear, and shadow.

The health of the system will never exceed the self-awareness of the person leading it. If the person at the top is afraid of vulnerability, the organization becomes allergic to feedback. If the person at the top is addicted to control, the culture becomes permission-based.

If the person at the top avoids accountability, blame becomes a leadership currency. And no amount of vision decks, DEI workshops, or performance frameworks will fix that. Because the problem isn't out there. It's in the mirror.

The Real Work

So, if you're serious about building something that lasts—if you actually want to lead, not just perform leadership—then you have to do the **internal audit** before the next strategic initiative.

Ask yourself:

- Where am I protecting my identity more than the mission?
- Where does my fear of being irrelevant cause me to shrink or sabotage others?
- Where have I let psychological fragility become operational constraint?

Because until you name these unconscious drivers, you will keep calling your patterns "strategy" and your sabotage "culture fit." And the cost? It's your credibility. Your team's trust. And the long-term viability of everything you've built.

Executive Blindness: Why Smart Leaders Miss the Obvious

The higher up you go, the harder it is to get real feedback. People stop telling you the truth. They filter their words. They watch your moods. They manage your ego because they've learned: **this person can't take it.** And so, you become trapped in a house of mirrors—seeing only what your unconscious allows, hearing only what your power permits. You stop noticing:

- That your trusted lieutenant is quietly manipulating the team.
- That your "collaborative culture" is really just fear-based inaction.
- That your leadership style has stopped being developmental—and become a personality cult.

You're not being strategic. You're being enabled. If you've gone six months without someone challenging you—you're not leading. You're being managed by your own myth.

Into the Mouth of Fear: A Leadership Reckoning

Leadership failure doesn't always arrive in a crisis. Sometimes, it creeps in silently, born from **covert fears** that masquerade as logic, dressed in the uniform of professionalism, justified by the language of "alignment," "stability," and "optics." I know because I've lived it.

Years ago, I stood at the edge of a 500-foot suspension bridge in Gatlinburg. A fear of heights knotted my gut. And I stepped onto that bridge anyway. Why? Because I knew this fear wasn't just about elevation—it was about **ownership**. It was about who I wanted to become, not just what I was willing to tolerate.

That moment catalyzed a deeper exploration into fear—not as a reaction, but as a system. **Fear stacking** was born from that moment: the deliberate act of confronting **multiple primal fears simultaneously** to force a psychological and physiological confrontation with the unconscious.

Because here's the brutal reality: You don't understand how deeply it can override your conscious mind, hijack your executive function, and manipulate your behavior—**without ever announcing its presence.**

Fear Is Not a Feeling—It's a System

We've been sold a lie in leadership circles. That fear is just a feeling—fleeting, personal, manageable through breathwork and mindfulness. But fear in organizations isn't always loud or visible. It doesn't announce itself with a trembling voice or a skipped heartbeat. It operates in the shadows. Subtly. Systemically. And often with a tone of professionalism so polished it passes as leadership.

In the corporate world, fear wears a suit. It shows up not as panic—but as silence in meetings where hard truths should be spoken. It reveals itself in the strategic use of buzzwords that obscure more than they clarify. It's there when a leader says, *"We're implementing these directives because the CEO has mandated them,"* rather than owning the vision themselves. That isn't alignment—it's abdication. It's the performance of leadership without the weight of responsibility. A deflection of accountability disguised as hierarchy. And most importantly, it's the clearest signal that fear has become part of the system's operational DNA.

Fear in organizations doesn't just visit. It embeds. It becomes a protocol. It rewards leaders who avoid direct confrontation in favor of behind-the-scenes triangulation. It encourages passive approval over principled resistance. It incentivizes the creation of PowerPoints instead of performance. Leaders—many of them well-meaning—learn to speak in polished tones, wrap mediocrity in mission statements, and redirect the discomfort of ownership upward. Not because they're cowards. But because the system has trained them to prioritize safety over substance.

Fear, at this level, is not emotional—it's architectural. It's structural. It has become the cultural water we swim in.

And like water, it adapts to every container. It finds the cracks in our values and seeps into them, reinterpreting courage as recklessness, confrontation as toxicity, and truth-telling as poor team fit. Eventually, the system stops even recognizing fear as fear. It becomes standard operating procedure. Emotional armor is mistaken for executive poise. The deferral of accountability is mistaken for humility. And empathy—real, vital empathy—is twisted into an alibi for lowered standards.

This is where the cultural infection takes hold. When leaders protect their own sense of security over the development of their people, the message sent—whether consciously or not—is simple: *comfort matters more than growth.* And from that root, an entire forest of dysfunction grows.

People learn to speak safely, not truthfully. They learn to interpret clarity as aggression. They learn to perform collaboration while secretly harboring resentment. Teams become skilled at smiling while walking past unresolved conflict. And leadership becomes less about shaping outcomes and more about managing optics.

This fear is not passive. It's instructive. It teaches the team that risk is dangerous, that voice carries punishment, and that safety is found not in doing the right thing—but in doing the unoffensive thing. Slowly, excellence gives way to compliance. Initiative is replaced by permission-seeking. Creativity becomes caged within what's "acceptable." And when that happens, even the most talented teams begin to decay—not because of external threats, but because **they have unconsciously chosen psychological safety over transformational truth**. And here's the most sinister part: you won't always see it coming.

Systemic fear doesn't need to scream to be heard. It doesn't need to fight to win. It just needs you to delay. To hesitate. To wait for approval before acting on principle. It thrives in cultures that value "alignment" over authenticity. **It wins when leaders choose to be liked over being effective**. It thrives where candor is optional and performance is redefined as presence.

I've seen this firsthand. I've led in systems where fear masqueraded as protocol, where every decision had to be cleared by multiple levels of leadership not for accountability—but for deniability. I've watched talented leaders shrink themselves to fit the mold of an organization that subtly punished courage. I've seen empathy weaponized as a shield from standards. And I've seen the cost—measured in stalled initiatives, ghosted goals, and high performers who silently exited because the culture had no room for honest effort that made people uncomfortable.

Fear, when covert, is more dangerous than incompetence. Because incompetence is obvious. It can be corrected. But covert fear is sophisticated. It's quiet. It operates through your best people, wrapped in the language of collaboration, and reinforced by policies that protect predictability over growth. And when it goes unchecked, it reshapes the very fabric of leadership into something that looks healthy on the surface—but is deeply, irreversibly compromised beneath.

So, let's call it what it is.

Fear is not a mood. It's not a private emotion. It's a system. And if you don't confront it, name it, and build the muscle to act through it—It will build your culture for you. Not the culture you intended. The one that lets you sleep at night. The one that protects egos, silences dissent, and trades potential for peace.

But peace without performance is decay in disguise.

The Body Doesn't Lie: What Your Fear Is Doing Without Your Consent

I once stood at the edge of an open helicopter door, 35 feet above the ocean's surface, rotor blades screaming above me, the wind howling like a thousand whispered doubts. The

training had been done. The logic was sound. My mind said, *"You're ready. You've got this."* And for a moment, I believed it. I jumped.

In the microseconds that passed, something happened. My legs twitched. Not once. Repeatedly. Involuntarily.

It was as if my body had stopped taking orders from me. My

conscious mind had been overruled. The command center had been hijacked by something older, deeper—more primal. And that was the moment it hit me with full force:

If fear can override your body's motor functions in real time, what else is it controlling in the background?

We often think of fear as emotional static—something you can "calm down" or rationalize away. But that moment taught me the brutal truth: **fear is not just emotional. It is operational.** It lives in the wiring. It lives in the subconscious and unconscious. And it doesn't wait for your permission.

And if fear can seize your body, unannounced and uninvited, it can just as easily seize your leadership. Let me ask you:

- **How many strategic pivots have been executed—not because the data demanded it, but because your skin got too hot under scrutiny?**
- **How often do leaders pull back from a hard conversation under the guise of "timing," when in reality they're just afraid of the backlash?**
- **How many performance standards have been softened, goals watered down, and values compromised—not from compassion, but from a survival instinct that whispers,** *don't rock the boat*?

These are not intellectual errors. They're somatic reflexes—leadership driven not by mission, but by muscle memory. Not by principle, but by protection. And the body knows. It always knows.

Our physiology is wired for one thing: survival. When the stakes rise, when visibility increases, when risk presents itself in the form of people, politics, or performance—the body doesn't wait to be consulted. It acts. It twitches. It stutters. It retreats. **And if you're not conscious of this process, it will steer you into decisions that feel rational but are rooted in fear's invisible calculus.**

We don't talk about this enough in leadership circles because it's inconvenient. It's not easily captured in a quarterly report. There's no Excel formula for self-deception.

But here's the truth: **You cannot outthink what your nervous system is trying to survive.**

You can't spreadsheet your way past the Shadow. You can't "align your KPIs" if you're unconsciously aligning your decisions with comfort over courage. Leadership—real leadership—demands something more primal, more difficult, more transformative.

You have to face it.

You have to descend into the inner operating system that's been running your show on autopilot. The part of you that's still bracing for rejection. The part that flinches when trust is required. The part that confuses performance with protection—and has built a career around avoiding psychic pain.

And don't fool yourself: this isn't about "fear of failure." That's the sanitized version. What we're actually afraid of is exposure. Of being unmasked. Of being seen as inadequate, unworthy, or unprepared. **So, we lead from behind armor. From image. From the curated persona that protects us from the full weight of vulnerability.**

But vulnerability is not a liability. It is the doorway to congruence. Because once you've stood at the edge of that chopper—once you've felt your legs twitch without your consent—you understand: **the enemy isn't fear. The enemy is unconscious obedience to it.**

So, the next time you make a leadership decision—pause. Ask yourself:

- Is this coming from principle, or from protection?
- Is this clarity, or camouflage?

- Is this the mission talking—or my muscle memory of pain avoidance?

Because that subtle internal shift—that deep inner audit—may be the most courageous act of leadership you ever perform.

Overcoming Fear: Cultivating Courage Through Confrontation

We talk about courage like it's a seminar topic. But courage doesn't come from reading leadership books. It doesn't emerge from podcasts or polished TED Talks. It doesn't bloom in comfort. **Courage is carved—blade by blade—by walking into the fire when every cell in your body begs you to run.** Courage is built by doing exactly what fear tells you not to.

- By walking into the meeting where knives are waiting behind smiles.
- By confronting the culture rot that's been metastasizing behind hallway pleasantries.
- By firing the person who poisons your team quietly, yet consistently—because you'd rather be resented for enforcing truth than celebrated for tolerating mediocrity.

That's real leadership. That's where fear stacking begins. I started fear stacking not as a theory—but as survival. As self-reclamation. Because I've lived the kind of leadership crucifixion most people only whisper about.

I've walked into rooms where I knew—*not suspected, not theorized, but knew*—that over half the room saw me as a villain. A traitor. A "toxic" force. Not because I failed. Not because I lied. But because I held a standard that forced others to see themselves clearly. And they couldn't handle that.

So instead, they chose the oldest defense mechanism in the book: **assassinate the character of the one who won't bend.** They didn't want accountability. They wanted a sacrifice. They wanted me to burn my reputation, my credibility, even my career—to cover their dysfunction in silence. And when I refused? They turned.

And still—I walked into the room. Head high. Eyes clear. Fully present. Because leadership isn't about applause. It's about alignment. I didn't cave. I didn't grovel. I didn't play the game.

I went all in. Go for broke. Every time.

Because if you cave once—if you betray your ethics once—it's never just a strategy. It becomes a habit. And the next time is easier. And before you know it, you're leading through compromise, not conviction.

Let me be clear: **People will always prefer a beautiful lie to a brutal truth.** That's not your failure. That's their fear. It's fear that makes them choose comfort over clarity. It's fear that makes them elevate cowards over truth-tellers. It's fear that makes them weaponize kindness to avoid confrontation—and then call it "culture."

But I'll tell you something they don't say in the HR handbook: **To those weak and timid souls who never grow—you are a devil just by existing.** Because you remind them of what they could be, *if they had the spine to evolve.* They'll try to erase you, isolate you, defame you—not because you're wrong, but because your presence demands self-confrontation. And they're not ready.

So don't bow. Don't apologize for your strength. Don't shrink to make them feel safe. Don't dull your edge to be invited to the table. **Stand.** Hold your standard. Hold your ethic. Hold your moral line with blood-and-bone intensity. Because if you break yourself to spare their feelings, you teach your people that weakness is virtue and truth is negotiable.

This is what fear stacking really is. It's not motivational theory. It's psychological warfare. It's spiritual conditioning. It's the daily discipline of showing up when you are misunderstood, misrepresented, and uninvited—yet still refusing to break.

You want to be a real leader? Then face the lie. Face the mob. Face the fear. And speak anyway. Because every time you do, you strip fear of its illusion. You train your nervous system to stop flinching. You become the kind of leader people *trust* when things get real—because you've already walked through hell, and refused to lose your name.

That's fear stacking. And the more you do it, the less power fear has. So, walk into the room. And don't just survive it—*own it.* **Go for broke.**

Jumping From the Sky: The True Meaning of Fear Stacking

Let's go back to the helicopter. Why jump out of a perfectly good helicopter into the open ocean. Not for fun. Not for a thrill. But because I needed to *feel* fear again. Not the polite version—the one that lives in performance reviews and behind-the-scenes politics.

No, I needed *real fear.* The kind that overrides your mind. The kind that shows up in your nervous system before your intellect catches up. That jump wasn't just about altitude. It was about awakening.

The bridge walk from Gatlinburg taught me what direct confrontation of fear could do. So, an idea rose from that even. What would happen if you're afraid of heights and add on more fears? What if you put two or three fears together in the same event. And then it hit me. By choosing to *multiple fears simultaneously*—and choosing to walk through them all at once could it perform a harder nervous system reset. Three fears were chosen and they are:

- The fear of falling.
- The fear of sharks.
- The fear of the ocean.

And here's the truth most people will never say out loud: **Hard fear stacking creates a full-on nervous system overload.** And when you survive it—it resets you.

The fear doesn't vanish. But *its grip changes.* It no longer drives the bus. It becomes background noise.

That jump rewired something in me. Thirty-five feet…no line, no parachute. Just me, a wet suit and a big risk if I landed wrong – massive problems. In the microseconds after I jumped – utter and complete terror took over. I've faced life and death situations and moved through them before, but when you just move through and don't realize its life and death it doesn't impact you the same. This – conscious decision to jump 3.5 stories from a helicopter into open ocean with an audience and my wife watching. Damned terrifying. And you know what – I chose it. I chose it to invoke terror in every cell in my body. I wanted fear – the mind killer – to take over, wash over me and for me to face it. I knew deep inside – there was only one way to face this demon of fear. And when I did – it happened. It recalibrated what I thought I was capable of. Not because the jump was graceful. Not because I felt in control. But because I did it *while fear was screaming at full volume in every cell of my body.*

And let me be clear—this path is *not for everyone.* This kind of fear stacking is *soul work in motion.* It's for the ones who know: *I'm struggling. I'm stuck. I'm fraying—and something has to change.* It's for the ones ready to claw their way out of the pit of internal compromise.

Because once you've stacked that kind of fear—felt it hijack your body, twist your breath, lock your knees—and *still moved?* Something incredible happens. You realize:

- I can grow.
- I can overcome.
- I can persevere—even in the presence of crippling, full-body fear.

That's not confidence. That's transformation. Its alchemical transmutation of your being. Fear stacking trains your system to walk into the storm instead of shrinking from it. It builds resilience that can't be taught—it must be *earned.* Not by studying fear. But by *feeling it, facing it, and forcing it to surrender.*

So, walk with me, friends. Stand beside me at the edge of your own jump—whatever it is.
Look the beast of fear in the face. He's mean. He's nasty. Let it glare. Let it threaten. Let it snarl. And when it does—**smile. And go at it. Go for broke.**

Because here's what I've learned, over and over: **Every time I go forward—every single time—fear flinches.** It pulls back. It gives up territory. It retreats in the face of someone who refuses to bow.

So, take the leap. Not blindly—but with clarity. With conviction. With open eyes and a war-ready heart. **Own your head. Own your space. Own your destiny.**

Because courage isn't the decision to jump—it's the discipline to do it while fear claws at your spine. And when you rise from that water—breathless, trembling, alive—you'll know: **Fear didn't leave you. You left it behind.**

Leadership Application: Where Is Fear Running the Show?

Let's stop pretending that leadership is about outputs, dashboards, and end-of-quarter metrics. That's management. That's operational theater.

Real leadership is psychological warfare. Not with your team—but with the voice in your own head that tells you to *flinch when the pressure hits.*

Your job as a leader isn't just to hit KPIs. It's to protect the psychological integrity of your people. But that *begins* with protecting your own. And that means getting violently honest about the ways fear is shaping your behavior.

So, pause. No titles. No optics. Just truth. Ask yourself:

- **Where am I deferring accountability—not because I'm confused, but because I'm afraid of confrontation?**
- **Where am I passing off ownership, not delegating—but disappearing, because I don't want to be the "bad guy"?**
- **Where am I "coordinating" instead of commanding—because I fear the resistance that comes with real clarity?**

Go deeper:

- **Where am I over-explaining decisions to earn buy-in that should already exist?**

- **Where am I hiding behind phrases like "alignment," "collaboration," or "consensus" when I really just don't want to deal with fallout?**

And here's the most important question you'll ever ask as a leader: **Where is fear making my decisions—and disguising itself as strategy?**

Because let me tell you from brutal, firsthand experience: **Fear is a master of disguise.** It dresses up in language that gets applause. It sounds like: "I just want to be thoughtful about this decision." "We're taking a collaborative approach." "Now's not the right time to push." "Let's see how things evolve."

But behind the curtain? It's a ghost pulling your strings. It's fear—wearing a mask of wisdom, hijacking your leadership while you call it caution.

And until you *name it*, it owns you. Until you drag it out of the shadows and say, *"You're not in charge anymore,"* it will keep writing the script for your leadership—and calling it maturity.

But here's the good news: The moment you name fear; **you cut its power.** Not all of it. Not forever. But enough to get your hands back on the wheel. Fear doesn't disappear. It just loses the right to steer.

So, if you're brave enough—if you're ready to evolve from positional leadership into principled command—here's your assignment:

- **Audit your fear.**
- **Name the rooms you avoid.**
- **Name the people you appease.**
- **Name the standards you've softened.**
- **Name the decisions you've delayed in the name of diplomacy.**

And then—**reclaim them.** Reclaim your clarity. Reclaim your authority. Reclaim your damn spine.

Because the team is watching. Not just your outcomes—your *courage.* And if you want them to follow you when the bullets fly, then show them a leader who doesn't negotiate with fear in the quiet moments. That's not leadership theater. That's leadership *truth.*

From Shadow to Steel

Jumping into the ocean from a helicopter didn't make me fearless. Let's be clear: I wasn't brave in that moment. I was *awake.*

I was face-to-face with the unfiltered presence of fear—not as theory, not as metaphor, but as a violent reality gripping my nervous system and daring me to flinch. What I learned in that fall wasn't about adrenaline. It was about *awareness.*

That leap showed me how much fear had disguised itself inside my leadership. It hadn't come dressed in panic. It wore the polished clothes of rationality. It spoke in the elegant language of *strategy.* It felt like prudence, like patience, like diplomacy.

But it was still a lie. **Fear doesn't just scream. Sometimes it whispers.** It says, "Let's wait for more data." "Let's get more consensus." "Let's not burn bridges." "Let's be reasonable." And that's how it wins—by sounding smart.

But the deeper truth is this: **Leadership isn't about controlling the narrative.** If you're being mentored to control the narrative, you're being lied to. Yes, you need to communicate, but if controlling the narrative is more important than being productive and meeting growth goals, you're faking it. And instead of faking it you should be focused on controlling *yourself and your fear*. Because if you can't confront fear in its rawest, most primal form—when it grips your lungs and tightens your throat—you'll never have the steel to confront it in its more insidious forms:

- When it hides behind a smiling stakeholder.
- When it lurks behind the excuse of "culture fit."
- When it coils inside a high performer who poisons the team from the inside.

If you can't face fear in yourself, you will never hold the line for others.

And that's what leadership is: *line holding*. It's standing firm when every part of you wants to retreat. It's looking at the easy out, the seductive compromise, and choosing truth anyway. Not perfectly. Not painlessly. But relentlessly.

So, if you're still reading this, if something inside you is rising and resonating—good. You're not done yet. Here's the antidote to fear. The one no course teaches. The one most executive retreat will never mention.

The Antidote: Radical Self-Confrontation

You don't need another coach to give you feedback. You don't need another productivity hack. You don't need another book telling you how to "influence stakeholders." **You need to sit in a quiet room with your shadow.** And ask the question most leaders run from: *"What part of me am I protecting when I pretend to lead?"*

Because that's where the real war begins. Not on the battlefield. Not in the boardroom. **Inside.** When you can name the part of you that is terrified of being irrelevant...When you can sit with the part that still craves approval...That still *needs* to be right...That still fears being *not enough*...

Then—and only then—can you stop performing leadership...**And start embodying it.** This is the transformation. This is the forge. This is where shadow becomes steel. You don't need to become someone else.

You need to *integrate* who you've been with who you're becoming. So, stand. Stare fear in the face. Smile back. And step forward. Not fearless. But forged. **Go for broke.**

Burn the Mask or Be Owned by It

Every leader wears a mask. That's part of the job. But the danger comes when **you forget you're wearing it**. When the role becomes identity. When the performance becomes the person. When the mission becomes a mirror for your ego's survival.

You can build the most articulate strategy in the world. You can hire brilliant consultants and architect pristine KPIs. But if you don't know where your ego ends and your leadership begins? It will all collapse. Because the organization can't evolve **faster than your self-awareness.**

Field Manual: Leading Through the Shadow
**Your greatest leadership threat isn't incompetence. It's unconscious sabotage —
yours.** The Shadow isn't evil. It's unacknowledged power — distorted through fear, ego, and unmet psychological needs. If you don't confront it, it will lead for you. You won't see it in spreadsheets. You won't catch it in personality tests. But your team already feels it. Here's how to start leading clean — from the inside out.

1. Name Your Ego Feeders

Directive: Identify what your ego demands from others to feel powerful.
Watch for:

- Needing to be the smartest in the room
- Avoiding feedback unless it's praise
- Surrounding yourself with loyalists instead of challengers

Action:

- Ask privately: *"What truth would threaten me if I heard it in public?"*
- Then go seek it.

2. Track Your Emotional Hijacks

Directive: Map the triggers that override your logic.
Watch for:

- Overreacting to criticism
- Avoiding high-talent threats
- Shutting down when control slips

Action:

- After every intense emotional response, ask:

"Was that about the moment — or about my own history?"

3. Confront Your Projection Patterns

Directive: Catch when you're assigning your Shadow to others.
Watch for:

- Calling someone "arrogant" when you feel insecure
- Labeling others "too sensitive" when you're avoiding vulnerability
- Framing feedback as "disrespect" when it threatens control

Action:

- Practice real-time internal calls:

"What part of me am I seeing in them?"

4. Deconstruct the Power Persona

Directive: Strip back the mask of leadership performance.
Watch for:

- Leadership language that sounds good but says nothing
- Values that shift to maintain popularity
- "Open-door" policies that repel actual truth

Action:

- Ask your team:

"What's something I say often that no longer carries weight?"

- Then stop saying it. Start proving it.

5. Build a Shadow Mirror System
Directive: Surround yourself with people who don't worship you — and won't protect your blind spots.
Watch for:
- Team harmony that feels too quiet
- Conflict avoidance in leadership conversations
- Executive reports who give you spin instead of substance

Action:
- Establish a **Shadow Contract**:

"If you see me slipping into ego, projection, or emotional manipulation — call it. Out loud. No punishment. Just truth."

Final Directive

You don't master leadership by performing it. You master it by confronting the war happening inside you. The Shadow doesn't disappear. But it can be trained. Integrated. Owned. And once it is —You stop leading for applause…And start leading from authority.

That's clean leadership. That's command through clarity. That's what the C-suite was supposed to be.

Chapter 14: Developing Your Shadow Literacy

"Until you make the unconscious conscious, it will direct your life and you will call it fate." – Carl Jung

Over two years, Bill cycled through 75% of his executive team. Not because they lacked skill. Not because the market was hostile. But because every time friction surfaced, Bill reached for peace like a life raft—and drowned his culture in the process.

He wasn't reckless. He wasn't toxic. He was *driven*. And deeply convinced that with the right mindset tools, he could *drive* his way through anything.

So, he journaled daily. He recited goals. He meditated on mantras like *"Punch through the barriers."* Bill shared "inspirational YouTube videos" preaching his mantras. And yet—his barriers never moved.

Because the real blockade wasn't external. It was **internal**. And it was winning.

You see, while Bill was busy visualizing breakthroughs, his *shadow* was silently **cutting his throat every single day**—whispering lies that looked like leadership. Those lies are:

- "Keep everyone happy."
- "Don't create tension."
- "If they're uncomfortable, you've failed."

Bill believed he was pushing through walls. But the truth? He was being puppeteered. He wasn't leading. He was performing. And his shadow—unseen, unchallenged—was the **puppet master.**

The board eventually confronted him: *"Bill, come on. What are you doing? Why can't you hire leaders who stay?"* But the question they *should* have asked was: *"Bill, when are you going to stop protecting the version of yourself that's burning this place down?"* He was, like so many of us, an **unconscious actor in his own downfall.**

In the previous chapter, we introduced the concept of the shadow its connection to fear. This chapter is about continuing to confront that part of leadership—the *inner terrain* that no title prepares you for. It is about building what I call **shadow literacy**: the ability to recognize, name, and integrate the hidden dimensions of yourself before they sabotage your impact.

What Is the Shadow—and Why Does It Matter?

Carl Jung, the father of analytical psychology, introduced the concept of the **shadow** as the repository of everything we reject, suppress, or deny within ourselves. It is not merely a dark corner of the mind filled with undesirable traits like anger, jealousy, fear, or pride; it also contains positive energies—ambition, power, creativity—that we were conditioned to fear or abandon. The shadow is built from the moments we were told to "sit down," "be nice," or "don't outshine others," internalizing aspects of our authentic nature were unacceptable. In this way, much of our vitality, strength, and even brilliance ends up locked behind walls of repression.

For leaders, the shadow is not an abstract psychological concept; it is a **living force**—an active, unconscious agent shaping conversations, decisions, and reactions in real time. It manifests in the sudden overreaction to critical feedback, the favoritism shown to the agreeable over the honest, the silent exclusion of high performers whose competence feels like a personal threat. When the shadow remains unacknowledged, it does not lay dormant. Instead, it drives behavior from behind the scenes, leading leaders to unconsciously protect their egos at the expense of their teams, their mission, and ultimately their own credibility.

Ignoring the shadow does not eliminate its influence. On the contrary, repression only deepens its control. A leader who cannot face their own insecurity might micromanage talented subordinates, slowly crushing innovation. A leader who buries their fear of failure may become risk-averse, stagnating the organization's ability to adapt in volatile conditions. Another, wrestling unconsciously with envy, may sabotage promising initiatives simply because they weren't their idea. The tragedy is not only personal; it radiates outward, poisoning cultures, derailing strategies, and severing trust. Teams can sense the dissonance even when they can't articulate it: decisions that feel arbitrary, rewards that feel political, risks that are feared instead of navigated.

In the age we now inhabit—marked by rapid transformation, rising complexity, and the collapse of outdated structures—the unexamined shadow is not merely a personal blind spot. It is an organizational vulnerability. It becomes the hidden hand that drives attrition among the best people, sparks costly misalignments, and erodes ethical judgment under the weight of unconscious fear. Leaders who fail to engage with their own shadow do not stay static; they regress, subtly at first, until one day the gap between who they are and who they claim to be becomes too wide to conceal.

Understanding the shadow is not about indulging in psychological introspection for its own sake. It is about survival, adaptation, and evolution. It is about reclaiming the buried parts of oneself—not to be ruled by them, but to integrate them into a stronger, wiser whole. Leaders who face their shadow transform its once-destructive forces into sources of authenticity, courage, and insight. They become less reactive and more deliberate, less manipulative and more magnetic. They are able to lead not from fear or defense, but from a deeply rooted center of self-awareness and integrity. And in a world that desperately needs resilient leadership, those who confront their shadows will shape the future—while those who deny them will be left to decay in the past.

Why Shadow Literacy Fills the Missing Gap

In understanding human behavior and leadership potential, modern frameworks often limit themselves to what can be easily observed, measured, and categorized. They speak fluently to the conscious mind—the surface-level thoughts, stated preferences, and deliberate actions that we know and can articulate. Some assessments attempt to reach a layer deeper into the subconscious, analyzing habitual tendencies, emotional reactivity, or automatic biases. Yet there remains a **critical blind spot** that even the most advanced tools rarely touch: the **unconscious**—the vast, unseen territory where the shadow and the archetypes dwell.

Human consciousness is not a monolith; it is fractured into three primary strata: **the conscious, the subconscious, and the unconscious**. Traditional personality assessments—no matter how sophisticated—primarily target the **conscious mind**. They capture the part of you that knows what it thinks, what it prefers, and how it wants to be perceived. Occasionally, they glimpse into the **subconscious**, that undercurrent of habits, emotional associations, and conditioned responses shaped by past experiences. But they almost entirely miss the **unconscious**—that primal depth where unacknowledged desires, repressed wounds, hidden fears, and archetypal patterns reside. It is here, in the unconscious, that much of human behavior is silently scripted, outside of awareness, yet devastatingly real in its impact.

Newer systems like THRIVE claim to bridge the conscious and subconscious more effectively, leveraging moments of heightened suggestibility—such as the hypnagogic state just before sleep—to influence internal narratives and behaviors. Programmatic techniques feed new ideas and affirmations into the subconscious, attempting to overwrite destructive patterns with intentional reprogramming. While these techniques can produce meaningful shifts at the behavioral and emotional levels, they still fall short of addressing the **deepest architecture of the psyche**. They can soothe the symptoms, but they rarely confront the architect behind the symptoms: the **shadow**.

By focusing exclusively on testing and coaching the conscious mind, leaders may unintentionally feed the very forces they seek to control. The shadow, denied acknowledgment, adapts like an insurgent pushed underground—its influence becomes less visible but more cunning. Conscious-mind interventions often polish the persona, refining the leader's ability to present a controlled, "improved" self. In the short term, this can yield apparent gains: more confident presentations, measured speech, and seemingly rational decisions. But beneath the surface, unintegrated fears, resentments, and unmet drives accumulate pressure. Over time, these repressed elements emerge in more destructive ways—sabotaging relationships, distorting judgment, and eroding authenticity—while the leader remains convinced, they are "fixing" the problem. This is the most dangerous form of self-deception: believing one is growing, when in truth the shadow is quietly strengthening its hold.

Carl Jung's primary insight was that the unconscious is not passive—it is **active**, filled with autonomous forces that exert **will** over the individual. The shadow, and the broader family of archetypes, are not inert. They **speak**, they **manipulate**, they **drive** our choices, often in opposition to our conscious goals. They are triggered by life's complexity—by situations that echo old wounds, unmet needs, unresolved fears—and they surge forward, often with startling force. Until the unconscious contents are brought into conscious dialogue, they rule from the darkness. No amount of surface-level programming can silence them. They must be **engaged**, **understood**, and ultimately **integrated**.

This is where **shadow literacy** fills the missing gap. Shadow literacy is the skill of recognizing when unconscious forces are at play—not simply labeling emotions or analyzing behavior, but **actively engaging with the deeper psychic figures that inhabit our inner world**. Jung's method of **active imagination** was a direct confrontation with these forces. It was a deliberate process of entering into dialogue with the shadow and other archetypes, uncovering their stories, their wounds, and their demands. It was not passive reflection. It was an act of courageous confrontation and integration—a path to **individuation**, the emergence of a truly unified and authentic Self.

Without shadow literacy, leaders risk living in self-delusion. They refine their conscious strategies and optimize their subconscious habits, but they remain vulnerable to the unseen currents that sabotage their efforts when the stakes are highest. They wonder why they self-sabotage, why relationships collapse, why ethical compromises creep in—never realizing these breakdowns are orchestrated by aspects of themselves they refuse to know.

In contrast, a leader fluent in shadow literacy does not seek perfection; they seek wholeness. They recognize that leadership is not just an outward act of execution, but an inward act of reconciliation. They integrate the disowned, the denied, and the dangerous—not to unleash chaos, but to harness its energy with conscious intent. They become whole, and in becoming whole, they become formidable. Shadow literacy is not a luxury. In the emerging world of complexity, ambiguity, and rapid change, **it is the missing discipline for authentic, resilient, transformative leadership**.

A Story of Shadow Illiteracy: How Archetypes Hijack Leadership

I've worked with many leaders over the years—sharp minds, strong credentials, commanding presences. But what separated those who built resilient teams from those who quietly hemorrhaged talent was not intelligence or strategy. It was whether or not they had the courage to confront their own unconscious drivers—their shadow.

Bob was a perfect case study.

On the surface, Bob seemed ideal. He led a critical division with charisma and an emphasis on "team harmony." Meetings were peppered with calls for collaboration, encouragements to "get along," and grand statements about "family culture." But underneath that polished surface, Bob was at war—with his own shadow.

Bob carried deep **trust issues** he never acknowledged. His leadership was less about building actual trust and more about **manufacturing the illusion of unity**. Any real conflict, any uncomfortable truth that could challenge the group's image of cohesion, was swiftly suppressed. Worse, manipulative behaviors and even overt narcissism from certain team members were not just tolerated—they were protected. Bob would rather shield dysfunction than risk breaking the fragile façade of "everyone getting along."

The result was a **toxic cycle**. Every critical issue—missed objectives, ethical concerns, obvious breaches of trust—was reframed through the lens of emotional appeasement rather than mission clarity. Meetings drifted into polite evasions. Problems were papered over with slogans about teamwork. No one ever said what needed to be said. And the narcissists? They thrived. They intuitively recognized Bob's soft underbelly—his shadow-driven need for approval and harmony—and exploited it mercilessly. They whispered to his unconscious fears and flattered his image of himself, steering outcomes in their favor while sabotaging the larger mission.

Confronting reality became a herculean effort. It would often take **weeks or even months** just to get Bob to acknowledge basic facts—problems that any emotionally mature leader would have addressed immediately. In the meantime, we were **bleeding time, morale, and opportunity**. Every cycle repeated itself predictably: the real issues went untouched, the manipulators grew stronger, and the mission drifted further off course.

This pattern didn't just happen once. It became a **chronic operating condition** over the span of years. And in environments like this, the highest performers—the ones who can smell dysfunction a mile away—don't stick around. They see the lunacy for what it is. They offer patience for a season. They give leaders a window to get their house in order. But when emotional volatility and erratic decision-making become the norm—when a leader refuses to engage their shadow—they leave. Quietly, decisively, permanently.

Because here's the harsh reality: **Life is too short to suffer under a leader who is driven by invisible wounds they refuse to heal.**

Shadow illiteracy isn't just a personal weakness. It's a **strategic liability**. It burns time, depletes talent, and slowly, inexorably, poisons the culture from the inside out.

Common Shadow Behaviors in Leadership

The shadow does not announce itself with grand gestures. It slips through the cracks—subtle, persistent, shaping leadership behaviors in ways that often seem justified on the surface but are corrosive underneath. Every leader carries a version of this. The form it takes depends on individual fears, unresolved wounds, and unintegrated parts of the psyche.

Here are some of the most **common shadow-driven patterns** that quietly erode leadership from the inside out:

Control Disguised as Competence

You tell yourself you're maintaining high standards, ensuring excellence, safeguarding quality. But beneath the rationalizations is a deeper truth: **you don't trust others to succeed without you.** Control masquerades as competence when fear whispers that if you don't tightly manage every variable, everything will fall apart. What you frame as leadership rigor is often just **an unconscious attempt to stave off anxiety and chaos**—at the cost of stifling innovation and suffocating team autonomy.

Anger Disguised as Passion

You pride yourself on your emotional investment, your fire, your intensity. You call it "passion." But when meetings end with people silenced, ideas crushed, and energy drained, it's not passion they're feeling—it's **fear**. When anger, masked as righteous intensity, goes unexamined, it becomes a battering ram. **People stop bringing their best ideas forward not because they lack courage, but because they've learned that survival requires silence.**

Favoritism Masked as "Protecting Culture"

You believe you're nurturing the organization's culture, choosing those who "fit" to advance and shielding the team from disruption. In truth, you're **rewarding familiarity over excellence**, reinforcing personal comfort over mission advancement. The shadow convinces you that loyalty is equivalent to contribution. That "trust" must be earned through personal rapport, not through demonstrated skill or courage. **This turns the culture into an echo chamber where challenge is seen as disloyalty—and where real talent quietly exits.**

Avoidance Wrapped in Compassion

You tell yourself you're being kind. You don't want to hurt feelings. You want to maintain a "positive" environment. But avoidance, dressed up as compassion, is often **fear in disguise**—a fear of being disliked, challenged, or exposed. True compassion requires confrontation when the mission demands it. **Avoidance sacrifices clarity on the altar of emotional comfort**, ultimately doing more harm than a difficult truth ever could.

Delegation That's Performative

You assign tasks. You hold meetings. You tell people, "I'm giving you ownership." But real power—decision-making authority, strategic voice, risk-taking leeway—**never actually leaves your hands.** Performative delegation leaves teams in limbo: they carry the burden without the authority. Over time, resentment builds. Initiative dies. **You wonder why no one is stepping up, not realizing you've trained them not to.**

These behaviors are not character flaws in the traditional sense. They are **defense mechanisms**—reflexive strategies your unconscious mind developed to shield you from old pain: the fear of failure, the shame of inadequacy, the terror of losing control or being exposed. They were built to protect your sense of self when you were vulnerable.

But here's the brutal reality: **These tools are expensive.** Every time you let them govern you, they exact a toll:

- **They drain trust.**
- **They kill momentum.**
- **They cripple innovation.**
- **They sabotage results.**

Left unchecked, shadow behaviors don't just hurt individuals—they **destabilize entire systems**. They create environments where mediocrity is safer than greatness, where emotional safety becomes an excuse for avoiding hard truths, and where the brightest minds walk away before their light can change anything.

Understanding your shadow behaviors isn't about self-flagellation. It's about liberation. When you expose them to the light, they lose their grip.
When you integrate them into conscious awareness, you reclaim the energy they once stole.
And when you lead with that wholeness, instead of your fear, **everything changes.**

Why Most Leaders Fail to See It

The strange paradox of leadership is this: **the higher you rise, the harder it becomes to see your own shadow**. Not because it disappears—but because the system around you adapts to it. At the top, leaders are rarely confronted with raw, unfiltered reality. They are surrounded by people—smart, capable, well-meaning people—who have quietly learned to **navigate around their leader's unconscious behaviors** rather than name them.

Over time, without ever making a formal agreement, the people around you begin adjusting themselves to survive your shadow. They learn which topics are too risky to raise. They learn how to frame concerns so they won't trigger defensiveness. They figure out when to stay silent, when to flatter, and when to simply give up trying to break through. The leader, meanwhile, remains largely unaware of the choreography happening around them. Everything seems fine. Meetings are polite. Reports are positive. Loyalty feels strong. **But it's all happening inside a curated reality—one carefully designed to avoid your unexamined reactions.**

This creates a **dangerous feedback loop**: Because no one is confronting you, you conclude that your leadership is effective. Because you believe everything is running smoothly, you become even less likely to question yourself. And because the system protects you from the friction of truth, your shadow grows stronger—operating unchecked, just beneath the surface of every decision, every relationship, every cultural signal.

The brutal, unspoken truth is this: **the more powerful you become, the more dangerous your unconscious shadow becomes if left unexamined**. Influence is a multiplier. Your habits, your fears, your blind spots—they don't just stay personal. They get scaled into organizational systems. They get written into policy. They bleed into hiring practices, operational assumptions, and cultural norms.

Over time, your shadow becomes not just a personal flaw, but **an institutional legacy**. It creates: A culture where truth speaking equates to dissent and is seen as disloyalty. A system where high performers are quietly edged out for being "too disruptive." A brand that projects innovation but is paralyzed by fear of risk.

It doesn't happen all at once. It happens one tolerated shadow behavior at a time. Leadership without shadow literacy is like piloting a ship by dead reckoning while the compass is broken—you will drift off course. You will fail to see the damage until it's far too late to correct.

Shadow literacy isn't a luxury for those who like psychological depth. It is **a survival skill** for any leader serious about building something that will endure beyond their own limitations.

The final, bitter irony? If you refuse to confront your shadow, **the people you leave behind will be forced to clean up what you refused to see**. And that—more than any title, metric, or headline—will become your true legacy.

Jungian Tools for Reclaiming the Repressed

The journey toward shadow integration is not casual work. It is a deliberate, courageous confrontation with the disowned parts of the psyche—the fragments you once buried for safety but which now seek expression through your leadership, your relationships, and your legacy. Jung provided multiple tools for this inner confrontation. Used carefully, they can transform your inner enemies into trusted advisors.

Below are three foundational exercises, followed by an important preparatory practice for deeper active imagination work.

1. The Mirror Exercise
Begin with a simple but unsettling question: Who triggers you the most in your organization? Pick three individuals. Don't overthink it. Trust your instinctive reactions.
For each one, ask yourself:
- **What specific behaviors do they exhibit that bother me?**
- **What emotions arise in me when I observe them?**
- **What part of myself feels threatened, dismissed, or diminished by them?**

Once you have your answers, **reverse the lens**: Could these individuals be reflecting parts of yourself that you've rejected or exiled? Very often, what we harshly judge in others is what we secretly disown in ourselves. The employee you label as "too ambitious" may echo your own stifled drive for growth. The colleague who "seeks attention" may mirror your buried desire to be seen and valued, a part of you that fears being labeled arrogant. When you shift from automatic judgment to deep inquiry, the trigger becomes a teacher. **Every emotional charge is a doorway to greater self-awareness.**

2. The Shadow Values Inventory
Take a sheet of paper and create two columns.
- **Column A:** List the values you publicly espouse—values you proudly associate with your leadership, such as transparency, collaboration, courage, accountability.
- **Column B:** Now, with brutal honesty, list the behaviors, decisions, or habits you engage in that contradict those stated values—especially the ones you quietly justify to yourself.

For example:
- **Value:** Accountability
  Contradiction: Avoiding direct feedback with certain high-conflict team members.

- **Value:** Transparency
  Contradiction: Withholding critical strategic context from staff under the guise of "protecting focus."

This is where your **shadow lives**—in the gap between aspiration and action. Do not shame yourself. Do not rationalize. **Simply observe.** Integration begins by acknowledging where your ideals and behaviors diverge. When your values and actions align, **trust grows**—within yourself, and across your teams. When they drift apart, **culture deteriorates**, often silently but irreversibly.

3. Archetype Journaling

This exercise invites you to bring your shadow into conscious dialogue through symbolic imagination. Imagine your shadow not as a vague feeling, but as a **personified character** within your inner world. Ask yourself:

- **What is its voice like? Calm? Angry? Mocking? Sad?**
- **What is it afraid of?**
- **What is it trying to protect?**
- **When did it first appear in your life story?**

Give your shadow a name. Sketch its image if you can. **Let it speak in your journal.** Write its story—not from your ego's perspective, but from its own. This is not fantasy or delusion. Jung taught that the psyche is composed of many parts—each with its own voice, its own survival logic, its own emotional truth. When you listen with patience and respect, **the shadow shifts from saboteur to advisor.** It stops leaking chaos into your leadership and starts offering you hidden strength, forgotten wisdom, and the power of true wholeness.

Preparing for Active Imagination: Meditation and Mindfulness First

Active imagination—the deliberate engagement of unconscious figures like the shadow or archetypes—requires preparation. It is not something to rush into blindly.

Before beginning active imagination work:

1. **Practice Mindful Grounding**

Spend 5–10 minutes in simple, structured mindfulness meditation:
  - Sit comfortably.
  - Focus your attention on your breathing.
  - Notice physical sensations, emotions, and thoughts without judgment.
  - Anchor your awareness in the present moment, like a tree rooting deeper into the soil.

2. **Establish Emotional Stability**

If you feel agitated, fragmented, overwhelmed, or emotionally raw, pause. Active imagination can stir powerful forces. Enter this space **only when you feel grounded and resilient**.

3. **Set a Clear Intention**

Before engaging any internal figure, set a calm, clear intention such as: *"I am here to listen and understand, not to judge or control."* You are not the ruler in the unconscious. You're a participant.

4. **Use a Time Boundary**

Especially when beginning this work, set a timer (e.g., 15–20 minutes).
Limiting the session time helps maintain psychological balance and avoids slipping into overwhelming emotional flooding.

Critical Caution

While active imagination can be profoundly healing, **it is not a substitute for professional psychological care**. It is always best to work with a professional. The information here is provided as reference only. If you do experiment with these techniques on your, here are some cautions. If you experience:

- Intrusive or overwhelming emotions
- Disassociation or loss of time
- Inability to "return" fully from internal exploration

Stop immediately and seek guidance from a licensed Jungian analyst, psychologist, or experienced psychotherapist trained in working with unconscious material. Self-directed shadow work is powerful—but **reckless engagement can cause real psychological harm. Respect the depth of the unconscious.** Approach with humility, preparation, and, when necessary, professional support.

From Shadow to Integration: The Emergence of Wholeness

Integration does not mean the elimination of the shadow. It means something far more courageous—and far more difficult. It means you **recognize** it. You **respect** it. You **reclaim** it. You stop pretending that the parts of yourself you fear, resent, or suppress don't exist. You stop fighting internal wars where nobody wins. Instead, you start walking into the darkened corners of your psyche with open eyes—and with open hands. You begin to say, without flinching:

- **"Yes, I have the capacity for arrogance—and I will watch it closely, without denial."**
- **"Yes, I desire power—but I will use it consciously, in service of others, not to feed my own emptiness."**
- **"Yes, I sometimes manipulate outcomes—but I will practice transparency even when it strips me of control."**

This is not about perfection. This is the soil of **mature leadership**. You are no longer at war with yourself. You are no longer terrified of the voices within you. You stop needing to dominate every room to affirm your existence. You stop needing applause to feel anchored. You no longer need to **perform leadership. You can simply be it.**

I can tell you this personally—this work is not theoretical for me. I have used active imagination for years. Not just as an exercise, but as a lifeline. It has opened me to patterns of my behavior that, frankly, I refused to acknowledge—patterns of pride, fear, avoidance, and rage that I had dressed up as "strength" or "standards."

It also revealed something critical: **when I am tired, exhausted, or stretched thin, the boundaries between my conscious, subconscious, and unconscious minds weaken.** The walls get thin. And when that happens, **archetypal forces surge forward more easily**—old fears, destructive drives, shadow figures trying to reassert themselves when my vigilance falters. This became visceral for me during one of the most intense moments of my life: **jumping from thirty-five feet out of a helicopter into the ocean.** [We covered this in a previous chapter.] That wasn't just a physical leap. It was a **symbolic one**—active imagination partnered with action.

And I will tell you something else most books on this topic may not: **Archetypes can be brutal.** They are not tame. They are not concerned with your ego's comfort. I have had archetypal figures—parts of my own unconscious mind—**say things to me meant to crush my**

soul. Not to be cruel, but to expose the rot beneath my illusions. To strip away falsehood. To force confrontation where I had built walls of defense. Let me explain this further.

For years, I openly said, half in jest, half in warning: **"There's a beast in me. I have to chain him, keep him under control, or he will act out."** And at times, under extreme stress, I would symbolically **unchain the beast**—unleash anger, force, dominance when I thought the situation demanded it. Ironically, now I know: **that beast was never a monster.** It was **my shadow**—misunderstood, exiled, screaming for acknowledgment. And every day he remained chained, he grew angrier.

And let me ask you: If you had been **chained and silenced for over thirty years**, how polite would you be when finally unchained? When I finally let the shadow speak—without judgment, without interruption—it was brutal. It accused. It raged. It demanded to be seen.

And yet, on the other side of that brutal honesty, **my life changed**. **My leadership changed.** Not because I became someone else. But because I became **more whole**—more aware of the full range of my humanity, not just the parts I liked or could show publicly.

I cannot overstate this: **If you take one thing from this book, let it be this.** Learn to practice active imagination. Learn to engage your shadow. Learn to pursue individuation—not as a hobby, but as a discipline, a sacred task. Because once you do, you will lead—not from fear, not from performance—but from the unshakeable ground of authenticity. And that is the rarest, most powerful force a leader can possess.

Your Shadow Shapes the Room—The Team Feels What You Can't Face

It's important to understand a hard, often uncomfortable truth: **Your team will feel your shadow—whether you acknowledge it or not.** You don't have to announce your fears. You don't have to disclose your insecurities. You don't have to admit your unresolved struggles.

They will know.

Not consciously, perhaps. Not in neatly labeled language. But at the **felt sense level**—through the subtle tensions in your meetings, the shifts in your tone, the way your eyes narrow when challenged, the decisions that don't match your stated values—**they will sense it.**
Your team will pick up on it when:

- **You're leading from ego**—seeking affirmation instead of seeking solutions, making decisions to protect your image rather than serve the mission.
- **Your decisions are driven by fear**—whether it's fear of losing control, fear of not being enough, or fear of confronting hard realities.
- **You're projecting unresolved emotion into policies and people**—punishing dissent under the guise of "cultural fit," micromanaging in the name of "standards," rewarding loyalty over courage.

And when they feel it, they will adapt. **Not by rising to their best, but by shrinking to their safest.**

- They'll **adapt**, not engage.
- They'll **stay silent**, even when the truth desperately needs to be spoken.
- They'll **comply**, hitting the minimum standard, instead of **contributing** with passion, creativity, and critical thought.

You might still retain your **title**, your **org chart**, and your **metrics** for a while. You might even mistake their polite compliance for loyalty. But make no mistake: **you will lose the culture**.

The culture will shift from vibrant to defensive. From proactive to performative. From courageous to cautious. And once that erosion begins, it is extremely difficult to reverse—because people lose not just their trust in leadership, but their trust in the system itself. This is why **shadow literacy is not merely a personal development exercise**.

It is **an organizational imperative**. Your shadow is not a private matter. **It is systemic the moment you lead.** If you refuse to confront it, you are asking your people to carry it for you—through their silence, their resignation, and their eventual exit.

But if you engage it—if you take responsibility for what lives within—you create a space where truth is not just tolerated but trusted. Where authenticity isn't just a branding slogan but a lived reality. Where people don't have to contort themselves around your blind spots—they can bring their whole selves to the mission. **That is leadership worth following. That is culture worth building.**

And it begins—with brutal, beautiful honesty—with you.

The Shadow Is the Gatekeeper to Greatness

Most leaders try to become "better" by polishing their outer skills—better communication, better time management, better strategy. But few realize that the key to transformational leadership is not improvement. It's **integration**.

To lead well, you must become whole. The shadow isn't your enemy. It's the part of you that was once hurt, scared, or silenced—and now wants to be seen. When you see it, speak with it, and own it…You step into the kind of presence that doesn't demand control—because it radiates clarity. You lead without needing to dominate. You create safety, not just for others—but for yourself. And in doing so, you stop the cycle. You stop being an unconscious actor in your own undoing. And you start becoming the kind of leader who can build something that lasts.

Field Manual: Becoming Shadow Literate

The most dangerous part of you is the part you won't face. Not because it's evil. But because it's *invisible*. The Shadow is not your weakness—it's your **unconscious power**. And when left unexamined, it doesn't disappear. It **drives**. It **leads**. It **decides**. Until one day, you're no longer the leader—*you're the puppet*.

This manual gives you the tools to see what's hiding, name what's been denied, and integrate the power you've buried. This manual dives deeper into strategies to begin the process of facing the archetypes in your unconscious driving your behavior. The most prominent archetype being your Shadow.

1. SHADOW TRIGGERS TO WATCH FOR

Use this as a **weekly self-check**. These patterns aren't quirks. They're signs.

Shadow Signal	Leadership Impact
You get disproportionately angry at "lazy" people	You're projecting a buried fear of your own fragility
You micromanage high performers	You unconsciously resent their autonomy
You shut down dissent	Your ego is mistaking disagreement for betrayal
You constantly need praise or approval	Your value is hooked to visibility, not integrity
You sabotage stability right before success	Your inner story believes you're not meant to win

2. SHADOW MAPPING EXERCISE (Do Monthly)

Objective: Find your blind spots and hidden drivers.
Take 15 minutes and write:
- "What do I least want people to say about me?"
- "What types of people do I silently judge or dismiss?"
- "Where do I overreact—emotionally, defensively, or in silence?"
- "Who triggers me most in leadership—and why?"

Then ask: *What do they reflect that I refuse to own?*
Your most frustrating relationships are often mirrors—not enemies.

3. SHADOW INTEGRATION PRACTICES

Integration isn't perfection. It's awareness + action.
Daily:
- Journal emotional spikes: "What emotion did I feel? What fear was under it?"
- Catch your auto-pilot reactions: "Was that a choice—or a script?"

Weekly:
- Invite a trusted peer to call out blind spots:
"Where am I harder to work with than I realize?"

Monthly:
- Reflect on one Shadow trait you've faced—and how it's now a strength.

"I once suppressed my need for control. Now I channel it into systems, not people."
You don't eliminate the Shadow. You partner with it.

4. SHADOW LITERACY AS A CULTURAL ADVANTAGE

What's true at the personal level is more dangerous at the organizational level.

Watch for team-level shadow patterns:
- "We avoid conflict." = We fear truth.
- "We only hire from top schools." = We worship prestige.
- "We have a family culture." = We avoid accountability.

Cultures inherit the collective Shadow of their leadership.
If you don't see it in yourself, you'll reproduce it in your systems.

FINAL DIRECTIVE: KNOW YOUR SHADOW OR BE RULED BY IT

You cannot lead people you secretly resent. You cannot protect a culture you subconsciously sabotage. And you cannot preach clarity if your own motivations are still hidden in the fog. **To become whole is to become dangerous**—*because you've met every part of yourself, and none of them are running the show.* Shadow literacy doesn't make you less human. It makes you *whole*. And whole leaders are the only ones strong enough to build something that lasts.

Chapter 15: Leadership Without You

"The ultimate goal of leadership is not to be needed—it's to build something that can thrive in your absence."

The first morning back, he was still dreaming about the beach. Salt air. Hammock sway. The quiet hum of his own breath—finally separated from strategy decks, investor calls, and cascading Slack pings. For the first time in years, the machine had run without him.

Or so he thought. He walked into the office with sun on his face and stillness in his chest. But by 10 a.m., it hit him like a record scratch at a dance party.

Nothing had moved. The product launch—paused. The hiring decision—deferred.
The cultural rollout—stalled in "alignment meetings." People weren't angry. They were *hesitant*. Everyone was waiting for him to come back… because *he'd never built them to move without him.*

At first, it stroked his ego: *"They need me. I matter."* Then the truth landed like a gut punch: *"They're paralyzed—because I never taught them how to move."*

He didn't just own the vision. He owned the decision grid, the emotional permission, the center of gravity. And when he left, he took *everything* with him. He hadn't built a team. He'd built a mirror. And without his reflection in it, the whole damn thing froze.

The Ego and the Endgame

There comes a moment in every leader's journey when the real question isn't, *"What more can I do?"* but rather, *"What would still work if I stepped away?"*

It's a confronting question—one that strikes at the core of your identity. Because for years, perhaps decades, your value has been tied to visibility. To the constant motion of doing, deciding, showing up, being central. You've been the face, the force, the final word. The leader everyone looks to when things get uncertain.

But now you're beginning to feel the fatigue. Or maybe you're contemplating what comes next—succession, sale, scale, or sabbatical. Whatever the trigger, one realization is emerging:
If everything depends on you, nothing can truly grow beyond you.

That truth isn't an indictment—it's an invitation. An invitation to build something that *lives*, breathes, and expands without requiring your constant presence. An invitation to create continuity, not codependence.
And that begins with this essential mindset shift: **Leadership is not what you control. It's what you leave behind.**

The Indispensability Illusion

At first, being indispensable feels like a badge of honor—a confirmation that you are not only needed but irreplaceable. Your team depends on you. Customers trust only you. Your inbox overflows with questions only you can answer. Every fire you extinguish becomes another tally mark for your worth. Every decision routed through your desk reinforces your identity as the **nerve center** of the business.

For a time, it feels like momentum. It feels like validation. It feels like power.

But slowly—almost imperceptibly—**indispensability mutates from an asset into a liability**. You begin to notice subtle, corrosive patterns:

- **Projects stall without your input.** Team members hesitate, waiting for your judgment before taking risks.
- **Employees defer instead of decide.** Initiative dries up because autonomy has been conditioned out of the system.
- **Innovation slows to a crawl**—not because people lack ideas, but because your full calendar is the bottleneck no one dares to bypass.
- **The culture mirrors your moods**—because you haven't built resilient systems or shared ownership. You've built a world where your energy, your presence, your approval dictates the operating rhythm.

This is the **leadership paradox of power**: **The more central you make yourself, the more fragile everything around you becomes.** At first, you think you're protecting the organization. You believe your involvement guarantees quality, alignment, excellence.

But over time, you realize something much darker: You have created a system that **reflects your limitations as much as your strengths**. And when the inevitable happens—When you burn out. When you get sick. When you need to scale. When you dream of stepping away—**The entire system freezes.** Not because your team lacks talent. Not because the mission lacks meaning. But because the architecture of the organization was built around **you**, not around the mission.

You were the scaffolding. You were the oxygen. And now, in your absence, everything suffocates. That is not strategy. **That is structural risk.**

It is a silent, slow-building threat that compromises succession, scales fragility, and ultimately dooms organizations to irrelevance once their "indispensable" leaders inevitably falter or depart.

True leadership is not measured by how much the organization needs you today. **It's measured by how little it needs you tomorrow.** If your systems, culture, and strategy cannot breathe without you, you have built an empire of dependency—not a resilient institution.

The work of real leadership—the painful, liberating, transformational work—is to **make yourself unnecessary**. Not because you don't care. But because you care enough to want the mission to survive and thrive **beyond your ego, beyond your shadow, beyond your presence**. The best leaders do not build monuments to themselves. They build engines of momentum that outlive their names.

Your Name Is Not a System

Take a hard moment of reflection. Ask yourself—honestly, without rationalization: **What parts of your organization only work because of your name?** Is it your personal relationships with investors who take your calls but would ignore anyone else? Is it your ability to step into internal conflicts and, through sheer force of presence, broker temporary peace? Is it your gift for translating mission and vision into action when clarity fractures across teams? Is it your authority—the unspoken reality that, when systems fail, people move only because **you said so**?

If the thread holding these critical functions together is **your personal credibility, authority, or energy**—then you're not operating with a real system. You're operating within **dependency architecture**. *And dependency architecture, no matter how strong it feels in the short term, is a ticking time bomb.*

Healthy, resilient organizations are not fueled by charisma. They are built on **values codified into action**. They run on **systems, processes, and cultures that are shared—not gatekept**. They are powered by **distributed authority**—teams capable of acting decisively without waiting for the gravitational pull of one individual to set them in motion. In resilient organizations:

- Accountability isn't enforced by fear of disappointing one leader—it's embedded into the fabric of peer expectations and role clarity.
- Conflict resolution doesn't require a heroic figure to step in—it flows from clear protocols and shared commitments to trust and transparency.
- Innovation doesn't hinge on one voice greenlighting the future—it emerges naturally from empowered teams who know how to act without waiting for permission.

Your name, no matter how respected, is not a scalable asset. It can open doors, yes. It can inspire, yes. But if the doors only stay open because you're standing in them—If the mission only advances when you personally push it forward—You haven't built an organization. You've built a shrine to yourself.

And shrines, no matter how beautiful, are dead places. Places of memory, not momentum.

The real work of leadership—the humbling, visionary work—is not to make yourself irreplaceable.

It is to make yourself unnecessary. It is to design something that runs with or without your name attached. Something that breathes and grows and evolves even when you're not in the room. Something that holds its shape when stress comes, because it was built not around your identity, but around enduring principles and scalable architecture.

The real legacy of leadership is not that people remember your name. It's that they remember what you built still works—long after you've gone. And if you can reach that place—if you can lead with that kind of humility, discipline, and vision—you won't just be respected. You will be *necessary for a season* and *honored for a generation*. Because you didn't just build influence. **You built endurance.**

Courageous Clarity: Not Just a Leadership Style—A Succession Strategy

In leadership, clarity is often misunderstood as simply good communication—clear instructions, organized meetings, polished vision statements. But true clarity is something deeper. It is not just a leadership style. **It is the immune system of your organization.**

Clarity is what governs behavior when you are not standing in the room. It is what anchors decisions when ambiguity descends and the easy answers evaporate. It is the silent force that guides conflict resolution, role expectations, ethical choices, and strategic action when external conditions are volatile and internal doubts are high.

Without courageous clarity, organizations drift. They revert to fear-based decisions, personal loyalties, territorial politics. Innovation stalls, conflict festers, and culture fractures under the weight of unspoken tensions.

But when you lead with clarity—when you infuse your mission, your systems, and your leadership bench with **courageous, principle-driven definition**—you are doing more than leading for today. **You are preparing your people for tomorrow.**

When you operate with clarity:
- You are **not just giving direction**—you are building **decision-makers**.
- You are **not just managing conflict**—you are teaching people how to navigate it without you.
- You are **not just enforcing values**—you are embedding them into the culture at a cellular level.

Clarity is what enables your team to:
- Act independently, without needing permission at every turn.
- Make decisions aligned with core values, even under pressure.
- Navigate ambiguity with confidence because the principles are stronger than the chaos.
- Carry the mission forward because it lives in them—not just in you.

This is why I call **clarity a form of succession insurance**. Without clarity, your absence creates drift. Factions form. Fear grows. Cynicism creeps in. The center does not hold because the center was **you**, not the mission.

With clarity, your absence creates growth. New leaders emerge—not as clones of you, but as carriers of the principles you instilled. The mission sharpens, adapts, evolves—because it was never built on your charisma alone. It was built on enduring truth.

Let me be absolutely clear: **Letting go does not mean you have become irrelevant.** It means you have **succeeded**. You have crossed the threshold that separates managers from architects, operators from builders, bosses from legacy-makers.

In a world where too many leaders mistake control for leadership, courageous clarity is the discipline that separates **temporary influence** from **lasting impact**. Real leaders build cultures that grow **stronger in their absence, not weaker**. And clarity is the blueprint that makes it possible.

The Psychology of Letting Go

Letting go is not a procedural act. It is a psychological reckoning. For many leaders, **their role is inseparable from their identity**. *Leadership isn't just what they do—it's who they believe they are.*

The adrenaline rush of making critical decisions, the validation that comes from being needed, the subtle comfort of being the axis around which everything spins—these are not surface-level gratifications. They are deeply wired emotional anchors. An anything rooted in emotion is nothing more than an out-of-control race car speeding towards an inevitable cliff of destruction.

Letting go threatens those anchors. It can feel like:
- **Losing control**—as systems start to function without your constant input.
- **Losing meaning**—as your visible daily contributions diminish.
- **Losing identity**—as the ego's craving for centrality no longer finds its daily fix.

These are not trivial losses. They can trigger fear, resentment, and even grief if unacknowledged. Because to a leader who has over-identified with their role, stepping back can feel like **death by irrelevance**.

And yet, if your goal is truly to build something that lasts—something that **outlives you**, **outgrows you**, **outshines you**—then you must move through this psychological passage. You must move from:

- **Possession** to **participation**.
- **Owner** to **architect**.
- **Conductor** to **composer**.

This transition is **profound**. It requires moving from the **front of the room**, where you direct the attention, to the **edge of the room**, where you **hold the space** but let others carry the sound. It demands moving from **voice**—the need to be heard—to **presence**—the need to empower.

It requires abandoning the heroic fantasy: the myth that you alone must hold everything together. And instead, embracing the humble, powerful truth: that your real work is to be the **gardener**, not the gladiator.

Gardening is not passive. It is deeply active—strategic, patient, messy, and alive. You till the soil of culture. You plant seeds of principle. You prune when necessary. You water trust, consistency, and autonomy. And then—you step back enough to let growth happen **without micromanagement and without egoic interference**.

When done well, this shift does not diminish your impact. **It multiplies it.** Your absence becomes not a vacuum—but a catalyst. Not a loss—but a legacy. Not a gap—but a garden that blooms larger than any one name could ever command. This is the psychology of true leadership evolution. Letting go is not the end of influence. **It is the beginning of transcendence.**

Four Strategic Shifts to Build Systems That Survive Without You

Let's walk through four transformative shifts that enable organizations to sustain excellence when you're no longer at the center.

1. Founder Energy → Framework Energy

Early-stage organizations are fueled by founder energy—intensity, adaptability, hustle. This is necessary in chaotic environments. But as the organization matures, that same energy becomes a limiter. What's needed now is **framework energy**—a system of rituals, cadences, decision rights, and feedback loops that allow the business to function predictably and flexibly without your constant direction. This includes:

- Documented SOPs (standard operating procedures) for key workflows.
- Defined roles and cross-functional responsibilities.
- Clear authority pathways: Who makes what decisions, under what conditions, with what data?

A system is not documentation alone. It's documentation that lives in daily action.

Ask yourself: If I disappeared for 60 days, what parts of the business would keep humming? What would stall? What would break? This is your diagnostic. Don't be ashamed of the answers. Use them to *architect freedom*.

2. Talent as Proximity → Talent as Multipliers

It's tempting to keep your best people close. To hold key talent in the inner circle. To give them access instead of **authority**. But proximity is not development. If your team relies on your voice to interpret vision, escalate tension, or drive execution, you haven't built leaders. You've built assistants. To build a resilient system:

- Elevate others into **distributed leadership** roles.

- Create succession depth in every domain—not just on paper, but in capability.
- Share your strategic thinking process, not just decisions.
- Develop leaders who can **extend** your thinking, not just repeat it.

The future belongs to those who stop guarding their influence—and start *multiplying* it.

3. Charisma as Culture → Clarity as Culture

Many organizations run on charisma. They function well when the founder is in the room. The vibe is right. The energy is high. The mission is alive. But charisma doesn't scale. It burns out. It bottlenecks. It can't be transferred. What you need instead is **codified clarity**:
- What are the core values—and how are they expressed in decisions, not just posters?
- What behaviors are rewarded, tolerated, and rejected?
- How are difficult conversations handled? How is conflict navigated?
- What does a "win" look like—across functions, teams, and time horizons?

Codify this. Make it explicit. Culture is not what you say when you're present. It's what people *do* when you're not.

4. Hero Leadership → Infrastructural Leadership

In hero leadership, the organization orbits around you. You're the fixer, the decision-maker, the visionary. It feels noble, but it's short-lived. In infrastructural leadership, you design the **ecosystem**. You build communication loops, empowerment layers, and resilience structures that allow things to function **without intervention**. The most powerful leadership move isn't doing more. It's building something that does not need you to do more. That's not abdication. That's architecture.

The Moment You Step Back

Eventually, it happens. A health issue. A family moment. A career transition. Or simply… the realization that it's time to hand off what you've carried. You will step back. And the system will respond.

It will either stand because you prepared it. Or it will fall because you were the system. That moment isn't just an operational test—it's a **spiritual reflection**. Did you build something that reflects your ego? Or something that reflects your essence? Will people say, *"We don't know what to do without them…"* Or will they say, *"They prepared us for this. Let's keep building."* The answer depends on what you do today.

Final Reflection: Legacy Is Systems, Not Stories

Your story matters. But your systems are what will live on. The point of leadership isn't to stay visible. It's to make sure what you've built is **durable**, **transferable**, and **evolving**. You are not the finish line. You are the *bridge*.

Build systems that work without your name. Build leaders who don't need your presence to act with principle. Build cultures that echo your values—not your quirks. That is the mark of real leadership. That is the gift you leave behind. That is legacy.

Field Manual — Leadership Without You

Objective: Build systems and leaders that thrive when you're not in the room.

1. Run the "Absence Audit" (Quarterly)

Ask your team:
- What would stall if I disappeared for 30 days?
- What decisions still require me—unnecessarily?
- Who has full authority—but still asks for my blessing?

If your name appears too often, you're not leading—you're presiding.

2. Empower Before You Exit

Create a succession map—not just for roles, but for:
- Decision authority
- Cultural stewardship
- Crisis response protocols

Define **what "done well" looks like**—then let others own it.

3. Systematize the Mission

Codify your values in actions, not slogans.
Design operating rhythms that don't need your intervention to maintain alignment:
- Weekly review cadences
- Decision matrices
- Transparent KPIs with owner accountability

4. Normalize Redundancy, Not Dependency

Create two-deep leadership.
Every major function should have:
- A primary driver
- A backup with 80% readiness

Build *organizational muscle memory*, not heroic reliance.

5. Build a Culture of Self-Trust

Ask your team:
"What would need to be true for you to make this call without me?"
Then go build that trust—through training, coaching, and removing ego.

FINAL DIRECTIVE: If your presence adds delay, fear, or paralysis—you're not building a legacy. You're building a cage.

Part III: Steel in the Fire — Execution, Conflict, and Culture Rebuild

You've seen the theater. You've stared down the shadow. Now it's time to lead for real.

This is where the nice words die. Where excuses don't make it past the first bullet point. Where "alignment" meets actual crisis—and only the prepared survive.

This is execution. This is how you setup winning.

It's not sexy. It doesn't trend. And it sure as hell doesn't get applause from people who benefit from the chaos you've been sent to clean up.

This final section is your crucible. It's about building what *lasts*—not what pleases. About hard calls, sharp boundaries, and the kind of clarity that costs you relationships, comfort, and sometimes… sleep. You'll face:

- **DEV (Decision-to-Execution Velocity)**—and why your mission is bleeding out while your team's still "processing."
- **Conflict Without Collapse**—how to hold the line without burning the village.
- **The Courage to Fire, the Wisdom to Keep**—when legacy turns to liability, and when loyalty becomes your greatest threat.
- **Feedback as a Force Multiplier**—not as a survey or a soft suggestion, but as a system of brutal clarity that builds culture under pressure.

This is where you stop hoping they'll get it. You *make sure* they do. It's not about being feared or loved. It's about being trusted when the storm hits. Because leadership isn't how you look when it's calm. It's who you are when the alarms are screaming—and you still have to choose.

This is where you rebuild. Where you become the one, they follow, not because they have to…but because they *trust* you've been forged in the same fire that forged them. No more masks. No more noise. No more delay.

Chapter 16 DEV — Decision-to-Execution Velocity

We had the momentum. Weeks of prep. Data aligned. Teams energized. A dozen small wins stacking toward the big one.

And then—**the meeting.** What should've been a greenlight turned into a slow, quiet death. Someone said, "Let's get a few more voices on this." Another, "Let's make sure Legal's in the loop." And then the nail: *"Let's circle back next week with a refined rollout."*

Next week never came. The whiteboard got wiped. The energy left the room before the people did. And just like that, what was once a surge of clarity became… nothing.

No explosion. No meltdown. Just emotional decay. I watched my best people—the builders, the believers—walk out in silence. No fire. No fight. Just that look. The one that says: *"You told us this mattered. We believed you. And now you're asking us to wait?"*

By the end of the month, two had transferred. One quit. The rest quietly stopped offering their best ideas. Not out of rebellion. Out of *resignation*.

Because nothing erodes trust faster than a leader who hesitates after declaring certainty. The Theater of Delay is real and it has a heavy price. That's the truth no one puts on the post-mortem. You don't lose the mission when you make the wrong decision. You lose it when you make *no* decision—when clarity isn't backed by motion. That's the moment I learned the rule: **If it doesn't move within 72 hours, it was never a real decision. It was theater.**

And the audience? They don't clap. They just stop showing up. That wasn't a failure of talent. It wasn't a strategy flaw. It was a **leadership stall**—a moment when we knew what to do but couldn't get ourselves to *move*. And that's what broke the team—not the decision, but the indecision *after* the clarity.

Because when action dies, **belief dies with it**. Not with a bang, but with silence. This is the slow erosion most leaders don't notice until it's too late. It's not the firestorms that wreck your mission. It's the fog. The delays. The deferrals. The stall-outs that become culture.

Leadership, in most modern organizations, has become a slow-motion performance. Decisions are made—then remade. Ideas are explored—then deferred. Ownership is "shared" until no one really owns anything. And through it all, meetings multiply. Slide decks expand. Postmortems get longer. And teams get stuck—**not because they're incapable, but because nothing ever truly moves.**

In a world that romanticizes clarity but fears commitment, **speed has become the most honest metric of leadership effectiveness**. This chapter introduces a metric few leaders track and even fewer know how to master: **Decision-to-Execution Velocity**, or DEV. Because in every high-functioning culture, **speed is truth.**

When Motion Dies, So Does Morale

Organizational failure rarely announces itself. It doesn't knock down the front door with a scandal or a budget collapse. **It seeps in—through the cracks of indecision, misalignment, and emotional fatigue.** And it begins with something deceptively small: **Loss of movement.**

When teams stop seeing decisions lead to momentum, they stop believing decisions matter. And when that belief erodes, so does leadership energy, execution drive, and eventually—*trust.* Let's unpack the specific dynamics that slowly destroy execution velocity and morale:

1. Endless Alignment Loops

Alignment is critical—until it becomes a substitute for action. The team keeps revisiting decisions:

- Not because anything has changed,
- But because *someone might still feel unsure,*
- Or because leadership is unwilling to move forward without universal comfort.

The result?

- Motion stalls.
- Meetings become rituals of indecision.
- Energy is spent *re-validating* clarity instead of *executing* against it.

This creates **cognitive fatigue** and **emotional erosion**—because people feel like they're endlessly circling the runway, never cleared for takeoff.

2. Passive-Aggressive Stakeholder Feedback

Here's how this plays out:

- A decision is made.
- Execution begins.
- A stakeholder, not present for the decision, expresses "concerns" through quiet channels or ambiguous signals.

No direct disagreement. Just… discomfort.

- "Did we think about…?"
- "Should we revisit…?"
- "I just heard someone was confused…"

Now the team's forward motion gets interrupted *not by accountability—but by optics.* Suddenly, work pauses—not to solve real problems, but to **appease political feedback** masked as input. This passive resistance introduces confusion, and more dangerously, *normalizes backtracking as culture.*

3. Waiting on Buy-In from Teams Who've Checked Out

Buy-in is vital. But what happens when you're asking for it from teams who **no longer believe motion matters?** This creates a recursive trap:

- Leaders delay action, waiting for emotional alignment from teams.
- Those teams, demoralized by past friction and broken promises, offer no real engagement.
- Leaders interpret the silence as lack of readiness—and delay further.

The organization becomes a stalled engine waiting for belief to arrive—while belief is waiting for motion to return.

It's a death spiral. And once you're in it, **trust no longer leads. Fear does.**

4. Leaders Punting Decisions Out of Fear
Decision-making becomes a **game of hot potato.**

- Nobody wants to own the wrong call.
- So, everyone waits for more input.
- Or escalates decisions upward.
- Or "delegates" them sideways.

And the longer a decision is delayed, the heavier it becomes. More eyes are on it. More complexity is imagined. More fear enters the room. Eventually, decisions become **emotional liabilities**—not leadership actions. And the team starts asking: "If they won't lead through this, why should we?"

5. Managers Confusing Empowerment with Consensus
The fear of being "too top-down" causes many mid-level leaders to believe **everyone must agree before movement happens.** So, before anything is executed:

- Everyone's input must be collected.
- Everyone's feelings must be processed.
- Every voice must be heard *at the same volume.*

And while that sounds inclusive, it's actually **a denial of leadership responsibility.** Because when empowerment is framed as *permission from the group*—**nothing moves.** People aren't leading. They're **co-managing hesitation.**

The Psychological Fallout: Internalizing Futility

As these patterns accumulate, something far more dangerous begins to form:
A corrosive internal narrative: *"Nothing I do actually moves this forward."* And once a team starts believing this?

- Initiative dies.
- Creativity shrinks.
- Courage disappears.
- Leaders become passive protectors of their calendar—not catalysts for change.
  The game is no longer *to advance the mission.* It becomes *how to survive the system.*

People stop trying to *lead.* They start trying to *navigate.* They don't ask *what's right.* They ask *what's safest.*

And this is the real tragedy: **The best people still care. But they no longer believe it matters.**

Final Conceptual Insight

Execution velocity isn't a luxury—it's a leadership responsibility. Because when motion dies, morale isn't far behind. Not because people are weak. But because people are smart—and they can sense when progress is no longer possible without politics. This is the battlefield most leaders miss: It's not the war of big decisions—it's the *quiet attrition of stalled ones.*

DEV: Measuring What Actually Moves

So, what is DEV? **Decision-to-Execution Velocity** is the time elapsed between a decision being made and *real, observable motion* beginning in alignment with that decision. It's not about long-term outcomes. It's about *immediate directional force.* You can measure it by asking:

- When was the decision made?
- Who owns the execution?
- What moved within 72 hours of that decision?
- Was that motion aligned, visible, and consequential?

DEV is not measured in updates. It's measured in **acceleration.** It tells you not only *what* is moving, but how **frictionless your culture is in converting clarity into coordinated action.** DEV exposes three things:

1. **Decision integrity** – Were we clear about what we're doing, why it matters, and who owns it?
2. **Execution readiness** – Does the team know how to move, what success looks like, and what guardrails exist?
3. **Leadership alignment** – Is there permission to act—or are people stalling, waiting to see how political winds blow?

If any of those three are missing, velocity dies.

The 72-Hour Rule: Clarity Without Motion Is Fiction

Here's the rule I teach: **If you can't show meaningful motion within 72 hours of a decision, the decision was never real.** It was a performance. It was a discussion with theater lighting. It was a page in a strategy deck that looked good during the offsite but never left the building.

And the moment your team starts seeing these decisions pile up without motion, they stop believing in your leadership altogether. Why 72 hours? Because three days is enough time to:

- Assign real ownership.
- Schedule the first milestone.
- Create a visible signal that execution has begun.
- Eliminate ambiguity about who's moving and how.

You don't need to finish the project in three days. But if nothing *moves* in three days? **Your clarity wasn't clarity. It was narrative.**

Leadership by Motion, Not Memory

Most leadership reviews are built on memory. Who was in the room. What we talked about. How the conversation felt. Whether the update sounded promising. Whether the leader "showed up."

But none of that moves the mission. Real leadership must be tracked by **how fast clarity turns into kinetic energy.** If you're not measuring that, you're measuring influence theater—not impact. If you're leadership coach is focused on anything else as the key, find a new coach. Here's what DEV reveals:

- Who brings clarity and moves teams.
- Who spins complexity and drags velocity.
- Where alignment is real—and where it's fake.
- Which decisions land—and which ones die in the hallway.

DEV doesn't care about feelings. It reveals **leadership truth through the speed of coordinated action.**

Velocity Dashboards: Operationalizing Speed as a Signal

To lead through DEV, you need a **dashboard that tracks momentum—not activity.** Here's what that looks like:

- **Time to decision confirmation** – How long does it take to go from discussion to "we're doing this"?
- **Time to ownership** – How long until someone is named as the decision's execution owner?
- **Time to first motion** – How long until the first task, milestone, kickoff, or deliverable begins?
- **Execution delta** – How aligned was the actual motion with the original decision intent?
- **Friction sources** – Where are decisions stalling and why? (People? Tools? Politics?)

Most dashboards show you throughput. This one shows you *friction.* DEV dashboards aren't about shame. They're about **velocity coaching.** They let you see:

- Which leaders create flow.
- Which teams absorb direction.
- Which systems empower speed—or choke it.

Without that visibility, you're leading through **vibes and wishful thinking.**

Why Leaders Kill DEV Without Knowing It

When momentum dies in an organization, it's rarely because someone wanted it to. It's not sabotage. It's not laziness. It's not a lack of vision.

Most DEV failure is emotional, not operational. It happens when leaders—especially good, well-intentioned ones—begin **choosing comfort over clarity**, and *approval over action.* And they don't realize what they're doing, because it *feels like leadership.* It feels inclusive. Thoughtful. Diplomatic.

But the effect? **Paralysis. Friction. Drift.** Here's how this invisible breakdown happens—one small fear at a time.

Delaying Final Decisions "To Gather More Voices"

On the surface, this looks noble. The leader says, *"Let's just get a few more perspectives before we finalize this."* But under the surface?

- The room has already aligned.
- The variables are clear.
- The decision is ready.

What's actually happening is *stalling*—because the leader doesn't want to bear the emotional weight of **being the one who closes the loop.** Inclusion becomes a shield. Clarity becomes a threat. And while the leader feels safe, the team enters limbo—still meeting, still analyzing, *but not moving.*

Keeping Projects in "Strategic Phase" to Avoid Accountability

Strategy is important. But at some point, **strategy becomes shelter.** Leaders may keep teams in ideation mode:

- To avoid naming risk.

- To delay owning outcomes.
- To sidestep the moment where execution reveals whether their vision *actually works.*

What looks like planning is really **procrastination with a PowerPoint. Clarity without commitment is a comfort zone.** And the longer you linger there, the harder it becomes to re-engage the energy needed to execute.

Adding Stakeholders to Avoid Confrontation

This is a classic political tactic disguised as collaboration. You've seen it before: A leader, afraid to say no to a powerful peer or challenging voice, **invites more people into the decision.** Not to get better input—but to spread responsibility. The logic is: *"If more people are involved, I won't be blamed for the decision."* But what actually happens is:

- Alignment fractures.
- Speed disappears.
- The decision becomes *nobody's to own.*
- ***Fear owns the room.***

This is fear, wrapped in the language of inclusion. And it's **organizational cowardice in a meeting invite.**

Revisiting the Same Issue Three Times

The meeting ends in alignment. The team starts to move. Then—suddenly—the topic is back on the table. Why? Because someone important wasn't happy. Or someone with a strong personality pushed back. Or the leader simply didn't want to deal with conflict. **This is how fear masquerades as thoughtfulness.** But every time you reopen a closed conversation without new information, **you train your team that nothing is ever final—and momentum is always reversible.** This is how trust dies: **Not through betrayal, but through the quiet erosion of decision integrity.**

Saying "We're Almost There" When No One Has Moved in Two Weeks

This is the soft lie leaders tell when they don't want to confront stagnation.

- The decks haven't changed.
- The work hasn't progressed.
- The blockers haven't been cleared.

But instead of naming the stall, they say: *"We're close." "Just a little more alignment." "Let's keep refining."* It sounds optimistic. But it's just another way to avoid the hard conversation about *what's really broken*. The work isn't "almost done." It's **stuck**—and everyone knows it.

The Hidden Driver: Fear in Disguise

All of these behaviors—every single one—have one thing in common: **They are fear, dressed as leadership.**

- Fear of being wrong.
- Fear of being disliked.
- Fear of backlash.
- Fear of responsibility.

But in avoiding discomfort, leaders stall progress. And worse—they rob their teams of momentum, clarity, and confidence. While leaders delay to feel safe, **their teams are burning energy, spinning in silence, and losing trust.**

DEV Demands Courage, Not Comfort

You cannot **lead with courage and delay at the same time**. You must choose. DEV—Decision-to-Execution Velocity—is not about rushing. It's about **leading decisively** through the emotional terrain of risk, responsibility, and reaction. When leaders choose comfort, motion dies. And when motion dies, morale follows. This is how organizations die—not with a bang, but with a slow, silent retreat from courage.

The Emotional Economics of Speed

Speed is not just a logistical advantage. It's not merely how quickly your teams move from decision to execution. **Speed is emotional currency.** When a team sees ideas turn into action—**quickly and visibly**—they experience more than momentum. They experience **meaning.** Why? Because *motion affirms belief.* It tells people:

- *"You're not wasting your energy here."*
- *"This place still works."*
- *"We may not be perfect—but we're moving."*

It's a psychological contract being fulfilled in real-time. And that's rare. Especially in systems where people have lived through **endless loops of false starts, broken promises, or chronic indecision.**

Why Fast Motion Builds Morale

When things move quickly:

- Morale rises.
- Energy compounds.
- Contribution feels *connected to consequence.*

Teams begin to believe their work has **impact**, and that belief is *far more valuable than any motivational keynote or cultural slogan.* **People don't burn out from hard work. They burn out from motionless systems.**

When decisions happen and results follow, the team internalizes a powerful message: *"What I do here matters."* That's more than morale—that's **emotional investment.** And emotional investment is the precursor to *sustained performance and cultural resilience.*

Why Slow-Motion Kills Belief

Most leaders assume that slowing down buys safety. But in reality, **slowness is often misread as indifference**.

- Delayed decisions signal uncertainty.
- Reopened conversations signal instability.
- Unfinished projects signal disorganization.

And for your team? It begins to feel like futility. They don't disengage because they're lazy. They disengage because **they no longer believe that anything they do will lead to change.** It's not that they've given up on the work. They've given up on *the system delivering what it promises.* *"Why care, if nothing moves?"* *"Why lead, if nothing sticks?"* *"Why try, if everything is always revisited?"*

These questions slowly dissolve ownership, initiative, and creative drive—*without a single resignation letter being submitted*

Momentum Restores Belief

And here's the irony: Most leaders try to restore belief through *words*. Through *vision decks*. Through *re-engagement campaigns*. But what your team really needs is not more inspiration. **They need to see something actually move.**

Even a small decision, followed by fast action, can reset months of emotional erosion.

- That project that's been stalled for three months? Ship it.
- That process everyone hates? Kill it.
- That initiative everyone said couldn't be fixed? Move on it—*today.*

When a team sees even one thing change *without delay,* something shifts in their minds: *"Maybe this place still works." "Maybe it's not too late to care." "Maybe I want to help again."* That's what speed does. Not just for deliverables—but for **trust.**

Belief Is What Retains Your Best People

Your top talent? They don't stay for safety. They stay for **momentum.** They stay because:

- Things are moving.
- The system still responds to leadership.
- Their decisions have consequences.
- Progress isn't an idea—it's *visible.*

They don't need you to have perfect strategies. They don't expect a frictionless path. They just need to see that **decisions matter and things move.** If you can deliver *that*, you'll earn more loyalty than any perks package, engagement campaign, or inspirational speech. You'll have a team that *believes again*—not because you promised something…

…but because they saw **you** *move.*

Final Reflection: If It Doesn't Move, It Doesn't Matter

You can have the best team, the clearest strategy, the most aligned values. But if nothing moves? You're not leading. You're narrating.

Decision-to-Execution Velocity is the pulse check of your leadership culture. It tells you who's leading, who's hiding, and who's pretending. So, ask yourself—now, right now:

- What's the most important decision we made this week?
- Who owns it?
- What moved in the last 72 hours?
- What friction still exists?
- And why is it still allowed?

Leadership is not about speaking well. It's about moving people toward a shared goal with urgency, clarity, and aligned action. No movement? No leadership. You've built motion. Now we build durability. Let's go.

Field Manual: Velocity as Truth

In the battlefield of organizational leadership, **speed is not a luxury**—it's a signal. It tells your team what matters. It reveals what's real. And it exposes what's been rotting behind all the polished presentations. This is your operational blueprint for enforcing **Decision-to-Execution Velocity (DEV)**—and killing the culture of stalling.

THE 72-HOUR RULE

DEV Principle: If nothing moves within 72 hours of a decision, it was a *performance*, not a pivot.

Field Actions:

- Every decision must generate a visible, irreversible action within 72 hours.
- Log the "first movement" next to every major decision (e.g., launched comms, updated KPI, task assigned with date).
- No "strategic hold" lasts more than 3 business days without a new, named owner.

Clarity without action is cowardice in a cape.

THE DEV DASHBOARD (Use Weekly)

Measure these five execution vital signs:

Metric	Question	Score Range
Time-to-First Motion	How fast did action follow clarity?	<24 hrs. = elite
Execution Delta	Gap between decision and what was actually done?	0–100%
Friction Source	Where is the drag (People / Politics / Clarity)?	Name it
Ownership Clarity	Who owns this execution and who's watching?	Clear / Fuzzy / Missing
Emotional Energy	Did speed increase or drain team belief?	Charge / Neutral / Drain

Review weekly. Red flags? Dig. *If you're not measuring motion, you're just watching theater in a suit.*

VELOCITY MINDSET SHIFTS

- **Done > Perfect** – You can refine in motion. But you can't correct what doesn't exist.
- **Speed = Safety** – Fast action builds emotional safety. Slow kills trust.
- **Visible Beats Verbal** – If they can't *see* it, it didn't happen.

Ask every team this, weekly:

"What moved this week—and how fast did we move it?"

If the answer takes more than 15 seconds, they're stalling.

LEADER BEHAVIORAL COMMANDS

Make these non-negotiable in your culture:

1. **Name the Next Visible Action** in every meeting.
2. **Assign a Single Owner** — no "collaborative execution."
3. **Set a Micro-Deadline** — not Q3, not "soon." Try: *"by Thursday at 3pm."*
4. **Enforce Post-Decision Silence** — once a call is made, the debate ends. Movement begins.

5. **Audit the Inaction** — if a call died, ask: "Was it fear, ego, or distraction?"
Stop tolerating intellectual theater disguised as strategic patience.

FINAL DIRECTIVE: MOVE OR BLEED

You will not be judged by the *brilliance* of your decisions. You will be judged by how fast your team moved when the moment was clear. Because in elite cultures: **Speed is truth. Friction is feedback. Stalling is sabotage.**

You don't need another decision-making model. **<u>You need movement.</u>**

Chapter 17 Conflict Without Collapse

We thought we were healthy. Meetings ran smooth. Everyone smiled. No one raised their voice. We called it "alignment."

Behind closed doors, though—different story. Deadlines slipped. Frustrations built. Side conversations multiplied like rats in the walls. One team lead pulled me aside and said, *"We're fine. It's just growing pains."* No one wanted to be the one to "rock the boat."

So, we didn't. We nodded in meetings we didn't believe in. We agreed to timelines we knew were lies. We watched underperformance get rationalized with words like *"grace,"* and *"let's be understanding."*

And then it broke. One Thursday morning, a mid-level manager snapped. The mask fell off. The dam cracked. She stood up in front of 12 people and said, "I'm done pretending this is working. We're behind, nobody says the truth, and the only thing consistent on this team is the silence." Nobody moved.

She had the courage to say what the rest of us had been swallowing for six months. But it was too late. People were already checked out. Resentments had calcified. Trust had rotted quietly—while we all kept smiling. That's when I realized: **The fire didn't destroy us. The delay did.**

We weren't avoiding conflict. We were avoiding reality. And reality doesn't care how "nice" your culture sounds when your house is burning from the inside. That moment didn't come out of nowhere. It came from every unsaid thing we buried under "team unity." Every truth softened into suggestion. Every frustrated glance that never made it into words.

We thought we were avoiding drama. But what we were really avoiding—was *honesty*. And when you avoid truth long enough, it doesn't disappear. It just comes back louder, meaner, and more destructive, just like our archetypes. Most organizations don't fall apart because of conflict. They fall apart because conflict was **never allowed to breathe**.

Because someone had a concern and stayed silent. Because a toxic pattern was named too late. Because the pressure built up behind polite language until it cracked into politics, triangulation, and hidden resentments. When conflict becomes a dirty word, cultures become emotionally dishonest.

People start performing. They manage impressions. They smile in the meeting and seethe in the hallway. They say "we're aligned" when what they really mean is, *"I'm afraid of what happens if I tell the truth."*

Conflict is not the enemy. **Avoided conflict is.**

The Myth of the Calm Culture

In many organizations, leaders believe they're leading a "healthy" team because things feel calm. No raised voices. No visible tension. No emotional explosions.

But calm is not always clarity. And quiet is not always health. **There's a difference between calm and numb.**

A team that avoids conflict doesn't prove emotional maturity—it often reveals **emotional suppression.** This kind of team isn't high-functioning. It's *highly conditioned* to stay inoffensive, careful, and deferential—**not because they trust each other, but because they've learned that truth is costly.**

When Avoiding Conflict Becomes Cultural Default

This internal shutdown doesn't happen all at once. It happens subtly—when people realize that naming friction, surfacing concerns, or challenging leadership invites more discomfort than it resolves. Here's how you'll know it's taking root:

- **Projects go sideways—but no one speaks up until it's too late.**
  Not because they didn't see the problems coming, but because **psychological safety was absent** when it mattered most.
- **Leaders mistake politeness for partnership.**
  Everyone nods in meetings. Everyone agrees. But *true alignment* is absent.
  Behind the scenes, doubt festers, execution falters, and trust erodes—not in big moments, but in **a thousand polite silences.**
- **Your highest performers quietly disengage.**
  Not because of burnout from work, but from **under-truth**—from spending too much energy **navigating politics instead of driving progress.**
- **Feedback loops grow longer, softer, and less useful.**
  What used to be direct becomes diluted.
  What used to be honest becomes euphemized.
  Everyone's playing the game of "safe communication," and the truth? It gets lost in translation.
- **The people most committed to the mission feel emotionally exhausted.**
  Because they can't push for what matters without walking on eggshells.
  They care deeply—but that care becomes *unsustainable* in a culture that punishes friction more than it rewards courage.

The Real Cost: Speed, Trust, and Execution

In emotionally muted cultures, three things quietly degrade:

1. Speed Dies

When truth is dangerous, decisions slow down. People wait for more signals. They hedge their language. They delay action. Not because they lack clarity, but because they lack *permission to act boldly.*

2. Trust Erodes

The irony? In the effort to "keep the peace," you **undermine psychological safety.** Because everyone knows what's not being said. And over time, people begin to distrust not just each other—but the *system itself.* "If I can't speak the truth without political consequence, then this is not a team. It's a stage."

3. Execution Fragments

Without honest friction, execution doesn't sharpen—it **scatters.** Teams start working in emotional silos. Cross-functional collaboration suffers. People choose comfort zones over ownership—and the result is **activity without impact.**

Why This Happens: The Cultural Addiction to Harmony

Most organizations don't collapse from conflict—they collapse from **the inability to handle it.** Because they've built a system where:

- Disagreement is coded as disloyalty.
- Directness is softened until it's meaningless.
- Accountability is filtered through layers of performative empathy.

And what begins as "kindness" becomes **cultural fragility.** The mission becomes **fragile to feedback.** The team becomes **fragile to tension.** The leadership becomes **fragile to challenge.** And in fragile cultures, one sharp truth can collapse the entire system.

Conflict Isn't the Threat—Suppression Is

The goal is not to eliminate conflict. **The goal is to build a culture that can *hold it.*** Conflict, when managed with clarity and care, is not corrosive—it's **constructive.** It's how real trust is built. It's how ideas sharpen. It's how good teams become *great ones.*

But when leaders equate peace with health, and silence with loyalty, they unknowingly create an organization where no one speaks **until it's too late.**

And that silence is far more dangerous than any argument could ever be.

Conflict Is the Crucible of Clarity

In fragile organizations, conflict is feared. In mature organizations, conflict is **functional.** It's not just tolerated—it's *leveraged.* Too often, leaders confuse calm for alignment and agreement for health. But the real strength of a team isn't shown in how well they avoid conflict—it's shown in *how well they move through it.* And the more they grow, the more critical that skill becomes.

Conflict, when done right, is how cultures evolve. It's not a crack in the foundation. It's a fire that forges strength and reveals what's real.

Conflict Tests Trust—It Doesn't Destroy It

Trust doesn't mean agreement. Trust means *truth without punishment.* So, when conflict surfaces—whether in direction, execution, or team dynamics—it doesn't mean trust is breaking. It means **trust is being tested** in the only way that matters: by whether the team can hold discomfort without breaking relationship.

Real trust is proven not in peace—but in pressure. If your culture can't hold tension without collapse, then what you have isn't trust. Its **emotional codependence disguised as collaboration.**

Conflict Sharpens Values, Not Dulls Them

Values aren't proven in hiring brochures or vision decks. They're proven when two people disagree—and choose to confront each other with clarity, dignity, and mutual accountability. In those moments:

- **Is honesty still safe?**
- **Is disagreement still productive?**
- **Do we protect the person without protecting the pattern?**

If so, then your values are *real*. If not, then your values are just stage props—and conflict will expose that, fast. Because values that can't survive disagreement aren't values—they're *vibes*.

Conflict Surfaces Misalignment Early

One of the most dangerous organizational trends is the quiet slide into **performance theatre**—when everyone smiles in meetings but leaves misaligned, misinformed, or misunderstood. Constructive conflict stops that before it metastasizes.

- It **reveals faulty assumptions** that would've wrecked execution later.
- It **flushes out hidden resistance** while there's still time to engage it.
- It **prevents passive disengagement** by making active participation *necessary*.

Conflict says: "*Let's disagree now, so we don't break later.*"

Conflict Shows Whether You're Fighting for Progress or Peace

Teams that avoid conflict aren't calm—they're **co-managed by fear.**

- Fear of discomfort.
- Fear of disapproval.
- Fear of power dynamics.

So instead of confronting issues, they perform "alignment." They keep the peace, not because peace serves the mission, but because it *feels safer than telling the truth*. But here's the thing: **You don't scale harmony. You scale truth.** And **truth only lives where tension can be named—without triggering collapse.**

The Real Skill: Naming Tension Without Breaking the System

This is where true leadership shows up. It's not in delivering the perfect strategy. It's not in crafting the most eloquent mission statement. It's in the *moment you say what no one else will—without burning the room down*.

Because truth doesn't kill culture. **Silence does.** When teams are trained to:

- Name tension early,
- Challenge ideas without challenging identity,
- And hold the line without holding grudges,

You create a space where **conflict becomes a crucible**—not a crisis.

Conflict Isn't the End—It's the Opening

Every conflict is a portal. Into deeper alignment. Into truer values. Into clearer roles. Into more honest leadership. But only if you're willing to *enter the fire instead of performing around it*. So, remember: **No culture scales without truth. And no truth survives without the ability to name tension, in real time, without emotional collapse.** Conflict isn't the enemy of your mission. Avoiding it is.

Constructive Conflict vs. Chaos: Know the Difference

Conflict itself is not the threat to your culture. In fact, it's essential. The real danger isn't conflict—it's **unregulated, unchanneled, and misread conflict.**

What breaks teams apart isn't disagreement. It's the failure to **differentiate between heat that sharpens** and heat that **scorches.** Between productive friction that brings alignment, and political chaos that fractures trust. That's why every high-functioning organization must teach its leaders and teams how to **tell the difference.**

Unregulated Conflict is Chaos in Disguise

Conflict becomes toxic when there are **no shared rules of engagement.** When emotion overrides ownership. When friction is allowed to fester underground instead of being brought to the surface with structure. You'll recognize *chaos conflict* when it shows up like this:

- **Blame loops** – People pass responsibility like a hot potato, focused on fault rather than forward motion.
- **Gossip-laced triangulation** – Feedback doesn't go to the person—it goes *around* them. Side conversations become a substitute for direct dialogue.
- **Escalated emotion without ownership** – Frustration builds, but no one takes action. People vent, but avoid stepping into resolution.
- **Constant rehashing of unresolved issues** – The same debate, relived across meetings, without new data or direction. What should be a post-mortem becomes a recurring trauma.
- **"Us vs. them" narratives** – Functions begin blaming other departments for friction. Silos strengthen. Trust weakens.

Chaos is not loud—it's *disorganized.* It's *reactive.* And it often masquerades as passion, when in fact it's *political fog.* And most dangerously? **It burns down culture without setting off alarms.**

Constructive Conflict is Focused, Honest, and Forward-Driving

On the other side is **constructive conflict**—the kind of tension that doesn't weaken culture, but *refines it.* In high-trust environments, teams are trained not to avoid conflict, but to **channel it.** They understand that pressure is part of performance. But it has to be pressure **with purpose.** Here's what *constructive conflict* looks like in practice:

- **Direct, respectful disagreement in the open** – No triangulation. No backroom brokering. Just clear challenges, shared transparently.
- **Disputes focused on ideas, not identity** – Nobody gets personally attacked. Feedback stays tethered to *what's being done,* not *who's doing it.*
- **Tension met with grounded presence, not posturing** – Emotion is acknowledged, but not weaponized. Teams don't "win" arguments—they seek *resolution and clarity.*
- **Feedback that includes next steps, not just frustration** – The conversation doesn't end with criticism. It ends with a *clear action or decision.*
- **Decisions made because disagreement surfaced early** – Conflict is invited *at the start,* not discovered *at the end.* This avoids breakdowns disguised as "last-minute concerns."

In environments like this, conflict doesn't slow execution—it *sharpens it.* Teams align faster, not because they avoid tension, but because they're **skilled at holding it.**

Why Leaders Must Train for This Distinction

When you don't teach your team how to discern between *constructive tension* and *chaotic dissent,* you leave your culture vulnerable to both **emotional suppression** and **emotional explosion.**

- Suppression looks like calm—until someone burns out or walks away without warning.
- Explosion looks like urgency—until you realize you've been reacting to politics, not strategy.

Both kill momentum. Both erode morale. Both fracture trust. But when conflict is channeled with clarity, **it creates alignment through heat—not illusion through performance.**

Conflict is Inevitable—How You Hold It Is the Choice

If you're building anything meaningful, conflict will come.

- Misalignment will surface.
- Frustration will rise.
- Strong opinions will collide.

And that's good. Because the goal isn't peace. It's *truth.* The goal isn't to avoid discomfort. It's *to build capacity to hold it without collapse.* That's what makes conflict a crucible—not a crisis. So, ask yourself:

- Are we building a team that fears disagreement?
- Or a team that knows how to fight *forward*—without burning down what we've built?

Because cultures don't die from tension. They die from being **untrained in how to hold it.**

Immunizing Your Culture Against Blame and Manipulation

Conflict doesn't always start with disagreement. Sometimes, it starts with *threat.* A perceived threat to identity, safety, belonging, credibility, or control.

And when an organization has not been structurally or emotionally prepared to **process and metabolize that fear**, it doesn't resolve—it **infects**.

- It infects strategy with emotional derailment.
- It infects trust with victimhood narratives.
- It infects communication with psychological triangulation disguised as concern.

What begins as one unresolved moment of tension **spreads like a virus**—mutating into gossip, passivity, and resistance. Not because people are bad—but because the system gave them no better pathway.

To prevent this, you don't need tighter control. You need **more maturity**—*baked into the system itself.* Here's how you build it.

1. Codify Conflict Early: Normalize Disagreement at the Source

The first and most foundational practice is to **name conflict before it shows up.**

If conflict is treated as a rare crisis, people will respond to it with fear or avoidance.

But if it's treated as a normal, expected part of collaboration, it becomes *less dramatic and more useful.* From the beginning—during onboarding, team charters, project kickoffs—say it out loud: **"On this team, disagreement is not disloyalty."** "If you're not challenging ideas, you're not contributing fully." "If something feels wrong and you say nothing, that's not professionalism—it's neglect." This isn't just about communication—it's about *creating a covenant of courage.*

- Put it in your onboarding decks.
- Practice it in retrospectives.

- Model it in leadership meetings.

Because **cultures are not defined by their values—they're defined by what is *rehearsed*.**

If your team never hears the permission to disagree, they'll eventually assume **you don't really want it.**

2. Tension Protocols > Emotional Escalation

When someone feels emotionally unsafe, they'll escalate in one of two ways:

1. *Silently disengage.*
2. *Loudly redirect the room toward their pain.*

Neither serves the mission. So, when emotional tension surfaces, you need **grounded structure—not emotional suppression, and not emotional chaos.**

Instead of:
- "Let's not go there."
- Or: "Tell us how you're feeling."

Ask:
- **"What's the specific behavior or pattern you're concerned about?"**
- **"How does this connect to the mission or performance expectations?"**
- **"Have you named this directly to the person involved?"**

This is not coldness. This is *emotional scaffolding*—the kind that supports safety *and* standards. It affirms that feelings are valid—but that *only those tethered to ownership and clarity can influence direction.* Without protocols, your team won't know the difference between:

- *Processing* and *performing.*
- *Sharing* and *stalling.*
- *Emotion* and *manipulation.*

Structure allows for humanity *without hijacking the mission.*

3. No Complaint Without Contribution

Blame culture thrives when pain is permitted to circulate without action. People start venting because it feels like the only path to validation. Feedback loops collapse into emotional spirals. And high performers begin to check out—not because they don't care, but because they're tired of swimming in fog. The remedy? **A single standard:** "No one complains without bringing a proposed path forward." This does three things:

1. It **forces emotional tension into constructive dialogue.**
2. It **reclaims agency.** The person becomes a *co-designer of the solution*, not just a narrator of the problem.
3. It **disarms chronic victimhood** by putting responsibility back in the room—where it belongs.

Because if you're not willing to contribute, *you're not ready to critique.*

This stops the team from turning into a therapy circle—and keeps it focused on *performance, progress, and partnership.*

Fear Doesn't Break Cultures—Unprocessed Fear Does

Every team will face emotional moments.
- Fear of change.
- Disappointment in leadership.
- Tension between functions.

- Breakdown in trust.

But the danger isn't the emotion itself. The danger is when **your system isn't built to hold it, metabolize it, and move through it.** When that happens, people seek:

- Sympathy over strategy.
- Control through confusion.
- Power through emotional escalation.

And unless you've built **a cultural immune system**, the whole organism gets sick—*not from malice, but from unprocessed pain.*

Codify conflict. Structure tension. Convert complaints into contribution. That's not just how you manage conflict. That's how you **build a culture immune to collapse.**

Psychological Safety ≠ Conflict Avoidance

In today's leadership circles, "psychological safety" has become one of the most cited, praised, and misunderstood concepts. At its best, it's meant to describe a culture where people feel safe enough to speak truth, take risks, own mistakes, and challenge power without fear of retaliation. But somewhere along the way, we **confused safety with softness.**

Now, in too many organizations, psychological safety has been misinterpreted as **emotional protection**—a buffer against discomfort, disagreement, and pressure. And that misunderstanding is not just misguided—it's *dangerous.*

What Psychological Safety Actually Means

True psychological safety is not about comfort. It's about **courage without penalty.** In a psychologically safe culture:

- I can say, *"This process is broken"* without being branded a troublemaker.
- I can challenge a leader's thinking without losing proximity or future opportunity.
- I can express emotion without that emotion being used as a character indictment.
- I can make a mistake—and the consequence is growth, not exile.

This is not indulgence. This is not the absence of standards. **This is the presence of trust that survives truth.**

What Psychological Safety Does *Not* Mean

Here's where too many teams get it wrong. Psychological safety does **not** mean:

- I'm shielded from confrontation.
- I never feel the heat of accountability.
- I get to opt out of feedback or hard conversations because I "feel unseen."

That's not psychological safety. That's **emotional fragility dressed as empathy.** When people use "safety" to avoid performance conversations, leadership tension, or strategic disagreement, they're not protecting the culture—they're *delaying its maturity.* And in the process, the team learns a dangerous message: *"Truth hurts the system."*

What Real Safety Requires

If you want to build *real* psychological safety, it starts with equipping your people to:

1. **Tell the truth without panic**

   That means disagreement isn't seen as disloyalty. Heat doesn't trigger crisis. Truth isn't delayed until it's "emotionally safe enough" to say.

2. **Receive feedback without collapse**
   This requires ego work. It requires trust in leadership. And it requires *practice*—because untrained teams collapse under pressure, not because they're weak, but because they've never been taught how to hold it.
3. **Repair conflict without weaponizing it**
   Safety isn't the absence of rupture. It's the ability to *repair rupture without turning it into performance, politics, or personal vendetta.*

These skills are not natural. They are **trained. Modeled. Rehearsed.** And only when they're embedded into the system can safety **coexist with performance**.

Safety Is a System, not a Feeling

Psychological safety isn't something you *feel*—it's something you *experience through repetition.* Through truth-telling without punishment. Through challenge without exclusion. Through ownership without collapse.

If no one speaks up, you don't have safety. If feedback is sugarcoated, you don't have safety. If conflict destroys trust instead of deepening it, you don't have safety. You have **politeness. Fragility. Avoidance.**

And those aren't virtues. They're warning signs. So, ask your team:
- Can people bring heat without being labeled difficult?
- Can someone fail without being frozen out?
- Can we disagree without dissolving?

Because safety isn't the removal of risk. It's the *resilience to hold risk—and still move forward together.*

What You, the Leader, Must Master

When conflict enters the room, people don't look to a handbook or an HR policy. They look to *you.* They track your breathing. They notice your tone. They read your face before they hear your words. They absorb your nervous system like an emotional Wi-Fi signal.

This is not metaphor. It's **mirror neuron science and group psychology.** Leaders set the emotional tone, not just with what they say—but with **how they regulate themselves in the presence of pressure.** If you can't hold the heat, they'll scatter. If you can, they'll stabilize—even in the storm.

Your Presence Becomes the Cultural Signal

In moments of rising tension—during disagreement, escalation, or emotional exposure—your team is subconsciously asking:
- *"Are we okay?"*
- *"Is this safe?"*
- *"Is this going to implode?"*

And they don't answer that by analyzing your words. They answer it by watching your *face, voice, pace, and posture.* That's why **your ability to self-regulate under stress becomes the most powerful leadership tool you own.** Not your strategy. Not your charisma. Not your facilitation skill. <u>**Your presence is the real intervention.**</u>

How to Lead Through the Fire

Here's what it means to be a calm container—not a reactive mirror—when conflict hits:

- **Breathe before you speak.**
  A single breath breaks the loop of reaction. It tells your body *you're not under threat.* That breath becomes *permission* for others to pause, too.
- **Don't match energy—regulate it.**
  If someone escalates, you don't meet them there. You *ground* them. Not by overpowering, but by modeling coherence.
- **Separate facts from feelings—in real time.**
  "This project was delayed" is a fact. "This always happens because no one cares" is an emotion. You must be the filter that parses both with clarity and compassion.
- **Ask grounded questions instead of defending.**
  Curiosity de-escalates. Defense inflames. Ask: "Can you help me understand what's behind that concern?" "What impact are you seeing that I might have missed?"
- **Name the pattern, not the person.**
  Targeting individuals invites shame. Targeting dynamics invites learning. Try: *"This keeps showing up across teams. Let's name it together and unpack what's underneath."*

A Real-Time Example

Imagine this moment in a tense meeting: Deadlines are missed. Fingers are pointing. Someone starts to spiral emotionally. You take a slow breath. You lower your voice. You say: "We've had multiple project stalls due to backchannel misalignment. Let's stop and get all voices on record. I know this feels uncomfortable, but clarity beats comfort every time." That sentence does more than reset the room. It *teaches the culture how to hold truth without burning down trust.*

The Deeper Insight: Your Body Is the Classroom

Leadership is often taught in frameworks. But leadership is learned—*in real-time tension.* And your team learns most by watching how you behave when it's hard to behave well. In that moment of pressure:
- Do you flinch?
- Do you defend?
- Do you dominate?
- Or do you *create space while staying clear?*

Because **that moment of presence teaches more than a dozen team-building sessions ever could. Your nervous system becomes the leadership curriculum.**

Regulated Leaders Build Resilient Cultures

If you want a team that doesn't collapse under conflict, **you have to show them how it's done.** They will follow your breath. They will mirror your mood. They will absorb your presence as a signal of whether it's safe to speak, stretch, and show up fully. So, master this:
- Stay calm in tension.
- Stay clear in confusion.
- Stay connected in disagreement.

Because **what you model becomes what they multiply.**

Conflict Is How Cultures Grow

If your team doesn't know how to fight, they'll never learn how to finish. Conflict is not a failure of leadership. It's a test of it.

The real question isn't, *"Will your team have conflict?"*
It's, *"What does your team do when the heat shows up?"* Do they spin? Do they hide? Do they politicize? Do they collapse? Or do they step into it—with honesty, clarity, presence, and purpose?

Build a culture that **names the fire, stands in it, and moves forward anyway.** You've faced the heat. Now we scale it. Let's go.

Field Manual: Holding Conflict Without Losing Culture

Conflict is not dysfunction. Suppressed conflict is. This manual gives you the tools to name the truth early, hold tension cleanly, and build a culture that can *disagree without disintegrating*. If your organization can't hold hard conversations—it cannot hold high performance. Period.

CONFLICT COMMAND PRINCIPLES

These five axioms guide conflict-resilient leadership:

1. **Silence Is Not Alignment**
   Smiles in meetings mean nothing. Ask what's not being said.
2. **Politeness Can Be Dishonest**
   Don't confuse "keeping the peace" with protecting the mission.
3. **Patterns Over Personalities**
   Address behaviors and dynamics, not identity or intent.
4. **Early Is Easier**
   Every week you delay truth multiplies the emotional cost of telling it.
5. **How You Hold It *Is* the Culture**
   Your nervous system is teaching your team how safe truth really is.

PRE-CONFLICT DETECTION CHECKLIST

Use this with your direct reports or leadership team monthly.

Signal	Question	Response
Energy Drop	Who's been quieter than usual?	[Name]
False Alignment	Where are we saying "yes" too quickly?	[Project/Team]
Avoided Conversations	What issue hasn't made it into the room yet?	[Describe]
Emotional Buildup	What tension are we managing instead of confronting?	[Describe]
Indirect Behavior	Where are side conversations replacing direct ones?	[Team/Dynamic]

If you see three or more of these at once—conflict is brewing in silence.

LIVE CONFLICT PLAYBOOK

When tension shows up, hold it clean. Here's the in-the-moment toolkit.

Step 1: Breathe, Don't Match *"Let me pause before I respond."*

Step 2: Name the Pattern, Not the Person *"I'm seeing a dynamic here where concerns are raised but not acted on. Let's explore that."*

Step 3: Ask, Don't Assume *"Can you help me understand what you're experiencing right now?"*

Step 4: Set a Truth Container *"We don't have to agree, but we're going to be honest—and we're going to do it without punishment."*

Step 5: Close with Commitment *"Here's what I heard. Here's what we'll do next. And here's when we'll check in again."* Don't end with "thanks for sharing." End with motion.

CULTURE-BUILDING RITUALS FOR CONFLICT SAFETY

Add these rituals to normalize healthy tension:

- **Red Flag Round**: In team meetings, ask: *"What's one thing we're not saying that we probably should be?"*

- **Pattern Naming Sessions**: Quarterly retros focused on dynamics, not deliverables. Ask: *"What patterns helped us this quarter? What patterns hurt us?"*
- **Pre-Mortem on Trust**: Before high-stakes projects, ask: *"Where are we likely to avoid hard truth in this process?"*
- **No Triangulation Rule**: If someone vents to you about someone else, ask: *"Have you told them directly?"* If not, don't solve it. Send them back to the source.

FINAL DIRECTIVE: TELL THE TRUTH—EARLY, CLEAN, AND WITHOUT APOLOGY

Your team doesn't need perfect harmony. It needs a system that can **hold the heat**. Because unresolved tension always becomes structural failure. And cultures that can't hold conflict—can't hold excellence. Conflict isn't the thing that breaks you. *It's the test that proves you're real.*

Chapter 18 The Courage to Fire, the Wisdom to Keep

"It is the mark of a wise leader to discern when to prune for growth—and when to shield against collapse."

There's a unique silence that falls over a room when you realize the person who once protected the organization is now *protecting themselves from the organization.* That silence is not peace. It's the moment before a necessary fracture.

I remember sitting across from a man I had once called indispensable. He had the institutional knowledge. He trained the interns. He held the history. He stayed late. He used words like "family" and "legacy" and "sacrifice."

And yet…The team avoided him. Innovation died in meetings he ran. He weaponized history to resist change. He criticized publicly and contributed privately—*just enough* to avoid accountability. But it wasn't what he did that made it hard.

It was who he *used to be.* I remembered the lean years. The shared victories. The late-night calls when we both swore, we'd build something lasting. And because I remembered that—I *hesitated.*

The Trap of Toxic Loyalty

What I didn't see at first was this: **I was paying emotional ransom.** I wasn't leading—I was negotiating with a ghost. Toxic loyalty doesn't shout. It whispers:

- "You owe me."
- "Without me, this place falls apart."
- "I've earned my place, no matter how I behave now."

And if you're not clear—if your own memory is louder than your current data—you'll believe it. You'll convince yourself that protecting the past is more important than protecting the future. And that's when you lose the culture. Not all at once, but inch by inch—through tolerated toxicity.

Sometimes, You See What You *Want* to See

One of the deepest leadership betrayals is the one we commit against our own perception. Because *sometimes,* we don't see clearly—*not because the truth isn't there,* but because the truth is *inconvenient.* Sometimes:

- You **want to believe someone is good** because acknowledging they've become manipulative is too painful.
- You **filter current behavior through past loyalty**, hoping they'll return to who they once were.
- You **rationalize harm** because you fear the political cost of calling it what it is.

And sometimes? The very person committing the harm will **accuse you** of the behavior they're actually guilty of—just to save face. I've seen it firsthand. I've watched people commit overt discrimination—then turn around and **accuse *me* of bias** the moment I moved to hold them accountable. Not because they believed it. But because **destroying my character was easier than confronting their own.**

The Hidden Threat: Legacy Leaders Turned Emotional Bullies

I've dealt with long-term team members who were once the backbone of the mission. People who had once carried real weight—but over time, transformed into **gatekeepers of fear.** They didn't use logic. They used intimidation. They didn't push for excellence. They *policed change.* They had one goal: **protect their position, no matter the cost.**

And the most damaging part? Other leaders *knew*—but lacked the political will to act. They couldn't muster the courage to walk someone who had once carried the torch.

But I knew. I knew what would come. I knew they'd try every trick—weaponize sentiment, play the victim, rewrite the narrative, fracture the team behind closed doors. I knew they'd paint *me* as the devil. And still, I moved. Because the organization needed the *release.* Not just for performance—but to **heal.**

And yes, people whispered. People questioned. People judged. I walked those halls, knowing half the room thought I was a traitor. But time—and outcomes—always prove the truth. You don't win those battles in real time. You win them by **playing the long game.**

Hard Decisions, Hard Truths

These are the kinds of decisions that separate **leaders from appeasers.** Not because you enjoy them. But because you **love the mission more than you fear the fallout.** Sometimes, to protect the culture, you have to walk someone who once built it. You have to absorb the slander. You have to hold the heat. And you have to keep walking—*with your eyes on the future.* Because leadership isn't measured by who you please—it's measured by what you protect.

The Unspoken Weight of Difficult Terminations

There's a quiet kind of pressure that descends on a leader when termination is on the table—not because it's the wrong move, but because it feels *emotionally misaligned with the story you've lived with that person.* This isn't just about performance reviews or HR protocols. Those are **procedural.** The real burden sits **in the soul of the decision**—in the tension between what's *right for the system* and what feels *wrong for the relationship.*

The questions swirl in the leader's mind, quietly and relentlessly:
- *What will this do to morale?*
- *Will others see this as betrayal?*
- *Am I losing part of the organization's story—someone who was here before we scaled, someone who "bled with us" in the beginning?*
- *Will this make people question my loyalty, my gratitude, my integrity?*

And behind all of that is a deeper, more disorienting question: *Am I betraying the past to protect the future?*

The Psychology of Letting Go

The real pain of difficult terminations is this: **You're not just releasing a person— you're grieving a version of them.** You're grieving:
- Who they used to be.
- What they used to bring.
- The memories they helped create.
- The image of them you carried for years, even when reality had already changed.

And in high-trust teams, especially legacy-driven ones, this loss feels *personal.* Because it is.

But here's the danger: **When you let sentimentality override clarity, you start leading the past instead of the present.** Every day you delay a necessary release:
- You send the message that **loyalty outweighs alignment.**
- You teach the team that **tenure is immunity.**
- You signal that **culture is secondary to comfort.**

And that erosion doesn't happen all at once. It happens in sighs behind closed doors. In muted Zoom calls. In the high-performer who quietly disengages. In the rising talent who starts planning their exit. In the tension that shows up in no one's words, but everyone's energy.

The Cost of Delay: Trading the Present for a Distorted Past

One of the hardest truths in leadership is this: **The longer you delay the right decision, the more damage it causes.** It's not loyalty you're preserving. It's *fantasy.* And worse—**that fantasy is now extracting rent from the team that's still showing up every day.**

Every day you protect someone for who they *used to be,* you abandon the people who are carrying the weight *right now.* You forfeit momentum. You stifle trust. You weaken execution. And all of it in the name of something that—deep down—you already know has changed.

Termination Is Not Always the Answer—But Avoidance Never Is

Let's be clear: Firing someone is not always the right call. Sometimes a hard conversation, a role shift, or a reset can bring a legacy contributor back into alignment. But when the truth is clear—when the damage is consistent, the behavior is corrosive, and the team is suffering? Then protecting that person becomes something else entirely.

It becomes leadership sabotage. Because you're no longer protecting a person. You're protecting your *image of yourself as a "loyal" leader.* And in doing so, you **sacrifice the integrity of the culture you're supposed to guard.**

Legacy is Not a Shield

We let him go on a Friday. Quietly. Cleanly. No drama, no backdoor references to legacy wins. Just clarity. We didn't send the usual "gratitude email." We didn't pretend it was mutual. For weeks, the room had been walking on eggshells around his energy. Every new idea got filtered through *"How will he take it?"* Junior staff deferred. Senior leaders deflected. The whole system bent subtly to avoid upsetting one person.

The day after he left, something strange happened. The next team meeting started… lighter. Not "celebratory." Not giddy. Just **free.** People spoke with less filter. Someone challenged a process that had gone unexamined for months. A junior analyst pitched a new idea and no one looked to the corner of the room to gauge the old guard's reaction—because that corner was empty now. By the end of the quarter, three stalled initiatives were back in motion. One team lead told me, *"I forgot what it felt like to breathe in this room."*

That's when I understood something: **You don't prune to punish. You prune to let what's healthy finally grow.** Removing one toxic protector didn't just solve a personnel issue. It unlocked the culture we'd been pretending we already had. The people who helped build the house *deserve our respect.* But when they begin burning it down to keep their seat at the table?

They no longer need protection. The culture does. Leadership isn't about being liked. It's about being *right*—in the long game. And sometimes that means walking the halls as the misunderstood one. The villain in the short-term story. The traitor in someone else's narrative.

But if you hold the line with courage and clarity? **Time and outcomes will always prove the truth.** You're not the destroyer. You're the protector. *Because sometimes, the most loving thing you can do for a culture is to remove what's silently killing it.*

The Wisdom to Keep: When Loyalty Still Has Life

It's easy to draw hard lines in leadership when someone is openly toxic, manipulative, or chronically corrosive. But what about those who are **deeply loyal but currently lost**? What about the long-timers who care—but are stuck? What about the once-high performers who now seem distant, defensive, or disengaged—not from entitlement, but from **burnout, fear, or uncertainty**?

Leadership requires discernment—not just decisiveness. Not every conflict is a sign that someone needs to go. Sometimes, it's a **signal that someone is struggling in silence**, unsure how to adapt to a world that's changing faster than they are.

This is where **courageous coaching** replaces reactive firing. But only if you know what to look for.

What to Look for in Someone You Keep

These aren't just "red flags vs. green flags." These are the **relational and behavioral signals** that someone is still willing to do the real work of rejoining the future—even if they're momentarily stuck in the past.

1. Willingness to Reflect

When confronted with tension or feedback, how do they respond?

- Do they pause and **look inward**?
- Do they say things like, *"I can see how I contributed to that,"* or *"That wasn't my intention, but I get the impact"*?

Or do they externalize everything?

- *"It's the new leadership."*
- *"Things aren't how they used to be."*
- *"This new generation just doesn't understand how we built this."*

The former shows humility. The latter reveals emotional entitlement. You don't need perfection—but you *do* need a willingness to self-interrogate.

2. Receptivity to Feedback

Hard conversations don't feel good. But some people **lean into them with curiosity.** They ask:

- *"What could I have done differently?"*
- *"How did that land with you?"*
- *"Can you help me understand the disconnect?"*

Others respond with:
- Defensiveness.
- Cynicism.
- Emotional weaponry.

They listen to respond—not to understand. They make it *your fault for confronting them.* Receptivity isn't just about hearing feedback. It's about **inviting it, metabolizing it, and changing because of it.** That's how you know someone is still *coachable.*

3. Pattern vs. Episode

Behavior always needs to be read over time. One outburst, one miss, one moment of disconnection? That's human. But if the behavior:
- Shows up across contexts,
- Persists after feedback,
- Or creates repeated harm despite coaching?

Then it's not an episode—it's a **pattern.** And *patterns don't change with time. They change with intention.* Good leaders don't react to episodes. They study patterns—and call them by name.

4. Do They Still Lift the Room?

Even when people are struggling, some of them still bring **energy, dignity, and care** to the spaces they inhabit. They might be slow to adapt—but they *don't sabotage.* They might be tired—but they *don't resent the mission.* They might be unsure—but they still *respect the process.* You can feel the difference. They show up with:
- Integrity.
- Quiet support.
- Respect for others' contributions—even if they're still grieving what's changed.

That's someone worth fighting for—if they're still willing to fight for *you, too.*

Transformation Over Tenure

Let's be clear: The goal is not to "let them stay." The goal is to see **if they can still contribute.** Staying is passive. Contributing is active. Staying says, *"Don't forget what I did."* Contributing says, *"I'm still willing to evolve for where we're going."*

That's the test. And it must be mutual. Because in a high-trust culture:
- Past service earns **honor**, not **immunity.**
- Tenure earns **dialogue**, not **a free pass.**

If someone is ready to step forward—even while grieving the past—they're still part of the future. But if they insist on being preserved like a relic, rather than transformed into a partner? Then it's not loyalty you're protecting. It's resistance you're funding.

Some People Are Worth the Work—But Only If They're Willing

As a leader, you will be called to make impossible decisions between protection and progression. But remember:
- **Some people need coaching, not termination.**
- **Some people need time, not removal.**
- **Some people are still aligned at the core—just temporarily out of rhythm.**

If they show you honesty, humility, and hope? Walk with them. Invest in them. Call them back to the table—not out of guilt, but out of *mutual trust.* But never forget: Staying is not the goal. **Contributing is.** And culture must always come before comfort.

Toxic Loyalty: The Hidden Rot of Team Culture

Let's stop sugarcoating it: **Some people stay too long.** They were once foundational. They were committed, reliable, respected. But at some point, they stopped growing. Then they stopped contributing. And eventually, they started **resisting anything that challenged their position.**

And yet—they stayed. Not because they earned it. But because **we lacked the courage to say: "What got us here won't get us there."** That's not just misalignment. That's *emotional hostage-taking.* And the cost isn't measured in quarterly performance—it's measured in **cultural erosion.**

How Emotional Entanglement Becomes Cultural Corrosion

Here's the trap: these individuals are often **woven into the team's emotional memory.** They remember the late nights. They know the original mission. They helped "build the house." And because of that, we:

- Excuse the attitude.
- Explain away the disengagement.
- Tolerate the disruption.

Not because it's right. But because we feel *guilty* detaching from the person who was once *loyal.* But here's the truth: **Loyalty is only as good as the present contribution it fuels.** If someone uses loyalty as a shield against evolution, they're no longer protecting the team. They're protecting themselves *at the cost of everyone else.*

What Toxic Loyalty *Sounds* Like

Toxic loyalty doesn't always scream. It often whispers. It postures. It guilt-trips. You'll hear it in phrases like:

- **"You wouldn't be here if it wasn't for me."**
  Translation: *I want credit for something I've long since stopped earning.*
- **"I've seen leaders like you come and go."**
  Translation: *I'm not listening—I'm dismissing.*
- **"This company's losing its soul."**
  Translation: *Change threatens my power, so I'll frame it as betrayal.*
- **"Back when we used to care…"**
  Translation: *Because I no longer feel essential, I'll weaponize nostalgia to undermine progress.*

These aren't reflections. They're *emotional manipulation tactics.* Legacy becomes leverage. Sentiment becomes sabotage.

The Dangerous Tradeoff: Comfort vs. Culture

Keeping these individuals isn't just a personnel decision—it's a message. It tells your team:

- "We value tenure over adaptability."
- "Resistance is rewarded if it's polite enough."

- "Change is optional if your resume is long enough."

And the people who get that message *loudest*? **Your best performers.** The ones who:
- Bring new energy.
- Challenge broken systems.
- Push for clarity, growth, and accountability.

They'll leave. Not loudly. But decisively. Because they'll realize: "No matter how hard I work, this system protects comfort—not contribution." And when that happens, **you've traded the future for the past.**

Loyalty Isn't Lifetime Tenure—It's Ongoing Alignment

True loyalty is not just about what someone *did*. It's about who they are *willing to become.*
- Loyalty evolves.
- Loyalty adapts.
- Loyalty contributes.

But when loyalty becomes *entitlement,* it stops being an asset. It becomes a rot—quiet, sentimental, defended. And if you don't address it? **Your culture will decay—*not because of betrayal, but because of tolerated stagnation.***

So yes—honor the past. But never at the expense of the people building the future. Because in the end, **culture is not sustained by memory. It's sustained by mission.**

How to Remove Without Triggering Collapse

Removing a deeply rooted individual from your organization—especially one who is seen as untouchable or irreplaceable—isn't just a management action. It's an *organizational procedure with cultural consequences.* This person may be wrapped in legacy. They may have social capital. They may be beloved, feared, or mythologized.

And over time, they've become **a symbolic node in your system**—a representation of the "old guard," of "how things used to be," or of perceive ed "protection." To remove them recklessly is to risk cultural whiplash. To do nothing is to preserve the rot and paralyze growth. The challenge, then, is to **extract without collapse.** To **disrupt without destroying.** To **honor the past without letting it hold the future hostage.** Here's how.

1. Quiet the Chaos – Prepare the System

Before the first conversation, before the announcement, before the fallout—**you stabilize.** Why? Because you're not just removing a person. You're extracting a **living dependency**—a root that may have its tendrils in workflows, emotions, policies, and backchannel influence. So:
- Document every mission-critical task, responsibility, and decision funnel they influence.
- Begin **quiet knowledge transfers**. Not in suspicion—but in systems thinking.
- Train rising leaders **in the shadows**. Let them observe, absorb, and adapt—before the spotlight hits them.
- Map **relational and operational interdependencies**. Who will feel the loss the most? Where will ambiguity creep in? Anticipate before it manifests.

The first goal isn't to remove. It's to **stabilize the ecosystem** so that removal doesn't ignite panic. Because every void you leave behind becomes a container for speculation, resentment, or chaos—**unless you've filled it with structure.**

2. Name the Shift – Control the Narrative

Once the decision is made, the next battlefield is **narrative.** And make no mistake—if you don't control the story, someone else will. Do not:

- Over-explain.
- Villainize.
- Collapse under pressure.

Instead:

- Acknowledge the individual's contributions *without pretending they still align.*
- Clarify the organization's evolving needs and future direction.
- Be **brief, clear, and grounded**—no spin, no sugar.

Try something like: "This was a difficult decision. We honor what they've given. But as our mission evolves, we must align talent with today's needs—not just yesterday's memories. This is about future-fit execution." Why this works:

- It honors history without romanticizing it.
- It speaks to progress, not punishment.
- It keeps the focus on *mission over emotion.*

Because in a moment of emotional volatility, **clarity is the most compassionate thing you can offer.**

3. Fortify the Culture – Lead the Emotions

After a high-profile departure, **you're not just managing operations. You're managing grief.** That grief will take many forms:

- For some, it's sorrow.
- For others, it's confusion.
- For many, it's **unspoken relief**—finally, the cultural blockage is gone.

All of it is real. And all of it must be *led.* Not avoided. So:

- Hold space for honest reaction without policing emotion.
- Reaffirm the mission—not as a pitch, but as a *re-centering anchor.*
- Allow people to ask questions, but resist the urge to answer every emotional undertone.
- Most importantly: **model the very leadership you expect from them.**

They're watching *how* you do this more than *what* you say. If you lead with:

- **Empathy and boundaries,**
- **Clarity and compassion,**
- **Stability and vision,**

You become the new foundation they attach to. **You become the root system that holds, even as another is removed.**

Extraction Is Not Just Removal—It's Realignment

Removing a legacy player is never just about performance. It's about realigning the organization's future with its present reality. Done poorly, it creates vacuum and fear. Done well, it becomes the *reset point*—a signal that this team is not just *changing,* it is *maturing.*

So don't just fire the person. Reinforce the system. Retell the narrative. Reground the team. Because when you do this right? The team doesn't collapse. **It exhales.**

Leadership Mirror: The Shadow in the Delay

There comes a moment in leadership when the real confrontation isn't across the table—it's inside the mirror. You've known what needs to be done. The behavior is chronic. The feedback loops are exhausted. The trust has been quietly eroding.

And yet, you hesitate. You delay. You stall under the weight of what feels like emotional complexity—but is often **internal avoidance** masquerading as compassion.

The question isn't just: *Why haven't you acted?* The deeper question is: *What in you is afraid to act?* This is where the work becomes personal. This is **shadow work**—the realm of the unconscious, where your leadership identity collides with your hidden fears, unmet needs, and unprocessed history. So, ask yourself, honestly:

- **Were you afraid of losing someone's approval?**
  Did the idea of disappointing them trigger an old wound—perhaps from your own childhood, your first boss, or a past betrayal?
- **Were you projecting your own fears of abandonment?**
  Did you stay loyal past the point of logic because you're terrified of being left behind? Of being misunderstood? Of becoming "the bad guy"?
- **Were you over-identifying with their story?**
  Did their struggle remind you of your own? Were you secretly hoping to save the version of *you* inside *them*?
- **Were you afraid of being seen as disloyal, ruthless, or cold?**
  Were you more attached to *how you'd be perceived* than to what the culture actually needs?

These aren't business questions. They're *identity questions.* And until you answer them, you'll keep confusing compassion with avoidance.

The Real Work: Confronting Yourself Before Confronting Others

Here's the brutal truth: the hardest part of firing someone isn't *confronting them.* It's *confronting yourself.* Because in every delayed termination, there's a hidden part of the leader that hasn't yet matured. A piece of you still hoping to:

- Be liked.
- Be rescued.
- Be absolved.
- Avoid being the villain in someone's story.

But leadership isn't sainthood. It's stewardship. And that means making the decision not for emotional ease, but for **cultural alignment.**

Executive maturity begins the moment you stop protecting your image—and start protecting the mission. And that moment rarely feels like a victory. It feels like grief. Like guilt. Like you're breaking a part of yourself. But that's not failure. That's **initiation.**

Shadow Work is Leadership Work

This is why great leadership is never just external. It's internal excavation. Because until you can face your own:

- Need for approval,
- Fear of rejection,
- Guilt over being "the bad guy,"

…you will *always* delay decisions that demand courage. This is the mirror.

And if you can look into it—without flinching—you'll stop leading from your shadow. This is why must confront the shadow in the C suite.

You'll start leading from *clarity*. Because real leadership is not the absence of fear. It's the ability to make aligned decisions *even when fear is present*. That's what separates **executive maturity from emotional performance.** That's what earns trust—not just from others, but from yourself.

The Paradox: Firing as an Act of Protection

When done with integrity, firing someone is not an act of cruelty.

It is an act of protection.

- Protection for the mission.
- Protection for the team.
- And often, protection for the person being let go—who may now be freed to grow in ways they never could under your roof.

The real courage of leadership is not in the firing itself. It's in facing the emotional turbulence *and still choosing clarity*.

Final Reflection

You are not called to preserve comfort. You are called to steward momentum, protect culture, and make hard choices that others avoid. And yes—sometimes that means firing someone who helped build the house. Because they are no longer fit to help shape the future. And the future deserves your clarity.

Leadership prompts for reflection:

1. Who on your team holds emotional power without performance?
2. Have you delayed a hard conversation because of fear, guilt, or nostalgia?
3. If you removed them, who on your team would *secretly feel relief*?
4. Are you protecting someone because of who they were—or who they are?

Field Manual: People Decisions Under Pressure

Leadership doesn't just shape strategy. It shapes *standards*. And few decisions test your standards more than who stays—and who goes. This manual exists for the moment when your gut knows the truth, but your fear still whispers: *"Maybe we can fix it."* Sometimes you can. Other times, you're just protecting decay.

LEADER'S TERMINATION READINESS SCAN

Ask these 5 questions before every critical people decision:

Question	Why It Matters
1. Would I hire them again today?	Loyalty is not a retention strategy.
2. If they left, would the culture feel relieved or wounded?	Your team already knows. The silence is data.
3. Are they co-creating the future—or clinging to the past?	Legacy protectors become legacy prisoners fast.
4. Am I keeping them because of contribution—or history?	Rewarding history over behavior erodes standards.
5. What would I tell a new hire if they acted like this person?	If the answer is "that's different," you're protecting hypocrisy.

If you're coaching behavior, you'd fire someone else for—your standards aren't culture. They're convenience.

TERMINATE OR KEEP? — LEADERSHIP DISCERNMENT MATRIX

Behavior Type	Action	Reason
High Skill + Low Trust	Investigate and clarify	Misalignment may be cultural or emotional.
Low Skill + High Integrity	Coach and protect	These are keepers. Invest in them.
High Skill + Toxic Energy	Remove swiftly	Skill without trust corrodes everything.
Low Skill + Low Ownership	Exit cleanly	You're not failing them. You're freeing the system.

Toxic competence is not a gift. It's a trap.

PSYCHOLOGICAL TRIGGERS THAT CLOUD JUDGMENT

Be honest. Which one of these is keeping them in the seat?
- "They've been here since the beginning."
- "They helped me survive the early chaos."
- "Everyone knows how much I trust them."
- "I can't handle the politics of removing them."
- "They used to be great."

Leadership isn't about what they *used to be*.
It's about what they're *doing to the mission right now*.

THE COURAGEOUS EXIT PROTOCOL

How to let someone go cleanly—with clarity, not cruelty:
1. **No Delay**: The longer you stall, the more confused the team becomes.

2. **No Spin**: Don't hide behind HR euphemisms. Communicate truth without drama.
3. **No Backchanneling**: End gossip by ending ambiguity. If they're gone, let them be *gone*.
4. **Close the Loop with the Team**:

"This was a leadership decision to protect the standards and future of this team."

Don't send an email full of gratitude if what you needed was accountability.

TRUTH BEFORE COMFORT

When you protect a person over the mission, you teach your team that performance is optional and that trust is a game.

You don't fire someone because they're bad.

You fire them because keeping them betrays the culture you claim to believe in.

And sometimes, the greatest act of leadership…

…is having the courage to **remove someone you like**

…for the sake of protecting **something** you *love*.

Chapter 19 From Feedback to Force Multipliers

"Feedback is the nervous system of a healthy organization. When it's working, you feel what matters. When it's broken, you don't know you're bleeding until it's too late."

The feedback came in sharp. An anonymous culture survey. 93 responses. Raw, unfiltered emotion. The message was unmistakable: *"We don't trust leadership to act on what we say." "We feel unheard, unseen, managed—not led." "We've been here before—nothing changes."*

The exec team reviewed the results in a closed-door session. Long faces. Nervous energy. A few voices called it an overreaction. One leader said, *"Let's not validate complaints we can't fix."* Another suggested, *"Maybe we just acknowledge it happened and move on."*

And that's what they did. A month passed. Then two. No town hall. No report-back. No discussion of the hard truths. Just… silence.

That's when the real damage began. People didn't riot. They didn't rage. They just started drifting. Ideas slowed. Meetings thinned. High performers began returning recruiters' calls. One senior engineer told a peer: *"They asked for honesty. We gave it. They buried it. I'm not doing that again."*

The survey hadn't killed the culture. The silence afterward did. Not because it proved leadership was evil or incompetent. But because it proved they *weren't listening*—at least not in a way that mattered.

You don't build trust by asking for input. You build trust by acting on it—or at the very least, by responding with courage. Even a hard "no," when delivered transparently, protects dignity.

But feedback without follow-through? That's a broken promise. And people don't forget it.

The Leadership Delusion of Feedback

Every leader wants to believe they are approachable. They convince themselves they've "created space" for people to be honest. They install surveys. Anonymous boxes. Town hall Q&As. Then they sit back and wait for the truth.

But what often comes through is either sterilized or radioactive: polite, pre-approved feedback that's been stripped of usefulness—or emotionally loaded venting with no path to resolution.

I've been there. I've launched well-intended feedback initiatives only to realize I wasn't hearing what people *really* thought—I was hearing what they thought I wanted to hear. And when real feedback *did* surface, it came in whispers, private DMs, or exit interviews.

That was the turning point. I realized feedback wasn't missing because people lacked opinions. It was missing because the **system itself discouraged truth.**

The Dangerous Myth of Anonymity

I remember the first time I was told to "just submit feedback anonymously." It was framed like a shield—**a noble act of speaking truth to power without consequence**. But deep down, it felt wrong. Cowardly, even. Not because people didn't have valid concerns, but because the system whispered something darker: "The only way you'll be safe is if you disappear."

Anonymity, pitched as protection, often becomes a crutch for weak leadership cultures. It silently teaches people that **being invisible is the safest path**. But safety without voice isn't safety. It's **institutionalized fear**. In reality, anonymous feedback often spirals into:

- **Vague criticism** with no accountability. ("Leadership needs to be better." Better at what? How? No one knows.)
- **Generalizations** that cannot be acted upon. ("Communication is bad." Which part? Who? In what context?)
- **Resentment-driven grievances**, not solutions. Anonymous forums become breeding grounds for blame, not bridges to change.

And worst of all: **It erodes trust.**

When leaders can't connect feedback to a face, a context, a lived experience—they don't know how to trust it. They start doubting the validity of the feedback itself. Eventually, they stop listening altogether. When this happens, the very process designed to "empower voices" becomes a mechanism for **mistrust and dismissal**.

Clarity is oxygen to a healthy organizational culture. People don't need to be invisible. They need to be **seen**, **valued**, and **safe enough to speak**. Here's what real leadership clarity demands:

- **Clarity of Roles**:
  People must know what is expected of them—and what they can expect from their leaders in return.
- **Clarity of Expectations**:
  Feedback isn't an attack. It's a *contribution to collective strength*. Leaders must model this truth loudly and consistently.
- **Clarity of Intent**:
  Feedback should be about **building**, not **punishing**. About **alignment**, not **accusation**.

If you build clarity into your culture, people don't need to hide. They don't need anonymous forms. They won't *want* them. They'll **stand in the light**, shoulder to shoulder with leadership, challenging what must be challenged, building what must be built. They'll know: "My voice isn't a risk. It's a responsibility."

If you lead, understand this: **Anonymity is a symptom. It is not a solution.** If your people feel they must be anonymous to be safe, you have a culture problem, not a feedback problem. Fix the **environment**, not the **tool**. Courageous cultures:

- **Encourage face-forward feedback**, even if it's uncomfortable.
- **Protect dissenters**, not just loyalists.
- **Model vulnerability at the top**, showing that feedback is welcomed, not weaponized.

You can't build resilient teams by making them hide. You build them by teaching them that **their voices matter more than their fears**. Ask yourself, if you're an emerging leader:

- Am I fostering clarity—or hiding behind the illusion of safety?
- When was the last time I invited feedback to my face—and thanked the person who delivered it?
- Am I building a culture where people *trust* enough to be seen?

Because leadership—**real leadership**—doesn't happen in the shadows. It happens **in the light**, where the strongest voices aren't hidden, but heard. Don't build your organization on fear. Build it on fearless truth.

Why Most Feedback Systems Get Hijacked

Let's not sugarcoat this: Most feedback systems aren't designed for **insight**. They're built for **optics**. For leaders to *appear* open, without truly **being** open. They don't seek clarity. They collect noise.

The result? A theater of engagement where real problems fester beneath a surface of sanitized "input." Meanwhile, the organization drifts toward irrelevance.

Three Unspoken Forces That Sabotage Feedback

Feedback systems don't fail because people are bad. They fail because **systems are blind** to human realities.

1. Power Always Distorts Feedback

No matter how many times you say, "We want your honest input," every employee is running a silent calculation: **"What is the cost of telling the truth here?"** Fear of retaliation. Fear of isolation. Fear of being labeled "difficult." These fears **bend** feedback away from candor—and toward survival. Until you confront the reality that **truth-telling feels dangerous in most organizations**, your feedback system is a stage play, not a truth serum.

2. Ambiguity Destroys Trust

When feedback channels are vague, undefined, or sporadic, people don't feel empowered. They feel ambushed—or worse, manipulated. A poorly structured feedback request sounds like a trap:
- **"Be honest!"** (*But what will happen if I am?*)
- **"Tell us what you think!"** (*Do you even know what you're asking for?*)

Without clear structures—defined goals, transparent expectations, safety protocols—feedback feels less like participation, and more like a social booby trap.

3. Inaction Erodes Honesty

The fastest way to kill a feedback culture isn't punishment. It's **silence**. When people summon the courage to speak—and nothing visibly changes—they learn a bitter lesson: **"My voice doesn't matter."** Not acting on feedback is worse than never asking for it. It teaches cynicism. It trains disengagement. It breeds high-performer attrition—and you won't even see it happening until it's too late. They'll nod. They'll smile. And they'll quietly leave.

How Feedback Systems Get Hijacked

It's rarely some evil executive plotting to suppress voices. It's **bad design**, compounded by **human nature**, fueled by **organizational blindness**. And the cost is staggering:
- **Strategic Blind Spots** — You lose visibility into what's broken until it breaks publicly.
- **Cultural Drift** — You think you're steering the ship, but the culture is steering you.

- **Innovation Paralysis** — People stop offering disruptive ideas because they assume no one's listening.
- **High Performer Attrition** — The best people leave not because of hard work—but because of unseen, unresolved barriers.

By the time you notice the symptoms, the real damage has already been done.

The Most Dangerous Feedback System

It's not the absence of a system. It's the **illusion** of one. The **most dangerous feedback system** is the one that **pretends to work** while quietly breeding fear, apathy, and decay beneath the surface. You don't fix this with a new survey. You fix it by **changing the emotional contract** between leadership and the people.

Reflection for Leaders

- **Do my people truly believe the cost of honesty is bearable?**
- **Have I built structured, transparent, and actionable feedback mechanisms—or vague, performative ones?**
- **When was the last time we visibly acted on feedback—and communicated it back to the people who spoke?**

Because **asking for feedback** is a leadership act. **Responding to feedback** is a leadership test. **Building on feedback** is leadership maturity.
Which one are you practicing?

Designing Feedback Systems That Produce Force, Not Fear

If you want a feedback system that fuels resilience—not resentment—you must treat it with the same rigor as any other mission-critical system. **Feedback isn't a "nice to have." It's a weapon against drift. A shield against mediocrity.**

But here's the catch: You don't get there by hoping. You engineer it—**intentionally**, **iteratively**, and **accountably**. Without that commitment, feedback will always decay into noise, politics, and fear.

1. Design Feedback as a Process, not a Personality Contest

In immature organizations, feedback mutates into **character assassination**:

- *"He's arrogant."*
- *"She's too emotional."*
- *"They're not a good culture fit."*

This isn't feedback. It's a **smokescreen** for judgment, bias, and political maneuvering. When feedback becomes subjective gossip, two things happen fast:

- Trust collapses.
- Power games thrive.

Real feedback is something different. It's built on three unbreakable pillars:

- **Observable Behavior**: What *specifically* happened?
- **Consistent Patterns**: Is this a trend, not a one-off?
- **Tangible Impact**: How did it affect the team, the mission, the outcome?

Example of garbage feedback: *"He's not collaborative."*

Example of mature feedback: *"In our last three planning meetings, Alex dismissed others' ideas without exploration. This has created hesitation among team members to share, slowing collaboration."*

See the difference? One attacks the person. The other diagnoses the behavior **with precision**. **Behavioral specificity is the language of high-trust, high-performance cultures.** If your feedback doesn't meet this standard, it's not feedback—it's sabotage.

2. Install Feedback Loops into Daily Operations

Feedback can't survive if it's quarantined to annual reviews, exit interviews, or anonymous surveys. If feedback isn't **part of the operating system**, it **dies of neglect**. High-performing teams **embed feedback into their daily cadence**:

- **After-action reviews** after every major decision: *What went right? What must improve?*
- **Micro-retrospectives** at the end of each sprint or planning cycle: *What did we learn? What friction emerged?*
- **Debrief rituals** after cross-functional collaborations: *How did our handoffs work? Where did trust grow—or erode?*

When feedback is **ritualized**, it **normalizes**. It stops feeling like a sniper attack. It starts feeling like **breathing**—natural, rhythmic, expected. **In DevOps, testing is baked into the pipeline. In elite teams, feedback must be baked into the flow.** No more "special occasions" for honesty. Honesty becomes the operating standard.

3. Train for Feedback Intelligence

Let's be clear:

- **Giving feedback well is a learned skill.**
- **Receiving feedback with maturity is a learned skill.**

Without training, people default to defensiveness, emotional shutdown, or passive aggression. And then leaders wonder why "feedback culture" sounds good on posters but crumbles in practice.

Train your people to:

- **Use frameworks** like Situation–Behavior–Impact (SBI) to bring surgical clarity to conversations.
- **Focus on shared mission goals**, not character attacks.
- **Turn feedback into dialogue**, not a drive-by shooting.
- **Ask for feedback proactively**, not just wait for it—and know how to act on it.

And leaders must be the first to model it. Because make no mistake:

- If you **deflect** feedback ("That's not really a problem"),
- If you **dismiss** feedback ("You just don't understand the bigger picture"),
- If you **punish** feedback (silent retaliation, lost opportunities),

You will kill the very system you're trying to build. **Your people will learn.** And what they will learn is silence. **The death of feedback is always slow at first. Then sudden. Then fatal.**

Leadership Close

Ask yourself, as an emerging leader:

- Have I engineered feedback into the operating system—or left it to chance?
- Do I demand behavioral specificity—or allow personality attacks?
- Am I training my people—and myself—to be literate in the language of feedback?

Because in a world moving at the speed of cognitive convergence, feedback isn't "soft skills." It's survival skills. You're either building **a force field of clarity**— Or sowing the seeds of slow, silent decay. **Which are you building?**

The Feedback System of High-Trust Teams

Let's get brutally honest: Most organizations don't fail because they **don't ask** for feedback. They fail because they **don't respond** to it. The pattern is depressingly familiar:

- A survey goes out.
- Reports get compiled.
- Leadership sends a polished "thank you for your input" email.
- Then... **silence**.

No action. No decisions explained. No momentum created. And whether leaders intend it or not, **the silence speaks louder than anything else**: **"Your input didn't matter."**

In that vacuum, trust withers. Hope corrodes. And the next time you ask for feedback, don't be surprised when you get shrugs—or worse, silence. Because every time you collect feedback and **fail to close the loop**, you **train your people** to stop telling you the truth.

High-Trust Leaders Close the Loop—Visibly, Relentlessly, and Honestly

In elite, resilient teams, feedback doesn't vanish into a black hole. It loops back **into dialogue, into decisions, into visible next steps. High-trust leaders know the drill**:

- They **acknowledge** what they heard.
- They **articulate** what actions they are taking.
- They **explain** what actions they aren't taking—**and why**.
- They **invite** continued conversation, not just one-way announcements.

Even when the answer is "no" or "not yet," real leaders **own the communication**: **"We heard your concern. Here's what we're doing about it. Here's what we're not doing—yet. And here's why."**

That moment—**naming the gap** between feedback and action—isn't a weakness. It's a profound display of **integrity**.

Integrity > Perfection

Your people don't expect perfection. They expect **honesty**. They expect **visibility**. They expect **respect**. Closing the feedback loop is not about always giving people what they want. It's about **respecting them enough to tell them the truth**. When you close the loop with transparency—even when delivering a hard "no"—you are saying:

- **"You were heard."**
- **"Your voice mattered."**
- **"You are part of how we move forward."**

And that's how trust is forged—not through grand gestures, but through consistent, visible integrity.

Leadership Reflection

If you're leading—or aspire to lead—ask yourself:

- Do I treat feedback as a transaction—or as the beginning of a relationship?
- Do I visibly close the loop every time—or only when it's convenient?
- Am I willing to say "no"—and explain it with respect?

Because here's the leadership truth no one tells you: **You don't build trust by agreeing with everyone. You build trust by honoring everyone.**

Feedback isn't finished when it's collected. It's finished when the loop is closed—and the relationship is strengthened. **That's leadership. That's culture. That's how high-trust teams are built—one honest loop at a time.**

From Feedback to Force Multipliers

When feedback becomes **systematic**, **behavioral**, and **reciprocal**, it undergoes a fundamental transformation. It stops being a **risk to manage**—And becomes an **accelerator to unleash**.

In military doctrine, a **force multiplier** is any factor that dramatically enhances combat effectiveness without proportional increases in resources. It might be:

- Advanced technology.
- Superior terrain.
- Elite training.
- Psychological advantage.

In leadership and organizational systems, the ultimate force multiplier is truth. A well-engineered feedback system is exactly that: a living, breathing strategic asset. It doesn't just react to problems. It actively multiplies your power to solve, build, and win.

What a Feedback Force Multiplier Actually Does

A real feedback system does not "gather opinions." It generates operational leverage. It:

- **Reduces friction** before it metastasizes into failure.
- **Surfaces innovation** from unexpected corners—because the next breakthrough may come from the quietest voice.
- **Accelerates learning** across all teams, turning every project, win, and mistake into compounding wisdom.
- **Identifies cultural drift** long before it becomes an existential crisis.
- **Retains top performers**, not through perks and pay raises alone—but by making them feel seen, heard, and respected at the deepest level.

In short: **It turns your organization into a precision-guided, continuously learning, self-correcting organism of execution.**

Feedback Isn't About Feelings—It's About Force

Let's be absolutely clear:

- Feedback isn't about making people feel good.
- It's not about protecting egos or dodging conflict.

It's about **building an adaptive organism**—an entity that:

- **Feels reality faster.**
- **Responds smarter.**
- **Learns quicker than the competition.**
- **Hardens itself against disruption without hardening against truth.**

Organizations that weaponize feedback correctly aren't just "nicer places to work." They are **lethal competitors**—learning, adapting, and executing at speeds that leave slower cultures in the dust.

Leadership Reflection

If you are serious about leading in a world that is only going to become more volatile, interconnected, and unforgiving, ask yourself:

- **Is feedback treated like emotional venting—or operational reconnaissance?**
- **Am I harvesting force multipliers—or hoarding liabilities?**
- **Are we building an organization that corrects itself faster than external threats can overtake it?**

Because in this era: **The team that hears itself most clearly—and acts most decisively— wins.** Feedback isn't a formality. It's the difference between fragility and force. Between decay and dominance. Between surviving—and surging. **Choose accordingly.**

Truth at Scale

Every growing organization reaches a tipping point. You can no longer rely on one-on-one conversations to surface the truth. You need *infrastructure*. You need systems that:

- Reward honesty.
- Clarify behavior.
- Protect dignity.
- And turn truth into momentum.

Because at scale, feedback isn't just about **fixing problems**. It's about **finding potential**. And when you get that right? Feedback stops being a function. It becomes your fuel.

Feedback isn't about feelings. It's about force. When done right, feedback becomes your organization's nervous system—sensing risk, exposing friction, and multiplying momentum.

But when feedback dies in silence, you don't just lose data. You lose **trust**. Do you have a feedback trust issue?

10 Questions to Diagnose Your Feedback Culture

1. Do your people feel safe giving *honest, direct* feedback to leaders?
2. Is feedback integrated into your daily, weekly, and quarterly rhythms?
3. Can your team distinguish between opinion and behavior?
4. Do you act on feedback—or archive it?
5. Are leaders trained to receive feedback without defensiveness?
6. Can employees trace feedback to action?
7. Do people give feedback *across* functions, not just up or down?
8. Is feedback framed around growth and alignment—not blame?
9. Do people who offer feedback get recognized, or avoided?
10. Is feedback tied to performance, retention, and strategic planning?

If you can't say yes to most of these—you have work to do.

This manual gives you the tools to close the loop, shift the culture, and build an environment where truth leads to traction—not trauma.

1. SYSTEM CHECK: Where Feedback Fails

Run this scan monthly across teams and orgs:

Symptom	Signal	Action
Anonymous surveys dominate	Fear of retaliation	Audit trust depth. Ask: *"What have we made unsafe to say out loud?"*
Feedback given → no visible follow-up	Loop breach	Publish "what we heard" and "what we're doing" within 7 days.
Leaders defer to HR to "own" feedback	Accountability evasion	Reassign ownership to direct-line leaders.
Only high-performers give input	Cultural disengagement	Ask quieter voices in private: *"What would make this place worth your best work?"*

2. FEEDBACK LOOP PLAYBOOK

Phase 1: Receive
- Ask for **specific, observable**, and **behavioral** feedback.
"What's one thing I could stop doing this week that would improve how we work?"
- Avoid anonymous intake whenever possible. Instead, build psychological safety for real names with real voice.
-

Phase 2: Respond
- Within 7 days of intake, deliver a *loop-back message*:
  - "Here's what we heard."
  - "Here's what we're acting on."
  - "Here's what we're not, and why."

o   "Here's how you can keep the dialogue open."
Even a **clear no** builds more trust than vague silence.

Phase 3: Reinforce

- In team meetings, embed feedback wins:
  - o   "This change came directly from your input."
- Highlight behaviors that reinforce feedback culture.
  - o   "She said it early, and that saved us weeks."

3. FEEDBACK CADENCE RITUALS

Weekly:

- Add "What's unclear?" or "What's not working?" to team check-ins.

Monthly:

- Leader 1:1s include "What's one thing I'm not seeing that I need to?"

Quarterly:

- Run a *Feedback Audit*: What was said? What was done? What was missed?

4. FEEDBACK FRAMING LANGUAGE FOR LEADERS

- **To create safety**:

"Nothing said here will be used as ammo. This is about upgrading our performance system."

- **To respond with clarity**:

"We heard you. And even though we're not acting on this now, it mattered that you said it."

- **To close a loop cleanly**:

"That issue is resolved. Here's the outcome. Here's how to track progress moving forward."

Feedback without loop-closure is not feedback. It's abandonment in disguise.

MAKE FEEDBACK A FORCE, NOT A FORM

Feedback isn't a form. It's a **force multiplier**. Done right, it:

- Surfaces hidden truth
- Accelerates execution
- Elevates trust
- Strengthens culture

But it only works when leaders treat input like **intelligence**—not inconvenience. **Don't just collect feedback. Convert it. Close it. Carry it.**

Closing Thoughts: The Battle Is Never Over—And That's the Point

If you've made it here, know this: You are already different than when you started. You have glimpsed truths that many leaders spend entire careers avoiding. You have stood face-to-face with the forces inside you—fear, pride, anger, desire—that most would rather chain in silence.

And you now know: the real work was never just about managing people or climbing hierarchies. It was—and always will be—about mastering yourself.

Leadership is not a static achievement. It's not a title you win, frame, and hang on a wall. It is a living relationship between your conscious values and your unconscious impulses. It is a daily confrontation between the mission you claim to serve and the comfort you are tempted to seek. It is a thousand micro-decisions when no one is watching—where clarity, courage, and character are either forged or faked. And the truth is this: **the battle is never fully over**.

There is no moment when the shadow vanishes. No summit where fear disappears. No final victory lap where ego no longer whispers. But that's not failure. That's growth.

The world you are stepping into is more volatile, more complex, more brutally fast than anything your predecessors faced. It will not reward leaders who perform for applause. It will reward those who can lead **from authenticity, not performance. From wholeness, not fragmentation.**

You don't need to be flawless to lead. You need to be *fearless enough to face yourself.* And if you keep doing that—one honest confrontation at a time— You will build not just businesses, not just teams, not just cultures.

You will build a **life** that can carry the weight of real leadership without collapsing. A life anchored in courage. A life ordered by clarity. A life worthy of the trust others will place in you.

The world doesn't need more leaders who seek power. It needs leaders strong enough to seek wholeness. And it needs them now.

Burning the script wasn't rebellion. It was return. Return to clarity. Return to leadership not shaped by fear, but by presence.

But clarity isn't permanent. It slips. Narrative loops return. It's an ongoing struggle to stay tuned to the frequency of truth and clarity to build successful organizations. For those interested, that's why I built the next step.

The Schippers Clarity Coach isn't advice. It's a mentor built on my knowledge and experiences to help think beside you in real time—to help you process decisions, stabilize your leadership, and hold focus when complexity pulls you back toward the script. For more information, go to https://www.irondogllc.com/ or go to www.amplifaidintelligence.com If you've burned the script...Now it's time to lead.

Appendices & Tools

Toxic Culture Audit

"Culture isn't what you say. It's what you tolerate."

Use this audit to assess your team's cultural health. Each section contains reflection questions and observable indicators. Scoring can be qualitative (discussion-based) or quantitative (rating 1–5: 1 = strongly disagree, 5 = strongly agree).

Section 1: Psychological Safety and Truth Flow

Are people safe to speak honestly—especially when the truth is hard?

Audit Items
- Team members openly disagree in meetings without fear of retribution.
- Leaders invite feedback and respond non-defensively.
- Mistakes are discussed as learning opportunities, not liabilities.
- There is no "shoot the messenger" dynamic.
- Feedback flows *up*, *down*, and *across* levels of the organization.
- Team members feel they can express concerns without being labeled negative, disloyal, or difficult.

Red Flags
- Silence in meetings.
- Passive agreement, then private dissent.
- Important issues regularly surface *after* decisions are made.
- Anonymous surveys are the only source of truth.

Section 2: Leadership Integrity and Accountability

Do leaders embody the values they expect from others?

Audit Items
- Leaders model transparency, consistency, and humility.
- Power is not used to intimidate, silence, or manipulate.
- Leaders acknowledge their mistakes publicly.
- There are no "untouchables" or double standards.
- Leaders actively address toxic behavior—regardless of seniority.
- Performance and values alignment are equally weighted in promotions.

Red Flags
- Leadership immunity to feedback.
- Culture of blame during failure but silence during success.
- Leadership defensiveness or gaslighting.
- A "favorites" culture where poor behavior is tolerated if outcomes are strong.

Section 3: Communication and Conflict Health

Is disagreement healthy—or avoided, politicized, or weaponized?

Audit Items
- Conflict is addressed quickly, directly, and respectfully.
- Disagreements focus on ideas—not personalities.
- Constructive debate is encouraged, not avoided.
- Gossip is discouraged through modeling—not policy.
- People feel equipped and supported to handle interpersonal issues.

- There is clarity on how to escalate unresolved conflict without drama or retaliation.

Red Flags
- Triangulation (people talking about others, not to them).
- Avoidance of key topics because it's "not worth the fallout."
- Team members walking on eggshells.
- Resentment being mislabeled as "professionalism."

Section 4: Values in Practice vs. Values in Theory
Do the stated values match the lived experience?

Audit Items
- Organizational values are referenced in daily decisions—not just the onboarding deck.
- Employees can name how values show up in behavior.
- Decision-making processes are guided by principles, not personalities.
- Incentives (bonuses, promotions, praise) reflect the values—not just output.
- Cultural "heroes" reflect the best of the values, not just results.

Red Flags
- Core values are vague, weaponized, or performative.
- High-output, low-integrity individuals are consistently rewarded.
- Values shift depending on who's in the room.
- Culture statements are divorced from operational reality.

Section 5: Growth, Burnout, and Boundaries
Does the culture support sustainable excellence—or extractive overachievement?

Audit Items
- Workload is monitored, discussed, and adjusted proactively.
- Boundaries (time off, weekends, communication expectations) are respected.
- Leaders model and encourage rest, reflection, and renewal.
- Burnout is addressed early, not punished when it explodes.
- "Always-on" culture is not glamorized.
- People are evaluated by long-term impact—not just short-term hustle.

Red Flags
- Chronic overwork framed as "commitment."
- Vacations interrupted or discouraged.
- Pride in exhaustion or being indispensable.
- People rewarded for saving problems that leadership allowed to persist.

Section 6: Inclusion, Belonging, and Equity
Do all people feel valued, respected, and safe to be themselves?

Audit Items
- Different perspectives are sought—not just tolerated.
- Microaggressions or biased behaviors are addressed, not ignored.
- Leadership reflects diversity—in background, thought, and identity.
- Decision-making doesn't favor proximity to power.
- There is psychological safety across demographic lines—not just among the "in-group."
- People don't have to conform to succeed.

Red Flags

- Dominant voices go unchallenged.
- Tokenism disguised as inclusion.
- Disproportionate attrition among underrepresented groups.
- Informal power structures that exclude or silence.

Scoring and Debrief
Suggested Scale (per section):
- 26–30: Culture is healthy and resilient in this area.
- 20–25: Mostly healthy, but there are growing cracks.
- 15–19: Structural vulnerability—issues are likely harming engagement and performance.
- Below 15: Urgent need for cultural intervention.

Reflection Questions:
- Where is our culture silently leaking trust?
- What are we tolerating that contradicts our values?
- What do people fear saying out loud—and why?
- Which of these red flags do we rationalize as "just how it is here"?

Next Steps: Action Planning
Once you've completed the audit:

1. **Host a Leadership Debrief** – Review the lowest scoring sections with your executive team.
2. **Engage Your Team** – Share what you've learned. Invite courageous feedback.
3. **Name a Cultural North Star** – Pick one principle or value to reinforce *visibly* for the next 90 days.
4. **Audit Quarterly** – Culture is not static. Reassess regularly to see how interventions are working.
5. **Reward Honesty and Repair** – Change begins when truth becomes more valuable than comfort.

Remember:
A toxic culture doesn't start with villains. It starts with avoidance. With tolerated dysfunction. With leaders too busy, afraid, or isolated to see what's really happening. This audit isn't about shame. It's about sight. Because once you see it, you can shift it. And that's how culture heals.

Narcissist Spotting Checklist

"Not everyone with confidence is a narcissist. But narcissists confuse confidence with superiority—and use charm as a weapon, not a gift."

1. Disproportionate Need for Praise and Attention

- ☐ They redirect group conversations to their own accomplishments, even when off-topic.
- ☐ They seem energized only when they're the center of attention.
- ☐ They frame ordinary achievements as exceptional or heroic.
- ☐ They react with visible frustration or withdrawal when not praised or publicly acknowledged.

Narcissistic individuals crave admiration as oxygen. They don't just enjoy being seen—they feel entitled to it.

2. Monologue Over Dialogue

- ☐ Conversations tend to orbit around their stories, experiences, or opinions.
- ☐ They rarely ask genuine questions—or listen with curiosity.
- ☐ They speak more than they listen in team settings or 1:1s.
- ☐ They interrupt, redirect, or "one-up" others' experiences.

Where there should be relational rhythm, there is domination. Narcissists turn communication into performance.

3. Lack of Empathy in Real-Time Moments

- ☐ They minimize or deflect others' pain, stress, or vulnerability.
- ☐ Their emotional responses often feel rehearsed, delayed, or out of sync.
- ☐ They struggle to validate others' experiences unless it benefits them to do so.
- ☐ They redirect emotional conversations back to their own challenges.

Narcissists may talk about empathy, but they rarely practice it in the moment—especially when it doesn't serve their narrative.

4. Charm as a Manipulation Tool

- ☐ They are intensely charismatic early in relationships—but the warmth feels conditional.
- ☐ Their compliments are often transactional or performative.
- ☐ They can turn on "polished charm" in front of authority or during high-visibility moments.
- ☐ Those closest to them often experience the *opposite* of how they present publicly.

Narcissists are excellent at seducing systems. Their charm is strategic, not connective.

5. Superiority Masked as Standards

- ☐ They frame feedback as "just having high expectations"—while demeaning others.
- ☐ They overvalue their ideas, solutions, and approaches—and minimize others'.
- ☐ They name-drop, status-signal, or overtly compare themselves to "less competent" peers.

- ☐ They resist collaboration unless they are in control or guaranteed credit.

Narcissists don't see themselves as part of a team—they see themselves as the team's gift.

6. Extreme Sensitivity to Criticism
- ☐ Even light feedback triggers defensiveness, blame-shifting, or withdrawal.
- ☐ They attack the messenger instead of reflecting on the message.
- ☐ They reframe errors as "misunderstandings" or blame systems/people.
- ☐ They struggle to say "I was wrong" without justification or caveat.

To a narcissist, being wrong is intolerable—because it threatens their self-constructed image of superiority.

7. Divide-and-Control Behavior
- ☐ They create subtle rivalries or "us vs. them" dynamics between teams or individuals.
- ☐ They privately discredit others to maintain influence or loyalty.
- ☐ They shift alliances based on who can serve their current goals.
- ☐ They withhold information to maintain control or remain indispensable.

This is the tactical narcissist—who doesn't just crave power, but manipulates relationships to keep it.

8. Disposable Loyalty
- ☐ They speak about "family" and "loyalty" but quickly discard people who challenge them.
- ☐ Past colleagues or direct reports often describe a "fall from grace" after the narcissist no longer found them useful.
- ☐ They tend to rewrite history after relationship breakdowns—positioning themselves as the victim or misunderstood genius.
- ☐ They surround themselves with yes-people, not truth-tellers.

To the narcissist, people are tools, not partners. Loyalty is transactional—not relational.

9. Image Management Over Integrity
- ☐ They care more about how things *look* than how things *are*.
- ☐ They spin narratives after failures instead of owning them.
- ☐ They use metrics selectively to enhance their own image.
- ☐ They seek proximity to power or prestige—even when it contradicts stated values.

A narcissist doesn't mind violating the truth—as long as they control the story.

10. Cultural Drain: The Hidden Cost
- ☐ High turnover in their teams (especially among high performers).
- ☐ Declining trust and emotional safety around them—even if performance is strong.
- ☐ Their direct reports often feel exhausted, second-guessed, or invisible.
- ☐ Team climate improves when they are on vacation or absent.

Narcissists can be high-output—but at high cost. Their presence often creates invisible burnout.

Scoring and Reflection

This is not a diagnostic tool for narcissistic personality disorder. It's a **cultural pattern awareness tool**. If 5 or more of these clusters show up **consistently** in someone's behavior:

- **Action is needed.**
- Begin with documentation, coaching, or a neutral 360° review.
- Watch not just how they treat you—but how they treat the least powerful person in the room.
- Trust your team's emotional signals. Toxic charisma often creates private fear and public silence.

Next Steps for Leadership Teams

- Consider implementing **shadow behavior tracking** during leadership evaluations.
- Ensure **feedback systems are anonymous, triangulated, and followed up with clear action.**
- Engage in **values-aligned hiring and promotions**—don't reward narcissists for short-term results that erode long-term trust.
- Provide **empathy development training and reflective coaching**—some behaviors may be unconscious, not malicious.

Closing Insight

"The narcissist isn't dangerous because they want to be seen. They're dangerous because they'll burn the team down to stay in the spotlight." Healthy leadership leaves room for others to rise. Narcissistic leadership makes others shrink to survive. Now that you see the signs—you can choose something different.

Decision-to-Execution Velocity Dashboard Template
"Speed isn't chaos. It's clarity moving with discipline."

The purpose of this dashboard is to measure and improve the **time, clarity, and effectiveness** of decision-making and implementation cycles across key initiatives or projects. Designed to surface:
- **Lag time** between decision and action.
- **Execution friction** caused by unclear ownership or misaligned communication.
- **Behavioral bottlenecks** in leadership and accountability layers.

Core Dashboard Sections
Each section contains metrics, sample questions, and scoring guidelines. This template can be used **weekly, bi-weekly, or monthly** in strategic operations reviews.

1. Time to Execute *How long does it take to move from decision to observable action?*

Metric	Target	Actual	Variance	Notes/Context
Avg. time from decision to first action	≤ 5 business days			
Avg. time from kickoff to 50% completion	≤ 3 weeks			
Avg. time from decision to KPI impact	≤ 45 days			

Reflection Questions:
- Are decisions being made in working sessions or deferred?
- Are action steps clear and time-bound during decision-making moments?

2. Clarity of Ownership *Does everyone know who owns what—and by when?*

Metric	Target	Actual	Variance	Notes
% of decisions with documented owner at time of decision	100%			
% of actions with named "first mover" assigned	95%			
% of initiatives with updated RACI matrix	100%			

Reflection Questions:
- Are multiple people "kind of" responsible?
- Is there visible role clarity—or passive diffusion of ownership?

3. Communication Efficiency *Is the strategy clearly understood by those who must implement it?*

Metric	Target	Actual	Variance	Notes
% of frontline stakeholders briefed within 48 hours of decision	$\geq 90\%$			
% of project owners who can articulate the "why" behind decisions	$\geq 90\%$			
% of communication cycles requiring clarification or rework	$\leq 10\%$			

Reflection Questions:
- Do we confuse "announcement" with "alignment"?
- Are teams acting on the *actual intent*—or a filtered version?

4. Execution Traction *How consistent and coordinated is the implementation effort?*

Metric	Target	Actual	Variance	Notes
% of action items delivered on time (within 10% of deadline)	≥ 90%			
% of initiatives showing weekly visible movement	≥ 85%			
# of reassignments or team resets due to leadership confusion	≤ 1			

Reflection Questions:
- Are sprints moving or stuck in the mud?
- What blockers repeat every week but never get named?

5. Feedback and Course Correction Loops
How quickly are we adjusting based on data and learning?

Metric	Target	Actual	Variance	Notes
Time from data signal to course correction discussion	≤ 7 days			
# of feedback-driven pivots implemented in real time	N/A			
% of teams actively using live dashboards/KPIs weekly	≥ 90%			

Reflection Questions:
- Are we learning in real time—or post-mortem?
- Do teams fear deviating from "the plan" even when it's wrong?

Red Flag Signals (Highlight These)

Signal	Description	Urgency	Action Owner	Notes
Decision made with no assigned owner		High		
Execution paused due to unclear roles		High		
Repeated strategy shifts without comms to teams		Med		
KPI movement misaligned with perceived success		Med		

Leadership Debrief Prompts
Use these at the end of each review cycle to provoke reflection, not just reporting:
- Where did clarity break down?
- What decisions are we still pretending we made—but didn't?
- What message did our pace send to the organization?
- Who absorbed the friction without complaint?
- Where is a great plan dying in execution silence?

Velocity Health Score (Composite Scoring)

Category	Weight	Score (1–5)	Weighted Score
Time to Execute	25%		
Ownership Clarity	20%		
Communication	20%		
Execution Traction	20%		
Course Correction	15%		
Total	100%		/5.00

Score Ranges:

- 4.5–5.0 → High Velocity – Sustain and scale
- 3.5–4.4 → Good – Watch for friction build-up
- 2.5–3.4 → Stalling – Requires process attention
- Below 2.5 → Broken Flow – Immediate re-architecture needed

Template Usage Suggestions
- Review **monthly** in leadership operating rhythm or transformation programs.
- Use a **shared dashboard** (Notion, Miro, Excel, Airtable) to update metrics weekly.
- Assign a **Velocity Owner**—someone who watches not the *what*, but the *how fast and how clearly*.
- Pair with a **"Decide → Do" tracker** to monitor follow-through on leadership decisions.

Feedback Fluency Framework

"Feedback fluency isn't just about saying the hard thing—it's about designing a system where truth can move faster than fear."

Purpose of the Framework

To move organizations beyond **feedback as a one-time event** into a dynamic, everyday language. Fluency means not just knowing how to speak—but knowing **when, why, and how to adapt** the feedback to context, personality, and strategic need.

This framework develops **organizational intelligence** in four integrated domains:
1. **Clarity** – What is being said?
2. **Safety** – Is it safe to say it?
3. **Actionability** – Can it be applied or tested?
4. **Integration** – Does it lead to meaningful change?

The Four Feedback Fluency Modes

Each mode reflects a distinct type of feedback exchange, with its own risks, rituals, and rules. Healthy feedback cultures can **navigate between these modes** seamlessly.

Mode	Description	Risk if Overused	Ritual to Anchor
Reflective	Self-driven inquiry: "What am I learning from my impact?"	Navel-gazing without action	Weekly team reflections, journaling
Relational	Interpersonal dialogue: "How are we showing up for each other?"	Avoidance of tension to preserve harmony	1:1 feedback rituals, peer calibration
Operational	Task + performance-focused: "What's working? What needs to improve?"	Feedback becomes only about output	Sprint reviews, scorecard retros
Strategic	Systems and structure: "What's the feedback telling us about the whole?"	Fragmented fixes without addressing root causes	Executive debriefs, learning loops

The Five Building Blocks of Feedback Fluency

1. Language Precision – *Say what you mean, without blame.*

- Use behavior-specific language: "In the last three meetings, I noticed…"
- Avoid identity-based judgments: Say "Your report missed key data," not "You're careless."
- Use **Situation–Behavior–Impact (SBI)** or **What–So What–Now What** models to structure feedback.

Practice tip: Run weekly "precision clinics" to rewrite vague feedback into specific, constructive language.

2. Psychological Safety – *Build the conditions for truth to flow.*

- Make feedback a **routine**, not a reaction.
- Reward honesty even when it's uncomfortable.
- Model emotional regulation in the face of critical input.

Culture cue: Leaders must be the first to say, "Here's what I missed this week," or "What's something I didn't handle well?"

3. Timing and Tempo – *Know when to pause, when to press.*
- Give feedback **close to the moment**, but not in the heat of reaction.
- Create predictable feedback **cadences** (e.g., "Friday Feedbacks," sprint post-mortems).
- Allow emotional digestion before diving into solutions.

Ritual: Use "Fast Feedback Fridays" to practice timely, bite-sized feedback with low stakes and high frequency.

4. Feedback Roles and Reciprocity – *Train both givers and receivers.*
- The **feedback giver** is responsible for clarity, courage, and compassion.
- The **feedback receiver** is responsible for curiosity, reflection, and responsiveness.
- Everyone is both—so build reciprocal skills, not one-directional rules.

Coaching prompt: After receiving feedback, train people to say, "What I'm taking from that is…", and "Here's what I'll try."

5. Integration and Follow-Through – *Close the loop or lose the trust.*
- Track feedback themes and measure what changes.
- Publicly acknowledge behavioral shifts in team members: "I noticed you implemented the feedback about pacing—well done."
- Feedback without follow-through trains people to stay silent.

System upgrade: Build a "Feedback → Action" tracker in team meetings or retros with status updates.

Common Feedback Dysfunctions and Fixes

Dysfunction	Signal	Fix
Feedback Theater	Feedback exists only in reviews or forms	Embed into weekly rituals, normalize informal exchanges
Defensive Culture	People react to feedback with shame, silence, or justification	Train emotional regulation, model leader vulnerability
Ambiguity	Feedback is vague or coded	Use observable behaviors + impact language
Feedback Hoarding	Feedback is only upward or one-way	Build peer-to-peer feedback circuits
Overcorrecting	People try to please feedback givers, losing authenticity	Normalize experimentation, reflection before implementation

Feedback Fluency Scorecard (Team Self-Assessment)
Rate each item from 1 (rarely true) to 5 (consistently true):

Fluency Indicator	Score (1–5)
Team members give feedback regularly without prompting	
Feedback is specific, not vague or personal	
Leaders invite and reward feedback—even when uncomfortable	
We have clear feedback rituals (e.g., retros, debriefs, 1:1s)	
Feedback leads to visible action and improvement	

Fluency Indicator	Score (1–5)
We reflect on *how* feedback was given—not just what was said	
Peer-to-peer feedback is common—not just top-down	
We address conflict with dialogue, not avoidance	
People say feedback is safe—even across power dynamics	
Feedback loops are closed and tracked	

Total Score: /50

- **41–50** – Fluent: Feedback is cultural oxygen
- **30–40** – Functional: Feedback happens, but inconsistently
- **15–29** – Fractured: Feedback exists, but fear, vagueness, or fatigue limits impact
- **Below 15** – Frozen: Feedback is symbolic, not systemic

Apply the Framework with These 3 Core Tools

1. Feedback Map Canvas

- Who needs feedback?
- What type (reflective, operational, relational, strategic)?
- What ritual or setting is best?
- What structure will I use (SBI, Radical Candor, etc.)?

2. Feedback Friction Audit

- Where is feedback getting stuck in our system?
- Who is NOT getting feedback—and why?
- Where is it most emotionally charged?

3. Feedback Action Tracker

- Feedback given → Response received → Follow-up behavior → Outcome
- Public wins? Patterns of improvement? Need for reset?

Final Insight

"Feedback isn't just a conversation. It's a cultural operating system."

When feedback becomes fluent:

- Learning accelerates.
- Trust deepens.
- Accountability becomes shared.
- The organization begins to think in real-time—not in reviews.

Fluency isn't perfection. It's practice. It's rhythm. It's feedback that moves with velocity and integrity—because truth deserves a clear voice.

Conflict Navigation Script Templates

Purpose: Help leaders break survival-based narratives without triggering ego defense, using data, system focus, and solution framing.

Step 1: Drop the Disruptive Truth (Fracture Initiation)

Start with a targeted statement that shifts from individual blame to systemic clarity.

"What I'm seeing isn't a leadership failure—it's a system running exactly how it's been designed: to avoid discomfort, not to drive performance." "This isn't about you failing—it's about your processes protecting comfort instead of outcomes." "The results aren't broken because of bad people. The system is designed to prevent truth from surfacing." This positions the problem as structural, not personal. You're disrupting the narrative without triggering ego defenses.

Step 2: Pause—Let the Narrative Break Begin

Silence here is tactical. It allows internal confrontation. Avoid rushing into explanations. Let their discomfort surface.

They will:

- Defend
- Rationalize
- Look for personal absolution

Step 3: Mirror the Defense Without Personalizing

Use reflective language to expose the systemic defense—not personal weakness:

"That defensiveness you're feeling right now—that's your system protecting status quo, not solving problems."

"Your impulse to explain away the issue? That's a comfort-based response, not a performance-based one."

By naming the behavior as systemic—not as their personal flaw—you lower identity threat.

Step 4: Anchor to a Single, Neutral Fact

Offer one piece of objective, verifiable data. Avoid judgment—focus on reality.

"Five projects have required your intervention in the last 60 days. Not because people failed, but because your approval bottleneck is designed that way."

"The last customer complaint wasn't caused by a bad employee. It was a missing process handoff."

Then pause. Let the data land.

Step 5: Shift to System Focus and Solution

Now pivot from confrontation to collaborative repair:

"This isn't about finding fault—it's about fixing the architecture."

"Let's solve the system so you're not stuck firefighting."

"The goal isn't to manage harder—it's to design better."

Present yourself as a partner in system repair, not a critic of their leadership.

Step 6: Solution Framing — Attack the System, Not the Person

At this stage, frame every statement around process and results, not personal leadership failings:

"What's broken is not you. What's broken is how authority is distributed." "Let's redesign the escalation points so success doesn't depend on your constant intervention." "If we shift the feedback loop, your team can self-correct without you as the bottleneck."

Step 7: Maintain Calm, Solution-Focused Authority

Hold steady. Never let the conversation slip into personal critique. Anchor yourself as the architect of system clarity. "I'm not here to blame. I'm here to help you reclaim your time and trust your system." "It's not about pushing harder. It's about engineering smarter."

Why This Works:
- **Identity Preservation**: Ego stays intact; the problem is structural, not personal.
- **Cognitive Reframing**: Shifts focus from "I'm failing" to "My system is misaligned."
- **Data Anchoring**: Facts prevent emotional derailment.
- **Solution Partnership**: You're positioned as an ally, not a threat.
- **System Optimization Focus**: Keeps the discussion tactical, productive, and forward-moving.

Example in Use:
Leader says: "My team just doesn't seem capable of handling this."
You respond (Step 1): "This isn't a capability issue—it's a system designed to centralize control and prevent autonomy."
Pause (Step 2). Mirror reaction (Step 3): "That urge to explain their behavior? That's the system defending itself—not solving the problem."
Data anchor (Step 4): "Your direct approvals have increased by 40% over the last 90 days."
Shift to solution (Step 5): "Let's adjust the decision gates to reduce friction. The goal isn't more oversight—it's better throughput."

Core Insight:

In your terms: Burn the Theater, but help them rebuild the stage. Let clarity destroy dysfunction—without destroying the leader. By targeting processes, using data, and offering partnership, you move the leader from threat response to system repair. Not "you failed." Instead: "The system is failing you—and I'm here to fix that with you."

The Compassionate Confrontation Matrix
A Tactical Framework for Breaking Survival Narratives Without Breaking People

Leadership isn't cruelty disguised as clarity. But neither is it comfort masquerading as kindness. The most transformative leaders master what I call **Compassionate Confrontation**—the discipline of telling hard truths without shaming, and dismantling fragile narratives without triggering identity collapse. This matrix offers a tactical guide.

Compassionate Confrontation Matrix

Leader State	Your Tactical Approach	Primary Focus	Risks if Mishandled
Denial / Defensiveness	Gentle Truth + Data Anchor	Disrupt Survival Narrative	Ego backlash / withdrawal
Shame Spiral	System Focus + Affirmation of Worth	Separate System from Identity	Emotional shutdown / disengagement
Confusion / Dissonance	Single-Fact Anchoring + Solution Frame	Reduce Cognitive Load	Overwhelm / paralysis
Anger / Projection	Calm Reflection + Emotional Labeling	Name Emotion, Not Accuse	Escalation / adversarial reaction
Vulnerability / Curiosity	Incremental Data + Partnership Language	Build Safety for Integration	Regression to defensiveness

Key Tactics Explained:

- **Disrupt Survival Narrative, Not Identity:** Attack the system. Name the structure. Never attack the person.
- **Anchor in Data:** One fact. Not a litany of evidence. Truth fractures faster in small doses.
- **Frame the Problem as Process, Not Personal:** "What's broken isn't you. It's how your system is routing authority."
- **Compassion Is Structure, Not Pity:** Compassion means building a psychologically safe container for the leader's narrative collapse—not excusing dysfunction.
- **Solution as Stabilizer:** After truth fractures, immediately present a forward path. Clarity without a solution induces panic.

Field Application Example:

Leader State: "My team just doesn't care about results."
Tactical Response (Using Matrix):

- Identify Denial + Projection
- Deliver Gentle Truth:
  > "What I'm seeing isn't apathy—it's a system protecting itself from failure."
- Anchor in Data:
  > "Four missed deadlines in two months—all traced to blocked decisions, not disengagement."
- Frame Solution:
  > "Let's redesign your handoff points so the system can move without depending on you."
- Reinforce Worth:
  > "This isn't your failure—it's your system's design flaw."

Final Reminder:
Your goal isn't to break the person. It's to break the system that's breaking them. Use Compassionate Confrontation to:
- Deliver truth with discipline.
- Dismantle narratives with respect.
- Build leaders without breaking them.

Because courage without compassion isn't leadership. It's brutality.

Daily Practice for Real Leaders: How to Lead Beyond Ego, Fear, and Theater

In the noise of leadership theater and survival-driven decision loops, most leaders forget one thing: **Your legacy is not a story. It's a system.** And systems are built or eroded every single day. The Legacy Tracker is a daily reflection tool designed to help leaders exit ego-driven patterns, confront survival narratives, and build operational clarity—not performance theater. Use this framework not as a checklist for perfection but as a brutal, honest mirror.

Legacy Tracker – Daily Practice

At the end of each day, confront yourself with these questions:

1. Where Did I Prioritize Comfort Over Clarity Today?

Examples:

- Avoided a necessary conversation to "keep the peace."
- Downplayed failure to avoid unsettling my team.
- Chose agreement over accuracy in a leadership meeting.

Note: Comfort feels like a win in the moment. It's structural decay over time.

2. What Fear Drove My Decisions Today?

Did I:

- Avoid feedback because I feared losing status?
- Withhold authority due to fear of execution errors?
- Say "yes" to avoid being disliked?

Note: Fear isn't weakness. Fear is the silent architect of failure if left untracked.

3. What System Did I Strengthen—or Weaken?

- Did my team solve problems without me?
- Did accountability tighten or slacken?
- Did the mission advance, or did I manage optics?

Real leaders engineer systems that survive without them.

4. What Truth Did I Tell?

- Did I name the real problem, or protect the narrative?
- Did I burn the mask—mine or someone else's?
- Did I confront dysfunction where it lived?

If your day ended without uncomfortable honesty, your system didn't advance.

5. What Will Outlive Me from Today's Decisions?

- Did I build something that can scale?
- Did I document, delegate, or design?
- Or did I preserve my role as the bottleneck?

Ego says: "They need me." Legacy says: "They don't."

Daily Closure Statement:

"My name is not a system. My survival is not the mission. My leadership is what remains when I'm no longer here." **Track your answers daily.** Because your legacy isn't written after you're one. It's engineered—every day—you choose clarity over comfort. That's leadership without theater. That's legacy.

About the Author

Dr. David Schippers, Sc.D., CISSP
Resilient Leader. Cyber Strategist. Shadow Walker.

Dr. David Schippers is not your typical leadership author. He didn't write this book from a corner office. He wrote it from the trenches—where sabotage wears a smile, performance is weaponized, and real leadership costs you something.

With over three decades in operations, corporate, consulting, cybersecurity, digital forensics, higher education, and executive leadership, Dr. D has seen firsthand how organizations fail—not because of market conditions, but because cowardice gets promoted and truth + clarity gets punished.

He holds a Doctor of Science in Cybersecurity, is a Certified Information Systems Security Professional (CISSP), and a licensed digital forensics investigator. As Vice President and Chief Academic Officer of a business school, Dr. Schippers rebuilt technical, business and doctoral programs, redesigned strategic systems, and faced the internal theater most institutions won't admit exists.

But that's not the whole story.

Dr. D's work doesn't stop at policy and protocol. He writes and speaks at the intersection of **leadership, cybersecurity, psychology, and shadow work**—teaching leaders how to face fear, name dysfunction, and build cultures that don't require masks to survive.

He's jumped from helicopters, walked through betrayal, led during crisis, and stayed when others literally ran.

And he's here to hand you the sword—not the script.

You can connect with Dr. D on LinkedIn at linkedin.com/in/daschippers, or through Iron Dog LLC, where he continues his mission to turn clarity into action and expose the high cost of leadership theater.

This book isn't just authored by him.
It's *forged* by him.

Because some battles require scars.
And some leaders are only born in fire.